STUDY GUIDE
With Computer Exercises
for STATISTICS FOR THE
BEHAVIORAL SCIENCES
THIRD EDITION

B. Michael Thorne
Mississippi State University

J. Martin Giesen
Mississippi State University

Mayfield Publishing Company
Mountain View, California

International Standard Book Number: 0-7674-1174-9

SPSS is a registered trademark of SPSS Inc.
Windows is a registered trademark of Microsoft Corporation.

Manufactured in the United States of America
10   9   8   7   6   5   4   3   2   1

Mayfield Publishing Company
1280 Villa Street
Mountain View, California 94041

CONTENTS

PREFACE

From our experience, only an occasional student in an introductory statistics course is able to grasp a statistical technique fully upon first presentation. For most students, *repetition* is the key to eventual understanding; that is, they must rehearse the new technique repeatedly, viewing it from as many different angles as possible. This *Study Guide* to accompany *Statistics for the Behavioral Sciences, Third Edition* provides the opportunity for such further practice.

The *Study Guide* is keyed to the text by chapter. Each chapter in the *Study Guide* begins with a statement of the corresponding text chapter objectives. Next, there is a brief review of the textbook chapter. The reviews provide an overview of the relevant chapter and act as a memory refresher.

Beginning with Chapter 3, the reviews are followed by a list of the symbols introduced in the chapter. After the symbols, the computational formulas from the textbook chapter are given. These are followed by a list of terms to define and/or identify. Some of the terms are defined in the reviews and others only in the text.

Fill-in-the-blank items keyed to the chapter topics follow the terms. Next, several problems similar to those found in the text are given, and space is provided for their solution. Answers to both the fill-in-the-blank items and the problems are given in Appendix 3. Beginning with Chapter 3, each chapter ends with a brief self-test, for which answers are provided in Appendix 3. The self-tests provide a final check of chapter mastery before students proceed to the next chapter. Exercises and examples using the SPSS statistical package in its Windows version precede the self-test in many chapters. These exercises are included for students in statistics courses in which the use of the SPSS-for-Windows package is either required or recommended. To get the student started on these exercises, Appendix 4 provides general instructions on the use of SPSS to compute statistical results. In addition, the appendix refers to Thomas Pavkov and Kent Pierce's *Ready, Set, Go! A Student Guide to SPSS for Windows,* which focuses on the types of problems covered in the text and in the *Study Guide.* Pavkov and Pierce's manual is available through your bookstore for an additional cost.

Although the *Study Guide* is designed especially for students using *Statistics for the Behavioral Sciences,* because of the chapter reviews and the listing of computational formulas, the *Study Guide* will also prove valuable to other students who need to refresh their skills. In addition, Appendix 1 repeats the brief math–algebra review from the text, and Appendix 2 contains the inferential tables from *Statistics for the Behavioral Sciences.* With the addition of the tables, this workbook serves as an effective stand-alone summary text.

CHAPTER 1

THE LANGUAGE OF STATISTICS

OBJECTIVES

The main objectives in Chapter 1 are

1. To define statistics.
2. To provide reasons for its study.
3. To provide a context (as a second language) for the study of statistics.
4. To offer advice on the need for organization in any approach to statistical problems and also to encourage regular class attendance.

CHAPTER REVIEW

Statistics are summary numbers, or indices, that result from the analysis of data. Statistics is also a set of tools concerned with the collection, organization, and analysis of numerical facts or observations. There are at least three good reasons for taking a course in statistics:

1. We are surrounded by statistics, and some statistical sophistication will make us more informed consumers of statistics.
2. A knowledge of statistics is necessary for an understanding of the specialized literature in the behavioral sciences.
3. Behavioral scientists need statistical techniques to deal with the variability that is inherent in observations made on living organisms. Statistics is the branch of mathematics that deals with variability.

   Although it uses numbers, statistics isn't completely mathematical. In fact, it can be viewed as a language, with new vocabulary to learn as well as "grammar" and "syntax," which are used to draw inferences and make decisions about hypotheses. As with a second language, the best way to learn statistics is by doing it, by practice and more practice.

Although statistics isn't strictly a mathematics course, some mathematical skill is necessary. If it has been a while since you had your last mathematics course, take time to read and work through Appendix 1 in your text or in this *Study Guide*. Among the tools you will need for the course, we recommend a good, but inexpensive, light-powered calculator; take the time to work through the instructions you receive with your calculator. In addition, be prepared to do homework and attend class regularly.

Finally, we recognize that many of you probably entered this course with a certain degree of anxiety. Although this anxiety is quite natural, it is to a large extent unwarranted. By regularly attending class, reading the text, and working problems outside the classroom, you will succeed in this course.

TERMS TO DEFINE AND/OR IDENTIFY

Statistics

Indices

Data

FILL-IN-THE-BLANK ITEMS

What Is Statistics?

Summary numbers resulting from data analysis are (1) _____. A set of procedures and

tools used to organize and interpret facts, events, and observations is called (2) _____.

Why Study Statistics?

Reasons for psychology students to take a course in statistics include the following:

1. We are surrounded by (3) _____.

2. It will help you become a more informed (4) _____ of statistics.

3. Psychology is defined as the scientific study of (5) _____ and cognition. Because what

   psychologists study is quite (6) _____, a knowledge of the branch of mathematics
   called statistics is necessary.

Goals for the Text

We have several goals for students using this text:

1. To help you learn the basic (7) _____, procedures, and logic of statistics.

2. To assist you in being a better (8) _____ of statistical information.

3. To improve your ability to read and understand the professional (9) _____.

4. To give you the (10) _____ to calculate and interpret statistics.

Statistics as a Second Language

Mastering statistics is much like learning a second (11) _____. In statistics there are conventions that must be learned, and the best way to learn them is by (12) _____. You will first be presented with a (13) _____ of statistics. Similar to your experience with a second language, in statistics you will probably always experience some (14) _____ and (15) _____. The best way to combat these feelings is (16) _____.

What You Need to Use This Book Successfully

To do homework, you will need (17) _____ and paper and an inexpensive light-powered (18) _____. In addition to doing homework regularly, good (19) _____ is essential.

PROBLEMS

1. List 10 examples of statistics you have encountered recently (a newspaper is a good place to start).

2. If you haven't already read the instructions that came with your calculator, do so now. Then use the memory function of your calculator to solve the following problems:

   a. $(25)(3) + (23)(5) + (22)(7) =$

b. $\dfrac{27}{5} + (13)(15) - (22)(7) =$

c. Find the square root of $\dfrac{14{,}332}{422} - 5.35^2$

d. $8 + 7 + 12 + 3 - 10 - 6 =$

e. $8^2 + 7^2 + 5^2 + 2^2 =$

f. $\dfrac{(29)^2}{7} =$

CHAPTER 2

DEFINITIONS AND SCALING

OBJECTIVES

The main objectives in Chapter 2 are

1. To define formally statistical terms such as variable (independent and dependent), population and parameter, sample and statistic, and sampling.
2. To define and illustrate the rules used for assigning numbers to objects or events—that is, to discuss measurement as it pertains to statistics.
3. To define and illustrate the two basic uses or divisions of statistics (inferential and descriptive).

CHAPTER REVIEW

A *variable* is anything that may take on different values or amounts. In research, two variables of interest are the independent variable and the dependent variable. The *independent* variable is the one manipulated or controlled by the researcher. The *dependent* variable in behavioral science is the measurement of behavior.

Population refers to a complete collection of objects or organisms having some common characteristic. A subset of a population is called a *sample.* A measurable characteristic of a population is called a *parameter,* whereas a measurable characteristic of a sample is called a *statistic.*

The process of selecting a sample from a population is called *sampling.* If a sample accurately reflects its parent population, it is an *unbiased* sample; an unrepresentative sample is called *biased.* In *random sampling,* each member of the population theoretically has a chance of being selected; random sampling is sometimes called *random and independent sampling* or just *independent sampling* because selecting one object or person for a sample has no effect (is independent of) the probability of selecting another object or person. *Sampling with replacement* means that each selected individual is returned to the population before the next selection; in *sampling without replacement,* the individual is not returned. In *stratified random sampling,* the population is divided into strata or groups, and random samples are taken from each strata.

Two basic types of data are measurement data and frequency data. *Measurement data* involve a true measurement process, whereas *frequency data* consist of counts, totals, or frequencies. Nominal scale data are generally frequency data, whereas ordinal, interval, and ratio scale data involve some form of measurement.

Scales of measurement are the rules used for assigning numbers to objects or events. From least to most complex, the measurement scales are nominal, ordinal, interval, and ratio. The *nominal scale* gives names or labels to different objects or events. Numbers on football jerseys are a nominal scale. *Ordinal scale* numbers serve both to identify and to rank-order the objects or events. An example of an ordinal scale might be the numbers 1–6 used both to identify finishers in a 5K race and to indicate their order of finish. In addition to providing categorizing and ranking properties, the *interval scale* has equal intervals between the scores. An example is the Fahrenheit temperature scale. Rating scales can cautiously be assumed to be interval-level measurement. A *ratio scale* is an interval scale with a true zero. Examples include time and weight. It is important to be aware of scales of measurement because some statistical techniques require particular scales of measurement.

Descriptive statistics are used to illustrate quantities of numerical observations. Examples include graphs and averages. *Inferential* statistical techniques permit us to make conclusions about a larger group based on some subset of it and tell us how confident we are in our conclusions.

TERMS TO DEFINE AND/OR IDENTIFY

Variable

Independent variable

Dependent variable

Population

Parameter

Sample

Statistic

Sampling

Unbiased sample

Biased sample

Random sampling

Random and independent sampling

Independent sampling

Sampling with replacement

Sampling without replacement

Stratified random sampling

Scales of measurement

Measurement data

Frequency data

Nominal scale

Ordinal scale

Ranking

Rank-ordering

Interval scale

Ratio scale

Descriptive statistics

Inferential statistics

FILL-IN-THE-BLANK ITEMS

Statistics: Some Basic Vocabulary

The general term used to designate anything that may take on different values or amounts is

(1) _____ . The (2) _____ variable is the one controlled and manipu-

lated by the experimenter; the (3) _____ variable in psychology is the measurement of
behavior. For example, suppose an experimenter wants to test the effect of different amounts of alcohol on
driving ability. She gives three different groups either 0, 1, or 2 ounces of alcohol, respectively. After a
suitable period, some characteristic of driving ability is measured in each participant. The amount of

alcohol given is the (4) _____ variable, whereas the measured driving ability is the

(5) _____ variable.

A complete collection of objects or organisms is called a (6) _____ , and a subset of

the collection is a (7) _____ . A measurable characteristic of the complete collection is

called a (8) _____ , whereas a similar characteristic of the subset is a (9) _____ .

A sample that is not representative of the population of interest is called a (10) _____

sample. One way to get a representative sample is to use (11) _____ sampling, a
sampling method in which each population member has an equal chance of being chosen. If individuals are

returned to the population after they are selected, this is called sampling with (12) _____ .

In (13) _____ random sampling, the population is divided into relevant groups, and random samples are taken from each group.

Scales of Measurement

The rules used for assigning numbers are called (14) _____ of measurement. Data derived

by some kind of true measurement process are called (15) _____ data, whereas data con-

sisting of counts, totals, or frequencies are considered (16) _____ data. The type of scale

that provides nothing more than a name or label is called a (17) _____ scale. If the scale

numbers are used both for categorizing and for ranking, the scale is called an (18) _____

scale. Equal intervals between numbers characterize the (19) _____ scale, and if the scale

has a true zero point, we call it a (20) _____ scale. Weight is an example of a

(21) _____ scale, whereas the Fahrenheit temperature scale is an example of an

(22) _____ scale.

Two Basic Uses of Statistics

(23) _____ statistics consists of techniques used to illustrate or describe the data, whereas

(24) _____ statistics is used to draw conclusions from the data. A graph is an example of

a (25) _____ statistic.

PROBLEMS

1. For each of the following brief descriptions, decide which is the independent variable and which is the dependent variable.

   a. Thirty people have been given one of three different kinds of drug, and their responses on a standard IQ test have been recorded.

   b. A social psychologist studies the problem-solving performance of individuals working alone or working in the presence of others.

   c. One group of third-graders solves simple multiplication problems with an odd-numbered answer. Another group of third-graders solves multiplication problems with even-numbered answers. The average number of seconds to solve the problems for each group is compared.

   d. In a study of visual acuity, participants view a standard stimulus under low illumination, moderate illumination, or high illumination. The length of time each participant takes to identify the stimulus is recorded.

2. Give the appropriate measurement scale for each of the following:

   a. weight

b. Social Security numbers

c. scores assigned by a rating scale of authoritarian characteristics

d. telephone numbers

e. highway speed limits

f. national college basketball ratings

g. judges' ratings of gymnastics performance

h. temperature centigrade

3. Tell whether each of the following is a parameter or a statistic. Explain your choice.

    a. the average weight of all left-handed boys at Fairlawn High School

    b. the average ACT (or SAT) scores of 15 randomly selected students from your statistics class

    c. the range in IQ scores of all inmates in the state prison in your state

d. the average income of a group of people selected by calling every 100th name in a small-town telephone directory

4. Read each of the following and tell whether a descriptive statistical technique or an inferential statistical technique has been used.

    a. A commentator on the nightly business report uses a pie chart to show how the average American family spends its money.

    b. A newspaper article describes how a study of 27 Alzheimer's patients concluded that patients benefited from lecithin and physostigmine injections.

    c. A study based on a small sample concludes that calories consumed in a morning meal cause less weight gain than the same calories consumed at night.

    d. Your statistics instructor gives the range of scores and the average score on the midterm test.

    e. A study shows that law students who take special review courses perform better on the bar exam than students who do not take the courses.

    f. A newspaper publishes a graph showing the performance of the stock market in the month of July.

CHAPTER 3

THE FREQUENCY DISTRIBUTION

OBJECTIVES

The main objective in Chapter 3 is to introduce a preliminary, but important, technique for organizing and describing data: the frequency distribution.

CHAPTER REVIEW

A first approach to organizing data is to arrange the numbers in order of value. By convention, we list the highest number first, followed by the next highest, and so on. The data can be condensed slightly by constructing a *frequency distribution* in which the scores are ranked from highest to lowest and the number of times each score occurs (its *frequency*) is listed beside it. Scores are symbolized by the letter *X,* whereas frequencies appear under the letter *f.*

A *continuous variable* is one whose measurement can take an infinite number of values; a *discrete variable* is one capable of assuming only specific values. Gaps in the measurement of a continuous variable are apparent rather than real; that is, the gaps are an artifact of the crudeness of measurement. Data from a continuous variable presented in the form of whole numbers have gaps between the numbers; these numbers with gaps are called *apparent limits. Real limits* close the gaps by subtracting a half unit from the lower apparent limit and adding a half unit to the upper apparent limit.

To compare frequency distributions from samples varying in size, we need to convert the frequencies to percentages; that is, we need to put them on an equivalent basis. The resulting distribution is called a *percentage* or *relative frequency distribution.* A *cumulative frequency distribution* is constructed by starting with the distribution's lowest interval and accumulating frequencies as you ascend. Thus, for any interval, the cumulative frequency tells the number of scores contained in that interval plus the sum of the frequencies in intervals below the one considered. Converting each of the accumulated frequencies to a percentage results in a *cumulative percentage distribution.*

SYMBOLS

Symbol	Stands For
X	a score
f	frequency of a score
N	sum of the frequencies, or total sample size
Cum f	cumulative frequency

FORMULAS

Formula 3-1. *Equation to convert frequencies into percentages*

$$\%age \ (percentage) = \frac{f}{N}(100)$$

f is the frequency or the number of times each score occurs; N is the number of observations or the sum of the frequency column in a frequency distribution.

Formula 3-2. *Equation to convert cumulative frequencies to cumulative percentages*

$$Cum \ \%age = \frac{Cum \ f}{N}(100)$$

Cum f stands for the cumulative frequency, which is the total number of observations up to and including the observations in the interval you're considering.

TERMS TO DEFINE AND/OR IDENTIFY

Score

Frequency distribution

Frequency

Continuous variable

Discrete variable

Apparent limits

Real limits

Percentage frequencies

Cumulative frequency distribution

Cumulative percentage

Cumulative percentage distribution

FILL-IN-THE-BLANK ITEMS

Introduction

The first step in organizing some data might be to arrange the scores by order of value, listing them from

the (1) _____ to the (2) _____ . The numbers constituting the data are

called (3) _____ and are symbolized by the letter (4) _____ .

Defining the Frequency Distribution

An arrangement in which the scores are listed in descending order and the number of times each score

occurs is listed beside it is called a (5) _____ _____ . The number of times

each score occurs is called its (6) _____ and is symbolized by the letter

(7) _____ . In order to further condense the data, scores occurring with a zero

frequency are often (8) _____ in constructing the frequency distribution.

Continuous variables and discrete variables: Real limits and apparent limits

A (9) _____ variable is one whose measurement can take an infinite number of values;

a variable that can take only specific values is called a (10) _____ variable. Data
from a continuous variable presented as whole numbers have gaps between the numbers, resulting

in (11) _____ limits. Closing the gaps by subtracting (12) _____ a unit from the lower limit and adding (13) _____ a unit to the upper limit results in

(14) _____ limits.

Percentage or Relative Frequency and Cumulative Frequency Distributions

One way to compare frequency distributions from samples of unequal size is to convert the fre-

quencies to (15) _____ frequencies. To do this, you divide each frequency by

(16) _____ and multiply the result by 100. N stands for the (17) _____

of the frequencies or the total sample (18) _____ .
   To construct a cumulative frequency distribution, start with the distribution's lowest interval and

(19) _____ frequencies as you ascend. For any interval, the cumulative frequency tells

you the number of scores in the interval plus the sum of the frequencies in all (20) _____

intervals. Cumulative frequency is symbolized by (21) _____ .

PROBLEMS

1. A group of students is given four brief presentations of a list of 15 nouns. A recognition test is given after a 20-minute delay. The number of nouns correctly identified by each student is listed next. Arrange them into a frequency distribution. Include a Cum f column and a Cum %age column.

6	15	12
8	15	14
12	13	13
15	15	13
13	10	15

2. Another group of students is given similar exposure to the same list of 15 nouns but is given a recall test rather than a recognition test of retention. The resulting scores are listed here. Construct a frequency distribution. Why would it be unnecessary to convert the frequencies in Problems 1 and 2 to percentages if you wanted to compare the two distributions?

0	1	2
1	1	4
0	2	2
0	1	1
3	2	1

3. To test their reaction times, 50 students from an introductory psychology class are asked to press a button when a green light flashes on. Their reaction times in hundredths of a second are as follows:

25	33	28	22	18
31	23	29	25	15
17	21	27	37	16
19	19	25	30	25
15	18	18	26	24
16	21	17	21	23
16	20	15	15	23
17	17	14	16	25
25	15	20	17	26
24	12	21	19	20

a. Construct a frequency distribution.

b. Add the real limits and a %age frequency column to your frequency distribution.

4. Find the real limits for each of the following scores:

Apparent Limits	Real Limits
a. 25	
b. 11.7	
c. 12.55	
d. 7.853	

5. A random sample of 20 depressive patients has been given the MMPI. Their scores on Scale 2 (Depression Scale) are as follows:

30	25	26	31
45	37	35	36
32	32	30	26
28	34	34	42
33	32	35	39

Construct a frequency distribution. Include a Cum f column and a %age f column.

6. For practice, some graduate students in a personality appraisal course administer the MMPI to 85 of their friends. Their scores on Scale 4 (Psychopathic Deviate) are shown in frequency distribution A as follows. Distribution B shows the Scale 4 results from 32 participants in a DWI (Driving While Intoxicated) class. What would you have to do to the frequency distributions in order to compare them? Add the appropriate column to each distribution.

Distribution A			Distribution B	
X	f		X	f
79	1		79	1
77	1		78	2
76	1		77	2
74	2		76	2
65	2		75	3
64	3		74	2
62	2		73	2
60	2		71	1
57	5		70	2
56	4		69	3
54	6		68	4
53	7		65	1
52	6		60	1
51	7		58	2
50	10		55	1
49	7		50	1
48	6		44	1
47	4		39	1
45	2			
44	1			
42	3			
40	2			
39	1			

7. A large number of students took a 50-item test in a section of introductory psychology. A frequency distribution of the results is shown here. Show the real limits, cumulative frequencies, and cumulative percentages. What is N?

X	f		X	f
49	1		35	8
48	6		34	3
47	6		33	1
46	11		32	7
45	13		31	3
44	16		30	4
43	8		29	3
42	15		28	4
41	16		27	1
40	13		26	3
39	9		25	2
38	5		23	1
37	3			
36	7			

USING SPSS—EXAMPLE AND EXERCISE

If you do not already know how to use SPSS, read and work through Appendix 4 before proceeding with the exercise.

The SPSS FREQUENCIES procedure can be used to produce frequency distributions with percentage and cumulative percentage columns in either an ascending or descending arrangement.

Example: We will use SPSS to produce a frequency distribution for Problem 3. The steps are as follows:

1. Start SPSS, enter the data, and name the variable **reaction.**
2. Click Statistics>Summarize>Frequencies.
3. Highlight **reaction** and move it into the Variable(s) box.
4. To produce a descending arrangement, click Format>Order by Descending values>Continue. The Frequencies dialog box and the Frequencies: Format dialog box should appear as follows:

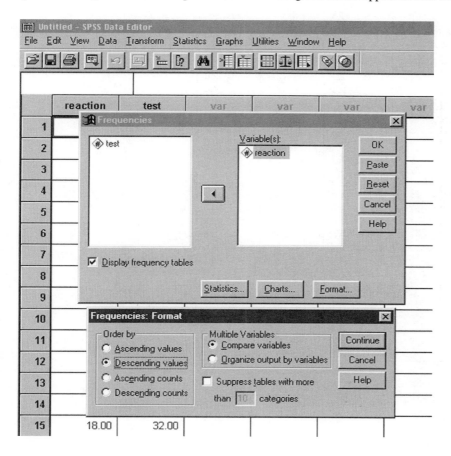

5. Click OK.

The output showing the complete frequency distribution for Problem 3 should appear as follows:

```
FREQUENCIES
  VARIABLES=reaction
  /FORMAT=DVALUE
  /ORDER  ANALYSIS .
```

Frequencies

Statistics

REACTION

N	Valid	50
	Missing	0

REACTION

		Frequency	Percent	Valid Percent	Cumulative Percent
Valid	37.00	1	2.0	2.0	2.0
	33.00	1	2.0	2.0	4.0
	31.00	1	2.0	2.0	6.0
	30.00	1	2.0	2.0	8.0
	29.00	1	2.0	2.0	10.0
	28.00	1	2.0	2.0	12.0
	27.00	1	2.0	2.0	14.0
	26.00	2	4.0	4.0	18.0
	25.00	6	12.0	12.0	30.0
	24.00	2	4.0	4.0	34.0
	23.00	3	6.0	6.0	40.0
	22.00	1	2.0	2.0	42.0
	21.00	4	8.0	8.0	50.0
	20.00	3	6.0	6.0	56.0
	19.00	3	6.0	6.0	62.0
	18.00	3	6.0	6.0	68.0
	17.00	5	10.0	10.0	78.0
	16.00	4	8.0	8.0	86.0
	15.00	5	10.0	10.0	96.0
	14.00	1	2.0	2.0	98.0
	12.00	1	2.0	2.0	100.0
	Total	50	100.0	100.0	

Note that the cumulative percentage column accumulates the percentages in ascending rather than descending order, which is the opposite of the way we taught the procedure in the textbook. In fact, it may be better for you to leave the frequency distribution format in ascending order (see step 4), because the cumulative percent column in the output is always ascending. If you do it this way, the SPSS frequency distributions will be perfectly inverted for all columns and will be easier to compare with the text. In a few cases, particularly in this chapter and the next one on graphing, SPSS does not have enough flexibility to produce the output that we described in the textbook. Because SPSS doesn't have the flexibility, we will have to be flexible for it.

Exercise Using SPSS

1. Use the data in the second column (scores from 35 to 23) from Problem 7 to construct a descending frequency distribution using SPSS. Note that you will need to enter each score as many times as indicated by the frequency. For example, 35 would be entered 8 times.

CHECKING YOUR PROGRESS: A SELF-TEST

1. Match the following:

_____ X	**a.** ranking of scores from highest to lowest with the number of times each score occurs listed beside it
_____ f	**b.** number of observations; sample size
_____ continuous variable	**c.** stands for scores
	d. number of score units in a class interval
_____ frequency distribution	**e.** number of scores through a given score or interval
	f. difference between highest and lowest scores
_____ real limits	**g.** variable capable of assuming only specific values
	h. variable whose measurement can take an infinite number of values
_____ N	**i.** formed by adding or subtracting half a unit
_____ cumulative frequency	**j.** number of occurrences of a score

2. Rounded to the nearest whole dollar, the amount of cash each student in a class had on a given day is shown here. Make a frequency distribution of these data. Give real limits and include a cumulative frequency column and a cumulative percentage column.

37	9	0	61	3	6
15	22	12	65	5	6
10	8	81	65	7	8
10	10	75	12	12	10
0	13	93	8	10	5
8	17	52	21	9	3
3	15	71	32	5	2

CHAPTER 4

GRAPHING DATA

OBJECTIVES

The main objective in Chapter 4 is to introduce and describe the following types of graphs frequently used in the behavorial sciences: the frequency polygon, the cumulative frequency curve, the histogram, the bar graph, the stem-and-leaf plot, and the line graph. Additionally, some graphing conventions are presented, and the shapes of frequency polygons are discussed briefly.

CHAPTER REVIEW

Before discussing specific types of graphs, two graphing conventions are presented. The first convention is the *three-quarters rule,* which states that the *Y* axis should be approximately three fourths as long as the *X* axis. The second convention is that the values on the *Y* axis generally should begin with 0, and the units on the axis should reflect reasonable deviations in the data.

The *frequency polygon* is constructed by plotting the scores on the baseline, or *X* axis, and plotting the frequency of each score along the *Y* axis. The axes of the frequency polygon are labeled with the word "Score" below the *X* axis and the word "Frequency" to the left of the *Y* axis. In addition, each graph should have a caption describing the source of the data. If you want to compare two or more sets of data on a single set of axes and the sample sizes differ, the frequencies must be converted to percentages before plotting.

One common and very important curve is the *normal* or bell-shaped curve. The normal curve is symmetrical, in contrast to *skewed curves,* in which a large number of scores are piled up at one end or the other end, with a tail at the opposite end. *Positively skewed curves* have a tail toward the upper end of the *X* axis, and *negatively skewed curves* have a tail toward the lower end of the *X* axis.

The *cumulative frequency* or *cumulative percentage polygon* can be plotted from a frequency distribution. In this curve, cumulative frequency (or percentage) is plotted over the scores. The cumulative frequency curve is useful for determining the relative position of any individual.

The only difference between the frequency polygon and the *histogram* is that dots are plotted over the score values in the polygon, whereas rectangular bars are plotted over the values in the histogram. The *bar graph* is a type of histogram used to plot categorical or nominal scale data. A bar is drawn over each category, with its height indicating frequency; the bar's width is arbitrary.

The *stem-and-leaf plot* has features of both the frequency distribution and the frequency histogram. To construct it, each data point is split into two parts: a stem (the first digit[s]) and a leaf (the last digit[s]). For example, a score of 155 has a stem of 15 and a leaf of 5. If a stem-and-leaf plot is rotated 90° counterclockwise, it becomes a histogram with digits over the scores (stems) rather than bars. Another useful feature of the stem-and-leaf plot is that it can be used to compare two groups of data.

In a *line graph,* an independent variable is recorded on the X axis, and some measure of the dependent variable is shown on the Y axis. The independent variable is assumed to be continuous, and a line is used to connect the plotted points.

TERMS TO DEFINE AND/OR IDENTIFY

Abscissa

Ordinate

Frequency polygon

Normal curve

Skewed curve

Positively skewed curve

Negatively skewed curve

Cumulative frequency curve

Histogram

Bar graph

Stem-and-leaf plot

Line graph

FILL-IN-THE-BLANK ITEMS

Introduction

An old adage states that a picture is worth a (1) _____ words, and recognition of the

truth of this leads to the discussion of (2) _____ as a descriptive technique. The graphs

discussed in the chapter are the frequency polygon, the (3) _____ frequency or per-

centage curve, the (4) _____ , the bar graph, the stem-and-leaf plot, and the

(5) _____ graph.

Rules for Graphing

To help prevent misrepresentation of data, a graphing convention is often used that states that the

(6) _____ axis should be approximately (7) _____ as long as the X

axis. This convention is called the (8) _____ rule. It is also important to begin the values

on the Y axis with (9) _____ and to be sure that the Y axis units reflect reasonable

(10) _____ in the data.

The Frequency Polygon

In a frequency polygon, the (11) _____ are plotted on the baseline or X axis, and

the (12) _____ are plotted on the ordinate or Y axis. Labeling of the axes is very

important: The word (13)" _____ " appears below the X axis, and the word

(14)" _____ " appears to the left of the Y axis. The graph should also have a

(15) _____ describing the origin of the data.

A comparison of distributions using the percentage or relative frequency polygon

If you want to compare distributions with unequal Ns on the same axes, you must first convert fre-

quencies to (16) _____ . Once you have done this, you can plot a percentage or

(17) _____ frequency polygon.

Shapes of frequency polygons

The (18) _____ or bell-shaped curve is an important symmetrical curve. Unimodal curves

with a high peak at one end and a long tail at the other end are called (19) _____ curves.

If the tail is to the right, the curve is (20) _____ _____; if the tail is to

the left, the curve is (21) _____ _____.

The cumulative frequency (or cumulative percentage) polygon

In the cumulative frequency or percentage polygon, the cumulative frequencies or percentages are plotted

over the (22) _____. The relative position of an individual may be determined from the

cumulative polygon by drawing a (23) _____ line from that person's score on the X axis

to the curve and then drawing a (24) _____ line from that point on the curve to the Y axis.

The point at which the (25) _____ line meets the Y axis gives an approximate number
(or percentage) of individuals scoring at or below the score being considered.

The Histogram

The histogram is like the frequency polygon except that a rectangular (26) _____ is drawn

over each score value on the X axis, with its height determined by the score's (27) _____.

Each bar is centered above a score value and extends (28) _____ between adjacent scores.

The Bar Graph

The bar graph is a type of histogram used to graph (29) _____ scale data. The bars don't

have to touch, and the spacing between them is (30) _____.

The Stem-and-Leaf Plot

To construct a stem-and-leaf plot, each score is divided into two parts: a (31) _____

and a (32) _____. The first digit(s) is the (33) _____ and the last

digit(s) is the (34) _____. For example, a score of 133 would have a stem of

(35) _____ and a leaf of (36) _____. Each stem is listed from

lowest to highest, a (37) _____ line is drawn to the right of the column of stems, and

then the (38) _____ are put beside the stems. If the plot is rotated so that the stems be-

come (39) _____ on the baseline of a graph, the result is a (40) _____ ,
with digits over the scores rather than bars.

The Line Graph

In a line graph, an (41) _____ variable is recorded on the X axis, and some measure
of the dependent variable appears on the Y axis. Because the independent variable is assumed to be

(42) _____ , a line is used to connect the plotted points.

PROBLEMS

1. You have gathered some test score data from a 50-item test in an introductory psychology class. In order
   to "curve" the grades, you decide to graph the data. The frequency distribution is shown here.

X	f
48	1
47	1
46	2
42	2
41	3
39	2
38	5
37	4
36	3
35	2
33	2
32	1
30	1
	$N = 29$

   a. Construct a frequency polygon.

b. Make a histogram.

c. Construct a cumulative frequency curve.

d. Construct a cumulative percentage curve and use it to find the approximate percentage of scores at or below a score of 35.

2. Before using behavior modification to reduce smoking, a confirmed smoker records the number of ciga- rettes smoked per day over a 2-week period. Use the appropriate graph to illustrate the data.

Day	f	Day	f
1	23	8	25
2	27	9	22
3	18	10	24
4	19	11	29
5	25	12	25
6	26	13	19
7	33	14	22

3. The highway patrol of an unnamed state keeps track on the number of people their officers stop for traffic violations who are wearing seat belts. They notice an apparent difference between weekdays and weekends in the proportion of people wearing seat belts. In a typical month, the number of people wearing seat belts out of the total number stopped is as follows: weekdays, 7,849 out of 11,542; weekends, 1,663 out of 3,192. Use the appropriate graph to show the results. Note that the sample sizes are different, so you will need to do something to put the groups on an equal footing.

4. The Registrar's Office of a small college records the number and type of requests for information it receives at its Information Desk. The numbers for a typical week are as follows: transfer of credit, 7; transcripts, 22; class availability/scheduling, 90; prerequisites, 12; other, 45. Illustrate these data with a bar graph.

5. The mean quality point average (QPA) has been determined by the semester after joining for the members of a campus social organization. Plot the result.

Semesters After Joining	Mean QPA
1	2.97
2	2.65
3	2.58
4	2.45
5	2.30
6	2.19

6. In a recent study, patients suffering from depression received one of three types of treatment: counseling alone, antidepressant medication alone, or a combination of counseling and medication. Their average level of depression (rounded to the nearest whole number) is assessed each month for 6 months. The data are given here. Plot the three groups on the same graph for comparison.

Month	Counseling	Medication	Counseling and Medication
1	17	16	18
2	15	10	12
3	14	9	11
4	13	11	9
5	10	10	6
6	8	9	4

7. Compare frequency distributions A and B on the same set of axes.

Distribution A			Distribution B	
X	f		X	f
25	1		25	6
24	3		24	7
23	3		23	8
22	4		22	10
21	5		21	7
20	6		20	4
19	8		19	3
18	7		18	2
17	7		17	2
16	6		16	1

a. Construct frequency polygons. The shape of Distribution A is _____ skewed; the shape of Distribution B is _____ skewed.

b. Plot the distributions as cumulative frequency curves.

8. The following numbers are first-lap speeds in miles per hour of 35 cars in the Indianapolis 500 race. Make a stem-and-leaf plot of the speeds. Then rotate the plot 90° counterclockwise so that it looks like a frequency histogram.

183	177	159	172	210
166	167	199	185	188
203	207	197	188	193
168	175	192	201	204
169	177	185	188	189
199	193	195	205	195
188	185	192	199	198

USING SPSS—EXAMPLE AND EXERCISES

If you haven't already done so, read Appendix 4 before proceeding with these exercises.

SPSS has a variety of graphing capabilities, both within certain procedures and independently under the Graphs menu. Unfortunately, the available choices for graphs may not correspond exactly to the ones requested in this chapter and described in the textbook. Thus, you may have to choose a graph that is an approximation to the one requested or one that may require you to draw a few lines to achieve the desired result.

Example: We will use SPSS to produce graphs for Problem 1. In this problem, part **a** requests a frequency polygon, and a histogram is requested in part **b.** SPSS won't easily produce either of these graphs exactly as we have defined them in the text. However, a good approximation for the frequency polygon is provided by an SPSS line graph constructed as follows:

1. Start SPSS, enter the data, and name the variable **test**. Again, remember that when we enter data from a frequency distribution, each score must be entered the number of times indicated by its frequency.
2. Click Graphs>Line>Simple>Summaries for groups of cases>Define.
3. Highlight and move the variable **test** into the Category Axis box and be sure "N of cases" is indicated in the Line Represents box. The Define Simple Line dialog box should appear as follows:

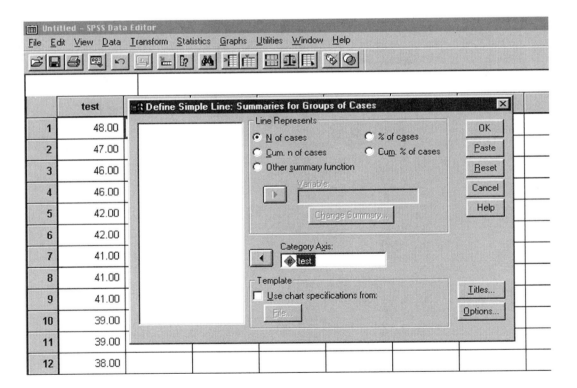

4. Click OK and the graph should appear in the output Viewer window.

5. To approximate a histogram for part **b,** click Graphs>Bar>Simple>Summaries for groups of cases> Define.
6. Move **test** into the Category Axis box and be sure "N of cases" is indicated. The dialog box should appear as shown in step 3 except that the box is labeled as Define Simple Bar rather than Define Simple Line.
7. Click OK and the graph appears in the output Viewer window.
8. To construct a cumulative frequency curve for part **c,** repeat steps 2–4 except choose "Cum. N of cases" rather than "N of cases" in the Line Represents box.
9. To construct a cumulative percentage curve for part **d,** repeat steps 2–4 except choose "Cum. % of cases."

Note that SPSS does not graph values with 0 frequency. For example, in the first graph in which we used an SPSS line graph to approximate the frequency polygon, you can see that the horizontal axis does not show the score of 31 and the line does not drop back to the X axis to indicate a frequency of 0 for that score. The same is true of the other graphs, and this is one way that SPSS approximates the graphs as we defined them in the text.

The output showing the four graphs for Problem 1 should appear as follows. (Again, note that SPSS does not plot scores with a frequency of zero.)

```
GRAPH
  /LINE(SIMPLE)=COUNT BY test
  /MISSING=REPORT.
```

Graph

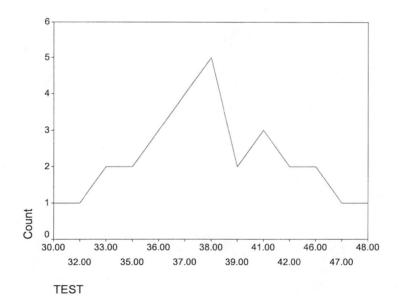

```
GRAPH
  /BAR(SIMPLE)=COUNT BY test
  /MISSING=REPORT.
```

Graph

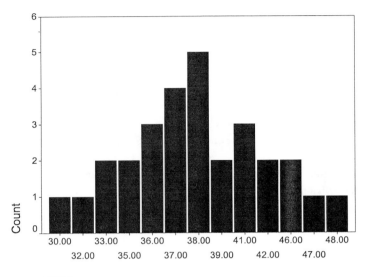

```
GRAPH
  /LINE(SIMPLE)=CUFREQ BY test
  /MISSING=REPORT.
```

Graph

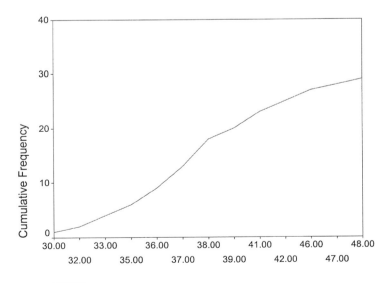

```
GRAPH
  /LINE(SIMPLE)=CUPCT BY test
  /MISSING=REPORT.
```

Graph

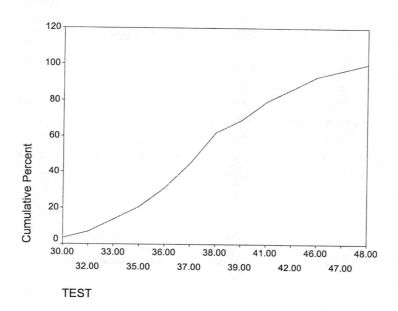

Exercises Using SPSS

1. Create a line graph using the data in Problem 2. Because of the way the data are provided, we have some special instructions for you to use to "trick" SPSS into giving the graph we want you to produce. Enter the data as a separate variable for **day** and as another separate variable for the frequency that you should call **freqcig.** The steps are as follows:

   a. Click Graphs>Line>Simple>Values of individual cases>Define.
   b. In the Define Simple Line dialog box, **freqcig** should be in the Line Represents box and **day** should be in the Category Labels Variable box.
   c. Click OK and the graph should appear in the output Viewer window.

2. Create a stem-and-leaf plot of the speeds of cars given in Problem 8. Again, we need to provide some special instructions for where to look for the stem-and-leaf plot in SPSS. The instructions are as follows:

   a. Start SPSS, enter the data, and name the variable **speeds.**
   b. The stem-and-leaf plot is a plot option under the Explore procedure. Click as follows:

   Statistics>Summarize>Explore.

   In the Explore dialog box, move **speeds** to the Dependent List and click Plots in the Display box (lower left).

Click Plots (lower right) to open the Explore: Plots dialog box. Be sure "stem-and-leaf" is checked and None is checked under Boxplots (it won't hurt if you leave it), then click Continue.

In the Explore dialog box, click OK and the output should appear.

CHECKING YOUR PROGRESS: A SELF-TEST

1. According to a graphing convention, which of the following is true?
   a. The X axis should be three fourths of the Y axis.
   b. The Y axis should be three fourths of the X axis.
   c. The two axes should be approximately equal.
   d. None of the above; there is no convention about the relative length of the axes.
2. True or False: Positively skewed curves have a tail toward the upper end of the X axis.
3. A histogram used to plot nominal scale data is called a
   a. line graph.
   b. stem-and-leaf plot.
   c. bar graph.
   d. frequency polygon.
4. The following are scores on a test in statistics. Make a stem-and-leaf plot.

66	88	89
86	91	88
76	89	76
74	55	95
93	54	80
80	90	29
65	92	69
86	92	84

5. The latency for rats to leave a lighted platform was timed on four trials. Their average latency in seconds over the four trials was as follows: Trial 1, 10.5; Trial 2, 4.6; Trial 3, 3.8; Trial 4, 4.1. Graph the data.

6. A marketing student tabulates all the cars that pass through an intersection according to country of manufacture. The data are as follows: United States, 43; Japan, 27; Germany, 10; Sweden, 3; Korea, 6; unknown, 4. Graph the data.

7. On the final exam in a typing class, students were required to type as many words as possible in a 1-minute test.

   a. Using the following frequency distribution, make a frequency polygon.

   b. Plot a cumulative percentage curve and use it to show about what percentage typed 65 or fewer words per minute.

X	f
75	1
74	1
73	2
72	2
70	3
69	2
68	4
65	4
64	3
63	2
62	2
57	1
55	1

CHAPTER 5

MEASURES OF
CENTRAL TENDENCY

OBJECTIVES

The main objective in Chapter 5 is to define, discuss, and detail methods for determining the three most frequently encountered measures of central tendency: the mean, the median, and the mode. Another objective is to describe the properties and the advantages and disadvantages of each measure.

CHAPTER REVIEW

Central tendency is the trend for scores in a distribution to be concentrated near the middle of the distribution. The measures of central tendency discussed in the chapter are the mean, the median, and the mode.

The *mode* is the most frequently occurring score in a frequency distribution. The mode is abbreviated *Mo;* a distribution with two modes is called *bimodal,* and both values are reported.

The *median (Md)* is a point along the score scale separating the top 50% of the scores from the bottom 50%. The median is the score value at the 50th percentile, with *percentile* defined as the score at or below which a given percentage of the scores lie. The procedure detailed for finding the median is the counting method.

The counting method is used for locating the median in a frequency distribution or in a simple array of scores ranked from highest to lowest. First, the total N is considered. If N is odd, the median is the score in the middle. For example, if there are 9 scores, the median will be the 5th score because there are 4 scores below it and 4 scores above it. If the total N is even, the median will be halfway between the two scores in the middle. Thus, if there are 10 scores, the median will be halfway between the 5th and 6th scores because there are 4 scores below the 5th and 4 scores above the 6th.

The *mean* ($\overline{X}$ for a sample, μ for a population) or arithmetic average is the sum of the scores divided by the number of scores. The mean is often called the balancing point in the distribution because if we sum algebraically all of the positive and negative deviations about the mean, the result is zero; that is, the positive and negative differences about the mean are in balance.

Four rounding rules are given in the chapter: (1) Round everything to hundredths; (2) if possible, round only the final answer; (3) in all preliminary calculations leading up to the final answer, maintain at least three decimal places; (4) if the digit in the thousandths place is less than 5, drop it and everything that follows it; (5) if the number in the thousandths place is 5 or more, round the preceding digit up.

The *mode* is the best measure in three instances: (1) when you need the quickest estimate of central tendency, (2) when you want to report the most frequently occurring score, or (3) when you have nominal scale data. The *median* is preferred when (1) you have a small, badly skewed distribution, or (2) there are missing or arbitrarily determined scores. The *mean* is the most useful of the measures of central tendency because many important statistical procedures depend on it. Also, the mean is the most stable of the measures from sample to sample. The sample mean is an unbiased estimate of the population mean.

In a symmetrical, unimodal distribution, the mean, median, and mode all have the same value. The mean is pulled in the direction of the tail in a skewed distribution, and the median will be between the mean and the mode.

SYMBOLS

Symbol	Stands For
Mo	mode
Md	median
$\overline{X}$	sample mean
Σ	capital sigma, indicates to sum the following values
$X - \overline{X}$	deviation of a score from the mean
μ	population mean, read "mu"

FORMULAS

Formulas 5-1 and **5-2**. *Equations for computing the sample mean*

$$\overline{X} \quad (\text{read ``ex-bar''}) = \frac{\Sigma X}{N} \quad \text{or} \quad \frac{\Sigma fX}{N}$$

Formula 5-1 tells you to add all the Xs or scores and then to divide the result by the total number of scores (N). In a frequency distribution, N is the sum of frequencies. Formula 5-2 tells you to multiply each score by its frequency before summing and dividing by N.

TERMS TO DEFINE AND/OR IDENTIFY

Central tendency

Mode

Bimodal

Multimodal

Median

Percentile

Mean

Deviations

Unbiased estimate

FILL-IN-THE-BLANK ITEMS

Introduction

Measures of central tendency are values near the (1) _____ of the distribution. The measures discussed in the chapter are the (2) _____ , the (3) _____ , and the

(4) _____ .

The Mode

The most frequently occurring score is called the (5) _____ , symbolized by

(6) _____ . The mode is the (7) _____ stable of the measures of

central tendency. A distribution with two modes is called (8) _____ , and both
values are reported.

The Median

The median is the score value at the (9) _____ percentile. A (10) _____ is the score at or below which a given percentage of the scores lie.

Locating the median by the counting method: Even number of scores

In a frequency distribution with an even number of scores, the median will be halfway between the

(11) _____ score and the (12) _____ score.

Locating the median by the counting method: Odd number of scores

If there is an odd number of scores, the median will be the (13) _____ score.

The Mean, or Arithmetic Average

The mean or arithmetic average is the sum of the (14) _____ divided by the

(15) _____ of scores in a distribution. In a frequency distribution, the

(16) _____ must be taken into account when the mean is determined. The symbol for the mean of a sample is (17) _____ , whereas the symbol for the corresponding population parameter is (18) _____ .

Rounding conventions

Rounding rules are as follows:

1. Round your final answer to (19) _____ .

2. If possible, round only the (20) _____ answer.
3. In all preliminary calculations leading up to the final answer, maintain at least

    (21) _____ decimal places.

4. If the digit in the thousandths place is less than 5, (22) _____ it and everything that follows it.

5. If the digit in the thousandths place is 5 or more, round the preceding digit (23) _____ .

The mean as a balancing point

The mean is called the (24) _____ point in the distribution because the sum of the deviations about it is equal to (25) _____ .

Comparing Measures of Central Tendency

The (26) _____ is useful for summarizing nominal scale data and for obtaining a rough estimate of the mean and the median. The (27) _____ is the best measure of central tendency when a distribution is badly skewed or when there are (28) _____ scores.

The mean is the most useful of the measures because most other (29) _____ procedures are based on it. Also, it is the most (30) _____ of the measures from sample to sample. Because the mean shows no systematic tendencies in relation to the population mean, it is called an (31) _____ estimate of μ.

Positions of Measures of Central Tendency on a Frequency Polygon

In a unimodal, symmetrical distribution, the mean, median, and mode will all be the (32) _____ . In skewed distributions, the (33) _____ is most affected and is pulled in the direction of the (34) _____ . The median will be between the (35) _____ and the mean in a skewed distribution.

Troubleshooting Your Computations

The most important thing to remember in locating the measures of central tendency is that your answer should be a value near the (36) _____ of the distribution. Also, if you are trying to find the mean in a frequency distribution, you must remember to take the (37) _____ into account.

To help prevent computational errors, you should perform all computations (38) _____ , being sure you get the same answer each time.

PROBLEMS

1. For the following distributions, try to give the three measures of central tendency without computing them. After you have done this, compute $\overline{X}$ for each distribution.
   a. 6, 10, 10, 14
   b. 7, 8, 9
   c. 1, 2, 3, 3, 4, 5

d.

X	f
20	1
18	2
16	4
14	2
12	1

2. Using the following distribution, find each of the three measures of central tendency. Show that the mean is the balancing point in the distribution—that is, $\Sigma f(X - \overline{X}) = 0$.

X	f
10	1
9	2
8	1
7	4
6	6
5	5
4	2
3	1
2	1

3. A neuroticism scale consisting of 10 items has been given to 50 individuals; higher scores mean greater neuroticism. The frequency distribution of their scores is as follows:

X	f
10	4
9	4
8	5
7	7
6	8
5	7
4	5
3	4
2	4
1	2

Find the mean, median, and mode of the scores.

4. A recall test of retention has been given after 25 students have studied briefly a list of 15 nouns. Determine the mean, median, and mode of the results.

X	f
6	2
5	0
4	6
3	5
2	8
1	3
0	1

5. The following data were obtained for 25 students given a recognition test of retention of 15 previously studied nouns. Find the median, mode, and mean.

X	f
15	7
14	6
13	4
12	2
10	3
8	1
6	2

6. ACT scores have been determined for 26 students in an honors introductory psychology class and are shown in the following frequency distribution. Compute the mean, the median, and the mode.

X	f
33	1
31	1
30	3
29	4
28	4
27	8
26	2
25	2
24	1
	$N = \overline{26}$

7. In a study of 15 rats, the latency to enter a darkened chamber has been recorded. If the animal didn't enter within 60 seconds, the trial was terminated and the animal received a score of 60. Determine the most appropriate measure of central tendency.

X	f
60	2
45	2
43	1
42	1
35	2
33	3
32	1
25	1
20	1
10	1

Omitting the nonresponders, determine all three measures of central tendency.

8. Using the rules for rounding, round each of the following. For each of your answers, cite the applicable rule.

    a. 1.4549 to hundredths

    b. 1.5551 to hundredths

    c. 3.66666 to hundredths

    d. 23.33333 to hundredths

    e. 7.825137 to hundredths

USING SPSS—EXAMPLE AND EXERCISE

From now on, we will assume that you have read Appendix 4 on using SPSS.

SPSS has several procedures that can provide measures of central tendency and dispersion. For example, Frequencies, Descriptives, or Explore could be used.

Example: We will use SPSS to obtain the three measures of central tendency (mean, median, and mode) using the data in Problem 6. The steps are as follows:

1. Start SPSS, enter the data, and name the variable **act.**
2. We will use Frequencies to obtain a frequency distribution and descriptive statistics.
3. Click Statistics>Summarize>Frequencies.
4. Move **act** into the Variables box.
5. Click the Statistics box to open the Frequencies: Statistics dialog box. There click Mean, Median, Mode under Central Tendency, and then click Continue>OK.
6. The statistics and a frequency distribution should appear in the output Viewer window. The output showing the descriptive statistics and frequency distribution for Problem 6 should appear as follows:

```
FORMATS ACT (F8.2).
FREQUENCIES
  VARIABLES=act
  /STATISTICS=MEAN MEDIAN MODE
  /ORDER   ANALYSIS .
```

Frequencies

Statistics

ACT

N	Valid	26
	Missing	0
Mean		27.8462
Median		27.5000
Mode		27.00

ACT

		Frequency	Percent	Valid Percent	Cumulative Percent
Valid	24.00	1	3.8	3.8	3.8
	25.00	2	7.7	7.7	11.5
	26.00	2	7.7	7.7	19.2
	27.00	8	30.8	30.8	50.0
	28.00	4	15.4	15.4	65.4
	29.00	4	15.4	15.4	80.8
	30.00	3	11.5	11.5	92.3
	31.00	1	3.8	3.8	96.2
	33.00	1	3.8	3.8	100.0
	Total	26	100.0	100.0	

Exercise Using SPSS

1. Using the data in Problem 3, use SPSS to obtain the mean, median, and mode of the scores.

CHECKING YOUR PROGRESS: A SELF-TEST

1. Match the following:
    _____ the measure used with nominal data
    _____ the most frequently occurring score in a distribution
    _____ the arithmetic average
    _____ the least stable measure of central tendency
    _____ the preferred measure of central tendency in a badly skewed distribution
    _____ the score at the 50th percentile
    _____ the measure of central tendency most affected by extreme scores
    _____ the sum of the deviations about it is zero
    a. mode   **b.** median   **c.** mean

2. Give all three measures of central tendency for the following distribution of golf scores after the final round of a tournament. Each score tells how a golfer finished relative to par; for example, a score of -4 means the golfer was 4 strokes under par.

X	f		X	f
-14	1		0	4
-12	1		$+1$	3
-11	2		$+2$	1
-10	3		$+3$	4
-8	3		$+4$	3
-7	2		$+5$	1
-6	2		$+6$	3
-5	1		$+7$	2
-4	3		$+8$	1
-1	5		$+17$	1

3. Find the mean, median, and mode for the following distribution of IQ scores.

X	f
147	2
142	3
137	4
132	6
127	5
122	8
117	4
112	3
107	2
102	2

CHAPTER 6

MEASURES OF DISPERSION AND STANDARD SCORES

OBJECTIVES

The main objective in Chapter 6 is to define and discuss the use of several measures of the spread or dispersion of some data. The measures of dispersion covered in the chapter are the range, the average deviation, the variance, and the standard deviation. Computational procedures are detailed for each of the measures. Standard scores or z scores are also defined, and their computation is discussed.

CHAPTER REVIEW

Several statistics are introduced in this chapter to measure the spread or dispersion of the scores around the mean in a distribution. The measures discussed are the range, the average deviation, the variance, and the standard deviation.

The *range* (R) is the difference between the highest and lowest scores in a distribution. It is useful in a descriptive sense because it is determined so easily. The major problem with the range is that it is based on the two extreme scores in the distribution. If the extremes are not representative of the distribution, the range will be unrepresentative as well.

The *average deviation* (AD) is the average of the deviations from the mean of the distribution of each score in the distribution. It is computed by dividing the sum of the absolute value of the deviations by the number of deviations. The absolute value of the deviations is used to prevent the sum of the deviations from always being zero, because of the property of the mean as the balancing point in the distribution that we discussed in Chapter 5. AD is introduced as a prelude to the variance and the standard deviation.

The *variance* is the average of the squared deviations. Population variance is symbolized by σ^2, and sample variance is symbolized by s^2. The numerator of the equation for the variance is sometimes called the sum of squares or *SS*. The sample variance (s^2) is an unbiased estimate of σ^2.

The *standard deviation* is the square root of the variance or the square root of the average squared deviation. Symbols for the population standard deviation and the sample standard deviation are σ and s, respectively. The standard deviation can be visualized as another unit of measurement on the baseline of a frequency polygon. A useful approximation of s can be found by dividing the range by 4.

A *standard score* or z score is the deviation of a raw score from the mean in standard deviation units. The sign of the z score tells the direction of the score relative to the mean: Negative z scores represent raw scores below the mean, and positive z scores indicate scores above the mean.

SYMBOLS

Symbol	Stands For
AD	average deviation
R	range
σ^2	population variance
s^2	sample variance
σ	population standard deviation
s	sample standard deviation
s_{approx}	an approximation of s; $s_{approx} = \dfrac{R}{4}$
SS	sum of squares or the numerator of variance
z	standard score or z score

FORMULAS

Formula 6-1. *Formula for calculating the range*

$$R \text{ (range)} = HS - LS$$

Formula 6-3. *Formula for computing AD from a frequency distribution*

$$AD = \frac{\Sigma f |X - \overline{X}|}{N}$$

To find *AD*, the first step is to subtract the mean from each score. Next, multiply the absolute values of the differences by their frequencies and sum the results. Finally, divide the numerator by N to find the average deviation.

Formula 6-8. *Computational formula for s^2, the sample variance*

$$s^2 = \frac{\Sigma X^2 - \dfrac{(\Sigma X)^2}{N}}{N - 1}$$

Formula 6-9. *Computational formula for s^2, the sample variance, for a frequency distribution*

$$s^2 = \frac{\sum fX^2 - \frac{(\sum fX)^2}{N}}{N - 1}$$

The numerator is the computational form of the sum of squares. To get it, sum the squared scores and subtract from this value the sum of the scores squared divided by sample size. Then divide the whole thing by $N - 1$.

Formula 6-14. *Computational formula for sample standard deviation*

$$s = \sqrt{\frac{\sum X^2 - \frac{(\sum X)^2}{N}}{N - 1}}$$

Formula 6-15. *Computational formula for sample standard deviation for a frequency distribution*

$$s = \sqrt{\frac{\sum fX^2 - \frac{(\sum fX)^2}{N}}{N - 1}}$$

s is simply the square root of the formula for sample variance.

Formula 6-17. *Formula for finding a z score from a raw score using sample statistics*

$$z = \frac{X - \overline{X}}{s}$$

Formula 6-19. *Formula for finding a raw score from a z score using sample statistics*

$$X = zs + \overline{X}$$

Formula 6-19 is obtained by solving Formula 6-17 for X.

TERMS TO DEFINE AND/OR IDENTIFY

Dispersion

Range

Average deviation

Absolute value of a score

Variance

Standard deviation

Sum of squares

Standard score

z score

FILL-IN-THE-BLANK ITEMS

Introduction

To describe a frequency distribution, we need to know a measure of the (1) _____ of the data in addition to measures of central tendency. Four measures discussed in this chapter are the

range, the average deviation, the (2) _____ , and the (3) _____

_____ .

The Range

The (4) _____ is the difference between the highest score in the distribution and the lowest score. The range is easy to determine but not very useful for further statistical procedures.

The Average Deviation

The average deviation, symbolized by (5) _____ , is useful as a prelude to the most

commonly used measures of dispersion, the (6) _____ and the standard deviation. In order to keep from obtaining zero each time the deviations around the sample mean are summed, we take

the (7) _____ _____ of the deviations before summing.

The Variance and the Standard Deviation

The (8) _____ is the average of the squared deviations, and the square root of the average

is called the (9) _____ _____ . The statistic based directly on the formula for the

population variance is a (10) _____ estimate of the population variance. To compensate for SD^2's tendency to (11) _____ the population variance, we have to modify the formula

slightly, which we did by dividing the numerator by (12) _____ rather than by N. Standard

deviation is the (13) _____ _____ of the variance.

   In addition to defining formulas, (14) _____ or raw-score formulas are introduced.

Raw-score formulas require fewer (15) _____ than the defining formulas and are easier
to use when computed with a pocket calculator.

   s can be visualized as a width measure on the (16) _____ of a frequency polygon. A

useful way to estimate the standard deviation is to divide the (17) _____ by (18) _____.

The numerator of variance is sometimes called the (19) _____ _____ _____, which is

the sum of the squared deviations about the (20) _____. It is symbolized by (21) _____.

Standard Scores (z Scores)

Values on the standard deviation scale are called either (22) _____ scores or (23) _____

scores. A (24) _____ is the deviation of a raw score from the mean in standard deviation

units. The (25) _____ of the z score tells us the direction of the score relative to the mean.

A (26) _____ z score indicates a raw score below the mean. To convert a z score back to a

raw score, multiply it by the standard deviation and add the (27) _____.

Troubleshooting Your Computations

In computing any of the measures discussed in the chapter, it is desirable to have a

(28) _____ for a correct answer. For example, if the distribution is large and

symmetrical, s should be approximately (29) _____ of the range. You must always

get (30) _____ numbers for the standard deviation and the variance. When com-

puting s, don't forget to take the (31) _____ _____.

PROBLEMS

1. Markus says that the AD of the following test scores is 2.5, but Karl says it is 1.45. Who is correct? What are R, s_{approx}, s^2, and s?

X	f
25	1
24	2
22	3
21	4
20	4
19	2
18	1

2. In a logic course, 23 students are given 10 word-analogy problems to solve in 5 minutes. The number of problems correctly solved is recorded for each student. The data are as follows:

X	f
10	1
9	2
8	1
7	4
6	6
5	5
4	2
3	1
2	1

a. Find R, s_{approx}, s^2, and s.

b. Plot a frequency polygon of the data and lay off the value of s on it. To simplify your graph, round s and $\overline{X}$ to the nearest whole numbers.

3. Scores on an experimental psychology test were as follows:

X	f
100	1
96	1
92	3
84	2
83	1
80	2
79	1
76	1
63	1
35	1

Find R, s_{approx}, s^2, and s. What is the z score for a raw score of 96? What score is 2 standard deviation units below the mean?

4. Using the following frequency distribution, demonstrate that $(\Sigma fX)^2$ is not equivalent to ΣfX^2. Compute R, s_{approx}, s^2, and s.

X	f
5	1
4	2
3	3
2	3
1	2

5. There are two applicants for the job as test pilot for experimental jet aircraft. Both applicants are given a reaction-time test and are found to have the same average times. Which applicant should get the job if consistency of reaction is an important criterion?

Applicant A		Applicant B	
X	f	X	f
1.04	1	1.04	1
1.03	1	0.85	1
0.95	2	0.84	2
0.88	1	0.80	2
0.85	2	0.77	3
0.78	2	0.75	3
0.74	1	0.74	2
0.70	1	0.72	1
0.65	3	0.70	2
0.60	4	0.57	1
0.55	2	0.55	2

6. Participants in an employee training program are tested after 1 week. By company policy, employees who score 1 standard deviation or more below the mean are required to take another week of training. Which employees must receive more training, and which are released from the program?

X	f
92	1
91	1
88	3
87	3
81	4
79	5
77	5
76	3
71	3
69	2
53	1
51	2
47	1
44	1
39	1

7. Using the following data, find s^2. Determine s and plot it on the baseline of a frequency polygon. For ease in plotting, round the mean and standard deviation to the nearest whole numbers.

X	f
28	1
27	1
26	3
25	5
24	5
23	2
22	1
21	1
20	1

8. Assuming a mean of 2.57 with a standard deviation of 0.83, answer the following questions:

a. What is the z score for a raw score of 3.75?

b. What is the z score for a raw score of 2.10?

c. How far from the mean in standard deviation units is a score of 1.3?

d. What score lies 1.75 standard deviation units above the mean?

e. What score lies 2.17 standard deviation units below the mean?

USING SPSS—EXAMPLES AND EXERCISES

SPSS has several procedures that can provide measures of central tendency and dispersion. For example, Frequencies, Descriptives, or Explore can be used. Using a Compute statement, z scores can be calculated, or they can be obtained "automatically" as an option under the Descriptives procedure.

Example: We will use SPSS to obtain the three measures of central tendency (mean, median, and mode), measures of dispersion (range, variance, and standard deviation), and z scores for all test scores using the data in Problem 6. The steps are as follows:

1. Start SPSS, enter the data, and name the variable **test.**
2. We will use Frequencies to obtain the measures of central tendency and dispersion.
3. Go to Statistics>Summarize>Frequencies.
4. Move **test** to the Variables box; uncheck "display frequency table" so the frequency distribution will not be calculated.
5. Click Statistics, select the measures of central tendency and dispersion that you want, and then click Continue>OK. This will give the descriptive statistics in the output Viewer window.
6. Next we will compute z scores using the Compute procedure. To do this we need to know the mean (symbolized by $M = 74.3333$ rather than $\overline{X} = 74.3333$, as we symbolized it in the text) and standard deviation ($s = 13.6403$) from the output. The formula for any z score is $z = (X - M)/s$ or $z = (X - 74.3333)/13.6403$. We will now put this formula in the Compute box.
7. From the Data Editor window, click Transform>Compute. Then enter "testz" in the Target variable box.
8. In the Numeric Expression box, move **test** in and use the keypad or type and edit so the expression appears as follows: (**test** − 74.3333)/13.6403.
9. Click OK. Check the Data Editor window and find the computed z scores.

Example: Repeat SPSS for the previous example using the Descriptives procedure. Although you will not be able to obtain the median and mode from this procedure, z scores can be computed automatically.

10. Click Statistics>Summarize>Descriptives, move **test** into the Variables box, and click "Save standardized values as variables." This causes the z scores to be computed.
11. Click Options and select the desired descriptive statistics that are available, then click Continue>OK.
12. The output Viewer shows the descriptive statistics. The Data Editor should show another variable **ztest** showing the z scores again, differing only in the number of decimal places displayed.

```
FREQUENCIES
  VARIABLES=test  /FORMAT=NOTABLE
  /STATISTICS=STDDEV VARIANCE RANGE MEAN MEDIAN MODE
  /ORDER  ANALYSIS .
```

Frequencies

Statistics

TEST

N	Valid	36
	Missing	0
Mean		74.3333
Median		77.0000
Mode		77.00[a]
Std. Deviation		13.6403
Variance		186.0571
Range		53.00

a. Multiple modes exist. The smallest value is shown

```
COMPUTE testz = (test-74.3333)/13.6403 .
EXECUTE .
```

	test	testz
1	92.00	1.30
2	91.00	1.22
3	88.00	1.00
4	88.00	1.00
5	88.00	1.00
6	87.00	.93
7	87.00	.93
8	87.00	.93
9	81.00	.49
10	81.00	.49
11	81.00	.49
12	81.00	.49
13	79.00	.34
14	79.00	.34
15	79.00	.34
16	79.00	.34
17	79.00	.34
18	77.00	.20
19	77.00	.20
20	77.00	.20

SPSS Data Editor window showing z scores obtained using the Compute statement (first 20 cases).

```
DESCRIPTIVES
  VARIABLES=test  /SAVE
  /STATISTICS=MEAN STDDEV VARIANCE RANGE MIN MAX .
```

Descriptives

Descriptive Statistics

	N	Range	Minimum	Maximum	Mean	Std. Deviation	Variance
TEST	36	53.00	39.00	92.00	74.3333	13.6403	186.057
Valid N (listwise)	36						

SPSS Data Editor window showing z scores computed using the Compute statement and using the z-score output option for the Descriptives procedure.

	test	testz	ztest
1	92.00	1.30	1.29518
2	91.00	1.22	1.22187
3	88.00	1.00	1.00193
4	88.00	1.00	1.00193
5	88.00	1.00	1.00193
6	87.00	.93	.92862
7	87.00	.93	.92862
8	87.00	.93	.92862
9	81.00	.49	.48875
10	81.00	.49	.48875
11	81.00	.49	.48875
12	81.00	.49	.48875
13	79.00	.34	.34212
14	79.00	.34	.34212
15	79.00	.34	.34212
16	79.00	.34	.34212
17	79.00	.34	.34212
18	77.00	.20	.19550
19	77.00	.20	.19550
20	77.00	.20	.19550

Exercises Using SPSS

1. Using the data from Problem 2, use the SPSS Descriptives procedure to obtain the mean, standard deviation, variance, and z scores for each score.
2. Using the same data and the necessary statistics from the previous exercise, employ the SPSS Compute procedure to calculate z scores again for each score. Use **correctz** as the target variable name.

CHECKING YOUR PROGRESS: A SELF-TEST

1. Match the following:

_____ z	**a.** symbol for the population standard deviation
_____ s	**b.** average amount that each score in a distribution deviates from the distribution's mean
_____ s^2	**c.** symbol for a standard score
_____ σ^2	**d.** symbol for population variance
_____ AD	**e.** numerator of the equation for variance
_____ SS	**f.** symbol for sample variance
_____ R	**g.** symbol for sample standard deviation
	h. symbol for the range of a set of scores

2. What does the size of a z score indicate?

3. What does the sign of a z score indicate?

4. Family size was surveyed in a large sociology class, and the results were as follows:

X	f
13	1
10	1
7	4
6	6
5	12
4	26
3	12
2	8

a. Find R, s^2, and s.

b. What is the z score for 6? 3?

c. What score is 1.5 standard deviation units above the mean? What score is 2 standard deviation units below the mean?

CHAPTER 7

PROBABILITY

OBJECTIVES

The main objective in Chapter 7 is to define and discuss intuitively what probability means in our everyday lives and elementary probability theory. This discussion is followed by a brief look at Bayesian statistics and a simple theoretical probability distribution—the binomial.

CHAPTER REVIEW

Probability theory is the key to testing statistical hypotheses. *Statistical hypotheses* are assumptions about populations based on sample results. Probability theory enables us to determine the amount of certainty we have in the conclusions we draw from our sample results.

The *probability* of an event is defined as the proportion of times an event would occur if the chances for occurrence were infinite. Another way to say this is that the probability of an event is the ratio of the number of ways the event can occur to the number of ways any event can occur. Although we constantly assess probabilities in our daily lives, there are times when our intuitive ideas about probability are incorrect. For example, the *gambler's fallacy* is the mistaken belief that the probability of a particular event changes with a long string of the same event. We often say that a team that has lost many times in a row is due to win, as though the string of losses had changed the probability of the team's winning.

To you as an individual, probability means probability, not certainty. Probabilities should be considered patterns or tendencies, not guarantees about what will happen to you personally. Theoretical probability, on the other hand, is the way events are supposed to work in terms of formal probability theory. Real-world, or empirical, probability is based on experience, whereas subjective probability is our personal probability, formed on the basis of our own perspective on the world. Bayesian statistics uses subjective probability as a starting point for assessing a subsequent probability. The Bayesian approach to making statistical inferences involves the use of these subjective, prior probabilities, which makes this approach controversial.

The *addition rule* states that for independent events the probability of either one event or another is equal to the sum of the probabilities of the individual events. The multiplication rule determines the probability of a series of events. The *multiplication rule* states that the probability of two or more independent events occurring on separate occasions is the product of their individual probabilities. *Conditional probability* is the probability of an event given that another event has already occurred. The multiplication rule can be modified to determine the probability of nonindependent events.

The binomial distribution—a simple theoretical probability distribution—is based on events for which there are only two possible outcomes on each occurrence of the event. Coin-flipping examples are often used to illustrate the construction of a binomial distribution. Two important features of the binomial are that when $p = .5$, the distribution is symmetrical, and as the number of trials increase, the binomial more and more closely approximates the normal probability distribution.

SYMBOLS

Symbol	Stands For
$p(A)$	probability of event A
$p(A \text{ or } B)$	probability of event A or event B
$p(A, B)$	probability of both A and B
$p(B|A)$	probability of event B given that event A has occurred

FORMULAS

Formula 7-1. *Equation for the addition rule of probability*

$$p(A \text{ or } B) = p(A) + p(B)$$

$p(A \text{ or } B)$ means the probability of either event A *or* event B, and it is equal to the probability of event A $[p(A)]$ plus the probability of event B $[p(B)]$.

Formula 7-2. *Equation for the multiplication rule of probability*

$$p(A, B) = p(A) \times p(B)$$

$p(A, B)$ is the probability of occurrence of both event A *and* event B, which is equal to the product of their individual probabilities. This equation is used when events A and B are independent.

Formula 7-3. *Equation for determining the probability of a sequence of nonindependent events*

$$p(A, B) = p(A) \times p(B|A)$$

When events A and B are not independent—that is, when the probability of B depends on whether A has occurred—then the multiplication rule must be modified as shown. $p(B|A)$ reads "probability of B given A."

TERMS TO DEFINE AND/OR IDENTIFY

Statistical hypotheses

Gambler's fallacy

Probability

Theoretical probability

Real-world probability

Personal (subjective) probability

Bayesian statistics

Addition rule of probability

Multiplication rule of probability

Independent events

Nonindependent events

Conditional probability

Binomial distribution

FILL-IN-THE-BLANK ITEMS

Introduction

(1) _____ _____ are guesses about populations based on sample results.

Although we can never be certain that our guesses are correct, (2) _____ theory will help us determine the degree of certainty we have in our conclusions. The essence of inferential

statistics is in using sample (3) _____ to attach a probability to the estimates of

(4) _____ parameters.

Thinking About Probability

One intuitive idea about probability is called (5) _____ _____, the mistaken belief that the probability of an event changes with a long string of the event. Formally,

(6) _____ is defined as the proportion of times an event would occur if the chances for occurrence were infinite. In other words, the probability of an event is equal to the number of times

the event can occur divided by the number of ways (7) _____ event can occur.

Probability and the individual

In terms of what will happen to you personally, probabilities should be considered long-run

(8) _____, and not (9) _____.

Theoretical probability; Real-world probability

(10) _____ probability is the way events are supposed to work in terms of formal probability theory. Probabilities based on past behavior and counting are called real-world, or

(11) _____ probabilities, and these are the basis for many assessments of chance

that affect our lives. This type of probability is sometimes called (12) _____

_____ probability because the occurrence of events has been tallied relative to the number of opportunities for the event to occur.

Subjective probability

Probabilities based on our own perspectives are called (13) _____ or

(14) _____ probabilities. Such probabilities are used in an area called

(15) _____ statistics. The classical approach to (16) _____ tells us to make our decision about our experiment's outcome on the basis of the data, without making any

prior assumptions. The (17) _____ approach, on the other hand, would have us use the data from our experiment to adjust our prior beliefs. The weak point of this approach is that prior probabili-

ties may be (18) _____ , and experimenters could reach different (19) _____ from the same data if they started with different prior beliefs.

Rules of Probability

The addition rule

For mutually exclusive, random events, the probability of either one event or another event is the

(20) _____ of the probabilities of the individual events. This is called the (21) _____

rule of probability. The formula for the rule is as follows: $p(A \text{ or } B) = $ (22) _____ .

The multiplication rule

The (23) _____ rule states that the probability of two or more independent events occur-ring on separate occasions is the product of their individual probabilities. The rule is shown symbolically as

follows: (24) _____ = _____ .

Events are (25) _____ if the occurrence of one event does not alter the probability of

any other event. (26) _____ _____ is the probability of an event given that an-

other event has already occurred, expressed symbolically by (27) _____ . The multiplica-tion rule for independent events can be modified to include nonindependent events. Thus, the probability for events A and B, where the probability of B depends on A, is found with this formula: $p(A, B) = $

(28) _____ .

More on conditional probabilities

(29) _____ probability can help us assess probabilities of events in our world by provid-ing a way to add information to probabilities we already know. On an intuitive level, if $p(B \mid A) = p(B)$,

then the occurrence or nonoccurrence of (30) _____ has nothing to do with the occurrence of

(31) _____ .

Bayesian statistics

Thomas Bayes initiated using (32) _____ to help establish a mathematical basis for statistical inference. The Bayesian approach to probability and statistics is (33) _____ , and it has not been widely adopted.

The Binomial Probability Distribution

The binomial distribution is based on events for which there are only (34) _____ possible outcomes on each occurrence. Two important features of the binomial distribution are that (a) when $p = .5$, the

distribution is (35) _____ , and, as N (the number of trials) increases in value, the distri-

bution more closely approximates the (36) _____ _____ _____ .

PROBLEMS

1. You've flipped a coin 9 times, and it has come up heads each time. There's no reason to believe the coin is biased. Do you think it's more or less likely that the next flip will produce another head? What is the probability of another head on the 10th flip?

2. Suppose you draw a single card from a standard 52-card deck. What is the probability of drawing the following cards?

   a. the ace of hearts

   b. an ace

   c. a face card (jack through ace)

   d. a heart

   e. a card that is not a heart

3. In a sock drawer, there are 6 brown socks, 12 blue socks, 4 red socks, and 8 green socks randomly mixed together. With your eyes shut, you take a single sock from the drawer. What is the probability of getting the following socks?

   a. a brown sock

   b. a blue sock

   c. a yellow sock

   d. a sock that is not red

   e. a red or a green sock

   f. a sock that is neither blue nor green

4. Suppose you answer a single question on a true–false test purely by chance.

   a. What is the probability that you will miss it?

   b. What is the probability that you'll get it right?

5. Suppose you have a multiple-choice question with four choices.

   a. What is the probability of guessing correctly?

b. What is the probability of an incorrect guess?

c. In terms of probability, which is easier, a multiple-choice question or a true–false question?

6. A slot machine has three identical reels with 10 different symbols on each reel. You pull the lever, and the reels spin independently until they stop. Assuming the symbols include stars, whistles, and clowns, what is the probability of getting the following?

a. three stars

b. two stars and a whistle

c. a star, a whistle, and a clown

d. the same three of any of the 10 symbols.

7. A box contains six pieces of currency: three $1 bills, two $5 bills, and one $20 bill. You can remove only one bill at a time. On two successive draws, *with* replacement, what is the probability of getting the following?

a. the $20 bill twice

b. two $1 bills

c. two $5 bills

d. a $1 bill and the $20 bill, in that order

e. $21 for the sum of the two bills

f. $6 for the sum of the two bills

8. Consider again the box from Problem 7. On two successive draws, *without* replacement, what is the probability of getting the following?

   a. $40

   b. $25

   c. $2

   d. $6

9. The psychology club conducted a lottery and sold 150 tickets. You bought 1 ticket, and your friend bought 3 tickets. There will be a first-place winner and a second-place winner.

   a. What is the probability that you will win first place?

   b. What is the probability that you will win first or second place?

c. What is the probability that you or your friend will win first place?

d. What is the probability that you or your friend will win something (either first or second place)?

e. What is the probability that both you and your friend will win something?

10. Suppose you obtain a biased coin with $p(\text{head}) = .6$ and $p(\text{tail}) = .4$. What is the probability of three heads in five flips? Of four heads in five flips?

11. A study was made of the relationship between personality type (extraversion/introversion) and whether a student held an office in a club or student organization. The results are summarized in the following table of probabilities:

Personality Type

		Extravert	Introvert	Total
	Yes	.28	.10	.38
Held Office	No	.24	.38	.62
	Total	.52	.48	1.00

a. What is the probability that a student will hold some office?

b. What is the probability that, given the student is an extravert, he or she will hold some office?

c. Does the added information about personality aid in predicting whether the student holds office?

d. Is personality type extravert or introvert (E–I) independent of holding office? Explain.

CHECKING YOUR PROGRESS: A SELF-TEST

1. An unbiased die is rolled 9 times, coming up 6 each time. What is the probability of its coming up 6 on the 10th roll?

   a. $\frac{1}{6}$

   b. less than $\frac{1}{6}$

   c. more than $\frac{1}{6}$

   d. none of the above

2. The probability of an event given that another event has already occurred is called which of the following?

   a. gambler's fallacy

   b. the addition rule of probability

   c. the multiplication rule of probability

   d. conditional probability

3. Your psychology instructor says that it is impossible for you to locate accurately sounds in your median plane (the plane that splits you down the middle) if you are blindfolded. To prove her point, you are blindfolded, and a clacker is used to make a brief sound either directly in front of you, directly overhead, or directly behind.

   a. What is the probability of correctly picking the location on the first presentation?

   b. What is the probability of picking the correct location by chance on three consecutive trials?

4. A fruit basket contains 1 apple, 2 oranges, and 3 large plums. *With* replacement, what is the probability of selecting, on three consecutive draws blindfolded, the following?

   a. 3 apples

   b. 2 oranges and 1 plum, in that order

   c. 2 oranges and 1 plum, in any order

5. Using the same basket from Problem 4, what is the probability of selecting, *without* replacement, the following on three consecutive blindfolded draws?

   a. an apple, an orange, and a plum

   b. 2 oranges and 1 plum, in that order

   c. 3 plums

6. A study of personality type (intuition vs. sensing) and the probability of holding student office was made. The results were as follows:

Personality Type

		Sensing	Intuition	Total
	Yes	.23	.15	.38
Held Office	No	.37	.25	.62
	Total	.60	.40	1.00

   a. What is the probability that a student has held some office?

   b. Given that a student is an intuitive type, what is the probability that he or she has held office?

   c. Does this added information about personality type aid in predicting whether the student has held office?

   d. In this problem, is personality type independent of holding office? Explain.

CHAPTER 8

THE NORMAL DISTRIBUTION

OBJECTIVES

The main objective in Chapter 8 is to discuss the normal distribution and to use the known characteristics of the standard normal curve to help us describe our sample distributions. Techniques for finding areas under the curve and for finding scores when areas are known also are discussed. Another objective is to learn to use the normal distribution to assign probabilities to scores and scores to probabilities.

CHAPTER REVIEW

The normal distribution is important because many empirical distributions are similar to it and because it is the limiting case for a number of other important distributions in statistics. Although there are many possible normal curves, each *normal curve* is symmetrical and unimodal, and the tails of each curve never quite reach the baseline. The *standard normal curve* is a special example of the normal distribution in which the mean is 0 and the standard deviation is 1.

Almost the entire normal curve is contained within 6 standard deviation units or *z* scores. A *z score* is the deviation of a raw score from the mean in standard deviation units, and we use *z* scores to enter Table A, a table containing areas under the right half of the standard normal curve (see Appendix 2). In the chapter, Table A is used to answer questions about sample distributions, assuming the sample was drawn from a normally distributed population.

Two types of problems are described in the chapter: finding areas under the curve and finding a score or scores when an area or areas are known. For example, to find the percentile rank of a score, the raw score is converted to a *z* score, and Table A is consulted to determine the total area below the raw score. Similarly, to find the area above a score, the score is converted to a *z* score and Table A is consulted. To find an area between two scores, both scores are converted to *z* scores, and the appropriate areas from Table A are added together or the smaller is subtracted from the larger. *Percentage area* is the same thing as percentage frequency. Thus, if you are asked to give the number of subjects associated with an area under the curve, you first find the area and then take that percentage of the total *N*. Percentage area can also be converted to probability by dividing it by 100.

If an area is known, the *z* score associated with it can be found in Table A and converted into a raw score using Formula 6-19. One type of problem in which scores are to be found asks for deviant or unlikely scores without giving the direction of the deviance. In this case, the percentage area must be split in half and each half denoted in each tail of the normal curve. Two *z* scores are found from Table A, and both are converted to raw scores. If the problem gives the area as a probability, convert it to percentage area (multiply *p* by 100) before proceeding.

Before working any normal curve problem, it is helpful to draw a normal curve and label it with any information you have. Then use the curve to try to decide what you are looking for.

FORMULAS

The formulas for this chapter are two of the formulas covered at the end of Chapter 6: the formulas for converting any raw score to a *z* score and for converting any *z* score back to a raw score.

Formula 6-17. *Formula for finding a z score from a raw score using sample statistics*

$$z = \frac{X - \overline{X}}{s}$$

Formula 6-19. *Formula for finding a raw score from a z score using sample statistics*

$$X = zs + \overline{X}$$

TERMS TO DEFINE AND/OR IDENTIFY

Normal distribution

Bell curve

Gaussian distribution

Probability distributions

Standard normal curve

z score

Percentile rank

FILL-IN-THE-BLANK ITEMS

Introduction

Because the normal distribution is useful in translating scores to probabilities, it is analogous to the

(1) _____ stone. Although the normal distribution is often attributed to German

mathematician (2) _____ , it was actually introduced by (3) _____ .

The normal distribution is important because many (4) _____ distributions are simi-

lar to it. (5) _____ distributions are those based on actual measurement. Also, the

normal distribution is important for inferential statistics because it is the (6) _____
case for a number of other important distributions. Examples of distributions that approach the normal
distribution with large sample sizes are the chi-square distribution and the sampling distribution of

(7) _____ .

Curves and Probability

All distributions of scores can be thought of as (8) _____ distributions. The area

under a portion of the curve represents the (9) _____ associated with the scores falling in that area. Determining that probability usually involves two steps. First, we convert our raw scores

to (10) _____ . Second, we use the z scores in conjunction with Table (11) _____

in Appendix 2 to determine an (12) _____ of the curve.

Characteristics of the Normal Curve

Each normal curve is (13) _____ ; that is, the two halves coincide. Each normal curve has

the same measures of (14) _____ tendency, and the (15) _____ of each

curve never reach the baseline. The (16) _____ normal curve has a mean of 0 and a stan-

dard deviation of 1. Almost the entire normal curve is bounded by (17) _____ standard
deviation units.

Review of *z* Scores

A (18) _____ is the deviation of a raw score from the mean in standard deviation units.

Negative *z* scores tell us that the raw score we are converting is (19) _____ the mean, and

positive values tell us that the raw score is (20) _____ the mean.

Using the Normal Curve Table

In Table A, the percentage area between the mean and any *z* score is found in column (21) _____.

The remaining area beyond the *z* score is contained in column (22) _____.

Finding Areas Under the Curve

Finding the percentile rank of a score

(23) _____ _____ is the percentage of cases up to and including the one in which

we are interested. The first step in working any normal curve problem is to (24) _____ the
normal curve and label it with the information given in the problem. To find the percentile rank of a score,

first convert the score to a (25) _____. Then obtain the appropriate area from either column B or column C in Table A.

Finding the percentage of the normal curve above a score

After the normal curve is drawn and labeled appropriately, the (26) _____ _____

is converted to a *z* score. Then the appropriate area is obtained from Table (27) _____. The *z* score

itself is found in column (28) _____.

Finding percentage frequency

When we find a percentage area under the normal curve, we can take that percentage of the total sample

size to find (29) _____ _____ subjects have scores in the area.

Finding an area between two scores

To find an area between two scores, both scores must be converted to (30) _____. Then

either the areas from Table A are (31) _____ or the smaller area is subtracted from the
larger to find the area between the scores.

Probability and areas under the curve

The percentage areas under the curve can be converted into probabilities by dividing them by

(32) _____. The range of probability is from 0 to (33) _____.

Finding Scores Cutting Off Areas

Finding the score that has a particular percentile rank

To locate a score associated with a particular area, first determine a (34) _____ from
Table A and then convert it to a raw score with Formula 6-19.

Finding deviant scores

When the problem asks for deviant or unlikely scores without specifying the direction of the deviance, you

are really being asked to find scores at (35) _____ ends of the distribution. The deviant

percentage must first be divided in (36) _____ before the graph can be correctly labeled.

Probability and deviant scores

If the problem of finding deviant scores is stated in terms of probability (e.g., find the scores that
are so deviant that their probability is .05 or less), the first step is to convert the probability to

(37) _____ _____. To do this, you multiply the probability by

(38) _____.

Troubleshooting Your Computations

As an aid to understanding and to determining whether your answer is appropriate, a small

(39) _____ _____ should always be drawn and labeled as completely as possible.

Then the obtained answer should be compared to the curve to see if it appears (40) _____.

A common error is to not have the answer in the correct final (41) _____.

PROBLEMS

1. Assuming that a national certification examination for a professional group has a mean score of 72 and $s = 14.5$, answer the following questions.

   a. What is the z score for a test score of 89.6?

   b. What is the z score for a test score of 61.5?

   c. What test score is 1.6 standard deviation units below the mean?

   d. What test score is 1.6 standard deviation units above the mean?

   e. What test scores are at least 1.5 standard deviation units away from the mean?

2. Use Table A in Appendix 2 to answer the following questions.

   a. What is the percentage area between the mean and a z score of $+0.57$?

   b. What is the percentage area between the mean and a z score of -0.57?

   c. Between the mean and what z score lies approximately 46% of the normal curve? Can your answer be both positive and negative?

   d. What z score cuts off the upper 10% of the distribution?

e. What area lies between a z score of $+1.28$ and a z score of $+1.96$?

f. What is the area above a z score of 1.96?

g. What is the total area between z scores of ± 2.58?

h. What is the area below a z score of -1.28?

3. For 55 graduating seniors who took the Miller Analogies Test (MAT), the following results were obtained: $\Sigma X = 2{,}942.5$, $\Sigma X^2 = 165{,}606.68$. Use the normal distribution to answer the following questions.

a. What is the percentile rank of a score of 71?

b. What is the percentile rank of a score of 35?

c. How many seniors scored between 31 and 45?

d. What is the score at the 95th percentile?

e. What is the score at the 15th percentile?

f. A university has found that scores on the MAT are highly associated with success in its graduate program in English. Specifically, seniors scoring below 41 on the test almost always fail to earn degrees, and for this reason the university will not admit a person with this score or lower. How many of the 55 seniors should not bother to apply?

g. What MAT scores are so deviant that they occur 15% or less of the time?

h. What MAT scores are so likely that they occur with a probability of .01 or less?

4. A blood pressure testing machine is stationed in a busy corridor in a large shopping mall. For 1 week, a medical student records the diastolic pressure reading of each person who uses the machine between the hours of 10 A.M. and 2 P.M., with the following results: $N = 124$, $\Sigma X = 9{,}771.2$, $\Sigma X^2 = 828{,}360.92$.

a. How many of the sample had scores of 110 or higher?

b. What was the probability of a score of 60 or less?

c. If the normal range for diastolic pressures is between 60 and 90, how many of the 124 persons had a normal reading?

d. Based on these data, what percentage of the population had readings as deviant as 110?

e. What readings were so deviant that less than 5% of the sample had them?

5. A national survey of speeds on interstate highways found that the average speed of 9,549 automobiles was 67.3 mph, with a standard deviation of 7.81 mph.

a. What speed is at least 1.5 standard deviation units above the mean?

b. How many cars from the sample of 9,549 had speeds at least 1.5 standard deviation units above the mean?

c. What is the percentile rank of a speed of 55?

d. What is the percentile rank of a speed of 75?

e. How many automobiles had speeds 2 or more standard deviation units away from the mean?

f. What speeds were so deviant that their probability of occurrence was .05 or less?

CHECKING YOUR PROGRESS: A SELF-TEST

1. How does the standard normal curve differ from any other normal curve?

2. True or False: Areas under the normal curve below the mean are always negative.

3. Applicants for a job take a standardized test of their job-relevant skills. Assume that the scores of the 520 applicants are normally distributed with a mean of 48 and a standard deviation of 8.2.

a. How many applicants scored higher than 65?

b. How many applicants scored lower than 40?

c. What is the percentile rank of a score of 44?

d. What is the probability of a score of 60 or higher?

e. What score would an applicant have to obtain to be in the upper 10% of applicants?

f. What scores were so deviant that less than 2% of the sample had them?

CHAPTER 9

CONFIDENCE INTERVALS AND HYPOTHESIS TESTING

OBJECTIVES

The main objectives in Chapter 9 are

1. To introduce the sampling distribution of means and the related distribution of *t* scores.
2. To derive and compute a range of values around the sample mean almost certain to include μ. This is called a confidence interval.
3. To develop a technique for testing a point estimate of $\mu;$ this is the one-sample *t* test.

CHAPTER REVIEW

The *sampling distribution of means* is derived by taking successive, same-sized random samples from some population, computing a mean for a measurable characteristic of each sample, and plotting the means on a frequency polygon. The *first property* of the sampling distribution is that its mean is the mean of the population or μ. The *second property,* which is a simplified version of the *central limit theorem,* is that the larger the size of each sample, the more nearly the sampling distribution will approximate the normal curve. The *third property* is that the larger the sample size, the smaller the standard deviation of the sampling distribution. The standard deviation is called the *standard error of the mean.*

When population parameters (μ and σ) are known, *z* scores are appropriate. However, we often do not know them, so they must be estimated from sample values. The sample mean ($\overline{X}$) is an unbiased estimate of

μ, and, as we defined it in Chapter 6, sample variance (s^2) is an unbiased estimate of population variance (σ^2). Recall that to obtain an unbiased estimate of σ^2, we divided the sum of squared deviations by $N - 1$ rather than by N. This expression, $N - 1$, is called *degrees of freedom* and is defined as the number of values free to vary after certain restrictions (e.g., the sum of the deviations equals 0) are placed on the data.

A *confidence interval* is a range of values within which the population mean almost certainly lies. The confidence intervals usually computed are the 95% and the 99% confidence intervals. Equations for the confidence intervals are derived in the chapter from the formula introduced in Chapter 6 to convert z scores to raw scores.

t scores are estimated z scores. They are used in place of z scores when population parameters are estimated from the sample. t scores correspond to the t distribution, and the t scores used in the confidence interval equations are determined from Table B (see Appendix 2), which contains values of t cutting off deviant portions of the distribution. In order to use the table of critical t scores, we need to know the *df*. For confidence intervals and the one-sample t test, $df = N - 1$. A confidence interval is an *interval estimate* of the population mean.

Another important use of the distribution of t is to test hypotheses about the value of μ. The seven-step procedure introduced for testing the null hypothesis is as follows:

1. **State the null hypothesis in symbols (H_0: $\mu = \mu_0$) and in words** in the context of the problem.
2. **State the alternative hypothesis in symbols (e.g., H_1: $\mu \neq \mu_0$) and in words.**
3. **Choose an α level,** the level at which you will reject or fail to reject the null hypothesis. Set $\alpha = .05$, if there are no specific instructions in the problem.
4. **State the rejection rule.** For example, the rule for a particular problem may be as follows: If $|t_{comp}|$ is $\geq t_{crit}$, then reject the null hypothesis. This is the rejection rule for a nondirectional hypothesis.
5. **Compute the test statistic.** In this chapter, the equation for the test statistic is $t_{\bar{X}} = \dfrac{\bar{X} - \mu}{s_{\bar{X}}}$.
6. **Make a decision by applying the rejection rule.**
7. **Write a conclusion statement in the context of the problem.**

For a directional test, H_0 is rejected if t_{comp} is of the same sign but is more extreme than t_{crit}.

A *Type I, or α, error* (a "false claim") is defined as rejecting the null hypothesis when it is really true. The probability of an α error is equal to α, the level at which we are trying to reject the null hypothesis.

Failing to reject H_0 when it is false is called a *Type II, or β, error* (a "failure of detection"). Lowering the value of α increases the probability of a β error.

The *power* of a statistical test is the probability that the test will detect a false null hypothesis. Factors affecting the power of a test are

1. The size of α. The smaller the α level, the less powerful the test will be.
2. The sample size. The larger the sample size, the greater the power of the test will be.
3. The distance between the hypothesized mean and the true mean. The greater the distance, the greater the power of the test will be.

In analyzing the results from large numbers of research studies, meta-analysis uses quantitative procedures to integrate the findings. Meta-analysis uses the *effect size*—the size of the difference between the null hypothesis and the alternative hypothesis in standardized units—results of studies rather than simply reporting whether or not the results were statistically significant.

Some researchers argue that hypothesis testing should be abandoned, claiming that the procedures are misleading and we should instead report confidence intervals and effect sizes. People opposed to hypothesis testing hold that many research studies don't have enough power to find what they are looking for, with a corresponding increase in Type II errors. This point is valuable if it forces experimenters to be more attentive to having sufficient power to detect an effect if it is present.

SYMBOLS

Symbol	Stands For
$\sigma_{\overline{X}}$	standard error of the mean
$\mu_{\overline{X}}$	mean of the sampling distribution of means, which equals μ
$z_{\overline{X}}$	z score for the sampling distribution of means
$s_{\overline{X}}$	estimated standard error of the mean
$t_{\overline{X}}$ or t	t score, which is an estimate of a z score
CI	confidence interval
df	degrees of freedom
$t_{.05}$ or $t_{.01}$	t scores from Table B cutting off deviant 5% or 1% of the distribution [occur with probability of .05(.01) or less]
H_0	null hypothesis
α	alpha level, the level at which we test H_0
H_1	alternative hypothesis
μ_0	specific value representing the "untreated" population mean
t_{comp}	computed t score
t_{crit}	critical t score from Table B
Type I, or α, error	rejecting true H_0
Type II, or β, error	failing to reject false H_0

FORMULAS

Formula 9-4. *Equation for estimated standard error of the mean*

$$s_{\overline{X}} = \frac{s}{\sqrt{N}}$$

The estimated standard error is found by dividing the sample standard deviation by the square root of sample size.

Formula 9-5. *Equation for $t_{\overline{X}}$, which is an estimate of $z_{\overline{X}}$*

$$t_{\overline{X}} = \frac{\overline{X} - \mu}{s_{\overline{X}}}$$

This equation is used to test hypotheses about the value of μ. It is the formula for the one-sample t test.

Formulas 9-6 and 9-7. *Equations for 95% and 99% confidence intervals*

$$95\% \ \text{CI} = \pm t_{.05} s_{\overline{X}} + \overline{X}$$
$$99\% \ \text{CI} = \pm t_{.01} s_{\overline{X}} + \overline{X}$$

$t_{.05}$ and $t_{.01}$ are the t scores cutting off the deviant 5% and 1% of the distribution of t, respectively. The values of t are found in Table B with $df = N - 1$.

TERMS TO DEFINE AND/OR IDENTIFY

Sampling distribution of means

Parent population

Central limit theorem

Standard error of the mean

Degrees of freedom

Estimated standard error of the mean

t distribution

Confidence interval

Critical values of t

Interval estimate

Null hypothesis

Alternative hypothesis

Nondirectional hypothesis

Directional hypothesis

Significant

α level

Rejection rule

Type I error

Type II error

Power

Meta-analysis

Effect size

FILL-IN-THE-BLANK ITEMS

Introduction

Intuitively, we understand that most of the statistics we are given are only (1) _____

because they are based on a sample from the larger group of interest—the (2) _____ .

In this chapter, we discuss the process of (3) _____ and how to determine the range within

which our (4) _____ should fall.

The Sampling Distribution of Means

The sample mean is an (5) _____ estimate of the population mean. The sampling dis-

tribution of means is derived by extracting successive random samples, all with the same (6) _____ ,
from some population. For each sample, the mean of some characteristic is computed and the

(7) _____ are plotted on a (8) _____ polygon. The resulting polygon

is called the (9) _____ _____ _____ _____ .
    The properties of the sampling distribution of means are as follows:

1. The mean of the sampling distribution equals (10) _____ .

2. The larger the size of each sample taken from the parent population, the more nearly the sampling distribution approximates the (11) _____ curve. This property is a simplified version of the (12) _____ _____ _____.

3. The larger the size of each sample taken from the population, the smaller the (13) _____ _____ of the sampling distribution. The standard deviation is called the (14) _____ _____ of the mean and is symbolized by (15) _____.

The equation for a *z* score based on the sampling distribution of means is (16) _____.

z scores obtained for a sample mean can be used in the same way as *z* scores for a (17) _____ _____.

Estimation and Degrees of Freedom

Often, we must estimate population values for μ and σ from our (18) _____. We can use (19) _____ to estimate the population mean and (20) _____ to estimate the population standard deviation. As you recall from Chapter 6, in the equation for our unbiased estimate of population variance, we divided the sum of squared deviations by (21) _____ rather than by *N* because of the tendency of the equation with *N* in the denominator to (22) _____ either the population variance or the population standard deviation.

$N - 1$ is referred to as (23) _____ _____ _____, which is defined as the number of (24) _____ free to vary after certain (25) _____ have been placed on the data.

At *t* score is an estimated (26) _____ and corresponds to a (27) _____ distribution. The mathematics of the distribution were derived by William Sealy (28) _____, who published under the pseudonym (29) _____.

Confidence Intervals

A (30) _____ _____ is a range of values around a sample mean within which μ almost certainly lies. The confidence intervals usually computed are the 95% and the (31) _____. The equations for the confidence intervals are derived from the formula used to convert (32) _____ to raw scores. Instead of z scores, the confidence interval equation requires (33) _____

obtained from Table (34) _____ .

For confidence intervals, $df =$ (35) _____ . The t distribution changes shape with

changes in (36) _____ _____ . Rather than being an exact estimate of the popu-

lation mean, the confidence interval is an (37) _____ estimate.

Hypothesis Testing: One-Sample t Test

The one-sample t test is a procedure for testing the (38) _____ _____ . The null

hypothesis, symbolized by (39) _____ , assumes a particular value for a population parameter—in

this case, for (40) _____ , the mean of the sampling distribution of means. The alternative to the null

hypothesis is that the value of (41) _____ is something other than what we have assumed it to be. If the

alternative hypothesis, symbolized by (42) _____ , doesn't specify the direction in which H_0 will dif-

fer from μ, we say it is (43) _____ . On the other hand, an alternative hypothesis stating

that μ will either be greater than H_0 or less than H_0 is called a (44) _____ hypothesis.
The seven-step procedure for testing the null hypothesis is as follows:

1. State the (45) _____ hypothesis in symbols and words.

2. State the alternative hypothesis in symbols and words.

3. Choose an (46) _____ level, which will always be set to .05 or .01 unless there are some special

   circumstances. Set $\alpha =$ (47) _____ , if there are no other instructions in the problem.

4. State the (48) _____ rule.

5. Compute the (49) _____ statistic.

6. Make a (50) _____ by applying the rejection rule.

7. Write a (51) _____ statement in the (52) _____ of the problem.

Directional tests

For a directional test, t_{comp} should have the (53) _____ sign as t_{crit}. In addition, with a directional test,

t_{crit} should be (54) _____ extreme than for a nondirectional test, because all of the probability is placed in (55) _____ _____ of the distribution. For this reason, directional tests are

(56) _____ powerful than nondirectional tests but hazardous if the (57) _____ of the

outcome cannot be predicted in advance.

Type I and Type II errors

The process of rejecting or failing to reject H_0 is sometimes called (58) _____

_____ _____. Rejecting H_0 when it is true is called a Type

(59) _____ or (60) _____ error. The probability of committing

this type of error is determined by the value we set for (61) _____. Lowering the

value of alpha will (62) _____ the probability of this type of error.

Failing to reject a false null hypothesis is called a Type (63) _____ or

(64) _____ error. Although the probability of this type of error is unknown, it is increased

by (65) _____ in the value of alpha.

The power of a statistical test

The (66) _____ of a test is the probability that the test will detect a false hypothesis, given

by the equation (67) _____ = _____. Factors affecting power are the

value of (68) _____ , the (69) _____ of the sample taken from the popu-
lation, and the distance between the hypothesized value of μ and the true value. Specifically, the smaller we

set α, the (70) _____ the power of the test will be. Also, the (71) _____
the sample size, the greater the power of the test will be. Finally, the greater the distance between the hy-

pothesized value of μ and the true value, the (72) _____ the power of the test will be.

Meta-analysis

The magnitude of the difference between H_0 and H_1, called the (73) _____ _____ ,
is the point of departure in the quantitative analysis of large numbers of research studies using

(74) _____. This form of analysis is more interested in (75) _____

_____ than in whether a significant effect is present in a study.

Should hypothesis testing be abandoned?

Some researchers say we should (76) _____ hypothesis testing because the

(77) _____ _____ in psychology experiments is really much higher than
most researchers think. Anti-hypothesis testers claim that a large percentage of studies don't have enough

(78) _____ to detect an effect even when the effect is present. As a consequence, Type

(79) _____ errors are committed at high rates, sometimes as high as 60%. This point is

valid if it forces experimenters to be more attentive to having sufficient (80) _____ in
their experiments.

Troubleshooting Your Computations

When the confidence interval has been computed, look at it to be sure that it is

(81) _____ in the light of your data. For example, the confidence interval

should contain the (82) _____ of the sample. Be sure to use (83) _____ rather
than N when finding the t score from Table B.

When computing t scores, the appropriate (84) _____ should be retained throughout
the computations. If the hypothesized mean is larger than the mean of the sample, the resulting value of t

should be (85) _____. Be sure that the absolute value of your computed t is larger than

the critical value of t from the table before (86) _____ H_0, if you're testing a nondirectional hypothesis.

PROBLEMS

1. Find $s_{\bar{X}}$ for each of the following samples.

   a. $N = 37, s = 5.3$

b. $N = 10$, $s = 2.5$

c. $N = 93$, $\Sigma X = 1{,}032.3$, $\Sigma X^2 = 12{,}801.45$

d. $df = 27$, $s^2 = 201.64$

e. $N = 25$, $s = 10.75$

2. Use Table B to answer the following questions.

    a. If $N = 10$, what t scores cut off the deviant 5% of the distribution?

    b. If $df = \infty$, what t scores cut off the deviant 1% and 5% of the distribution? Are they similar to the z scores cutting off 1% and 5%? Explain.

    c. For $N = 47$, what t scores cut off the deviant 5% and 1% of the distribution?

    d. Why do the critical values of t decrease with increases in df?

    e. According to the text, what critical values of t do you use when the exact df observed are not given in the table?

3. Find the 95% and the 99% confidence intervals for each of the following data sets.

   a. $N = 257, \Sigma X = 5{,}140, \Sigma X^2 = 106{,}912$

   b. $N = 26, \overline{X} = 10, s = 2$

   c. $N = 42, \Sigma X = 441, \Sigma X^2 = 4{,}914.42$

4. As part of its hiring procedure, a large company administers a standardized personality scale to job applicants. Fifty-four applicants for a quality control position have a mean score of 54.2, with $s = 16.1$, on the dimension of Conscientiousness. Assume that μ for Conscientiousness is 49.8.

   a. Determine whether applicants for the quality control position demonstrate higher Conscientiousness scores than the general population.

   b. Based on this sample of applicants, what is the 95% confidence interval for μ?

   c. What is the 99% confidence interval for μ?

5. A sample of 49 participants works at a perceptual task on which they have to correctly identify the shape of a stimulus after exposures of short duration. The number of correct identifications on 50 trials is recorded and the average is found to be 29.6, with $s = 7.3$.

   a. Construct the 95% confidence interval for μ.

   b. Construct the 99% confidence interval for μ.

6. Assume that the 327 students who have taken statistics at a large university constitute a population. Each student has been given a math achievement test with the following results: $\mu = 53.7$, $\sigma = 10.5$. On the basis of this information, answer the following questions.

   a. What is the standard error of the mean for samples of size $N = 25$?

   b. One sample of 25 students has been drawn from the population, and the average test score has been found to be 55.1, with $s = 8.5$. What is the estimated standard error?

   c. Test the null hypothesis using the sample described in part **b**.

   d. It is possible that you made an error in your decision in part **c**. If so, would it be a Type I or a Type II error?

7. The average rested worker at a calculator production plant can assemble 106 pocket calculators an hour. During the last hour of their shift, 26 workers assemble an average of 97.4 calculators, with $s = 17.2$. Is the performance of these workers significantly worse at the end of the shift?

8. In 20 years of coaching basketball, Coach Williams has kept records of her teams' performance making free throws during games. Her records indicate that the average player makes 71.1 shots out of 100. Not satisfied with that performance, Coach Williams hires a sports psychologist to work with the team to improve concentration and visualization at the foul line. At the end of the year, Coach Williams discovers that the 12 players on her team averaged 77.6 successful free throws per 100 attempts, with $s = 8.41$.

   a. What is $s_{\bar{X}}$ for the sample?

   b. Find the 95% confidence interval. Is 71.1 within the interval?

c. Test the hypothesis that $\mu = 71.1$.

d. Did working with the psychologist significantly improve free-throw shooting?

9. At a large high school, 537 seniors take the ACT with the following results: $\mu = 22.5$, $\sigma = 4.1$. Assuming that the 537 seniors constitute a population, answer the following questions.

    a. Suppose that 50 samples of size $N = 10$ have been drawn with replacement from the population. The mean of the resulting sampling distribution is found to be 22.73, with $s = 4.05$. What is $s_{\bar{X}}$ for this sampling distribution?

    b. What is $\sigma_{\bar{X}}$? How does it compare with $s_{\bar{X}}$ computed in part **a**?

    c. Suppose we draw another sample of size $N = 10$ from the population and find its mean to be 20.85, with $s = 3.73$. Test the hypothesis that this sample was drawn from the original population with $\mu = 22.5$.

    d. What is the 95% confidence interval for μ based on the sample in part **c**?

USING SPSS—EXAMPLE AND EXERCISE

SPSS has a specific, easy-to-use procedure for computing the one-sample t test.

Example: We will use SPSS to work Self-Test Exercise 7. The steps are as follows:

1. Start SPSS, enter the data, and name the variable **hypochon.**
2. Statistics>Compare Means>One-Sample T Test.
3. Move **hypochon** into the Test Variables box and enter 49.2 as the Test Value. Note that the Test Value is μ_0, the hypothesized value for μ for the null hypothesis.
4. Click OK and the solution should appear in the output Viewer window.
5. To obtain the 95% CI for μ, we must trick SPSS a bit and enter a Test Value of 0 and click OK.
6. Only the CI values should be read from this portion of the output.

Notes on Reading the Output

1. The column labeled "Sig. (2-tailed)" gives the exact p value for the computed $t = 2.425$. This means that $p = .034$, and we need not look up the critical values for t at the .05 or .01 levels. Our rule for rejecting H_0 can now be based on whether "Sig. (2-tailed)" or $p \le .05$.

2. The 95% CI is the CI on the difference between the sample mean and the hypothesized mean. In order to obtain the correct CI, we must re-run the analysis with a Test Value set to 0. This portion of the output will give the correct CI, but the t value will not be correct and should be ignored.

The solution output for the data of Self-Test Exercise 7 is as follows:

```
FORMATS hypochon (F8.2).
T-TEST
  /TESTVAL=49.2
  /MISSING=ANALYSIS
  /VARIABLES=hypochon
  /CRITERIA=CIN (.95) .
```

T-Test

One-Sample Statistics

	N	Mean	Std. Deviation	Std. Error Mean
HYPOCHON	12	58.4167	13.1665	3.8008

Sig. (2-tailed) is the exact p value for the computed $t = 2.425$ and $p = .034$.

One-Sample Test

	Test Value = 49.2					
					95% Confidence Interval of the Difference	
	t	df	Sig. (2-tailed)	Mean Difference	Lower	Upper
HYPOCHON	2.425	11	.034	9.2167	.8511	17.5822

```
T-TEST
  /TESTVAL=0
  /MISSING=ANALYSIS
  /VARIABLES=hypochon
  /CRITERIA=CIN (.95) .
```

T-Test

One-Sample Statistics

	N	Mean	Std. Deviation	Std. Error Mean
HYPOCHON	12	58.4167	13.1665	3.8008

Only the 95% CI is correct for the following output.

One-Sample Test

	Test Value = 0					
					95% Confidence Interval of the Difference	
	t	df	Sig. (2-tailed)	Mean Difference	Lower	Upper
HYPOCHON	15.369	11	.000	58.4167	50.0511	66.7822

Exercise Using SPSS

1. We have conducted a study of the verbal skills of females. The task was to unscramble 20 sentences within a 10-minute period. (*Example:* free are things best the life in—The best things in life are free.) Each of the 20 participants received a score indicating the number of sentences she unscrambled correctly. Several previous studies over the last 2 years have indicated that females averaged a score of 9.0 on the task. Using SPSS, test the hypothesis that this year's sample performed differently than in the past. Also provide a 95% CI for the population mean for this sample. The data are as follows: 15, 15, 14, 14, 13, 13, 13, 11, 11, 11, 11, 10, 10, 9, 9, 9, 8, 8, 6, 3.

CHECKING YOUR PROGRESS: A SELF-TEST

1. The probability that an inferential test will detect a false null hypothesis is called the
   a. central limit theorem.
   b. power of a test.
   c. Type I error.
   d. Type II error.
2. If the null hypothesis is rejected when it shouldn't be, it is called a
   a. power.
   b. Type I error.
   c. Type II error.
   d. standard error.
3. If the null hypothesis is not rejected when it should be, it is called a
   a. power.
   b. Type I error.
   c. Type II error.
   d. standard error.
4. What are the properties of the sampling distribution of means?

5. A local school district employs a standardized reading test for all students entering the 9th grade. The mean score on this test is 27.4. Last year, the district instituted a reading program in the 6th through the 8th grades. The 217 students entering the 9th grade this year have a mean reading score of 28.2, with $s = 8.56$.

   a. Has the program improved reading?

   b. What is the 95% CI for μ?

6. A social psychologist finds that in a typical 15-minute conversation with a spouse, a person performs 32.1 nods of the head. In a sample of 13 couples experiencing marital difficulty, the average number of nods is 22.6, with $s = 7.6$.

a. Did marital difficulty reduce nods?

b. What is the 99% CI for μ?

7. The Hypochondriasis scale of the MMPI yields $\mu = 49.2$. The counseling center of a university routinely administers the MMPI to students seeking counseling. The hypochondriasis scores of the 12 students seeking counseling during the first week of the term are listed below.

X
42
76
59
62
52
57
63
50
48
72
81
39

Find:

a. $\overline{X}$

b. s^2

c. s

d. $s_{\overline{X}}$

e. What is the 95% CI for μ?

f. Do students seeking counseling evidence more hypochondriasis than would be expected from test norms?

CHAPTER 10

SIGNIFICANCE OF THE DIFFERENCE BETWEEN TWO SAMPLE MEANS

OBJECTIVES

The main objectives in Chapter 10 are

1. To introduce the sampling distribution of differences and the related distribution of *t* scores.
2. To develop a technique for testing the significance of the difference between two independent sample means.
3. To develop a technique for testing the significance of the difference between two dependent sample means.

CHAPTER REVIEW

The chapter begins with the derivation of the sampling distribution of the differences for independent samples. First, pairs of random samples are taken from a population, and means for some characteristic are computed. Next, the difference between the pairs of means is determined. A frequency distribution of the differences is constructed, and the distribution is used to plot a frequency polygon. The distribution is called the *sampling distribution of the mean differences.*

The properties of the sampling distribution of the mean differences are (1) its mean is equal to 0; (2) the larger the size of the samples drawn from the population, the more closely the sampling distribution approximates the normal curve; (3) the larger the size of the samples, the smaller the standard deviation of the sampling distribution. The standard deviation is called the *standard error of the difference between means* and is symbolized by $\sigma_{\bar{X}_1 - \bar{X}_2}$. Both raw-score and defining formulas for estimating the standard error of the differences are given. The estimated standard error is symbolized by $s_{\bar{X}_1 - \bar{X}_2}$.

As in Chapter 9, hypothesis testing involves computing how far from the mean of the sampling distribution our observed difference in sample means lies in estimated standard error units. We first compute a t score and then compare the computed t score with values known to cut off the deviant 5% (or 1%) of the distribution of t for samples of a given size converted to degrees of freedom. The t score or t ratio is the ratio of the difference between a pair of sample means to the estimated standard error of the differences. The degrees of freedom for the t test for independent samples is $N_1 + N_2 - 2$, and the critical values again are found in Table B.

A *two-tailed* test looks at both ends of the distribution of the test statistic, t in this chapter. Only one end of the distribution is considered in the *one-tailed* test. The end considered in the one-tailed test is the one predicted by the experimenter before conducting the experiment. The one-tailed test is a more powerful test if the outcome of the experiment is in the predicted direction. If you can reasonably predict the outcome's direction before data collection, use of the one-tailed test is warranted because it is more powerful. To determine the one-tailed probabilities, halve the probability values in Table B.

Assumptions required by the two-sample t test for independent samples are that the populations from which the samples are drawn are normal, that the population variances are homogeneous (equal), and that the samples are independent. The first two assumptions apparently can be violated with little effect upon the conclusions made with the test. This property of a statistical test to give valid conclusions even when its assumptions are violated is called *robustness*. If you fear violation of the assumptions, it is recommended that you use fairly large samples of equal size.

The power of the test can be increased by using dependent samples. Dependent samples can be formed by using *matched pairs* of unrelated individuals in which subject pairs, matched as closely as possible on relevant characteristics, are selected. Then, one member of each pair is assigned to one treatment group, and the other member is assigned to the other group. Another procedure for obtaining dependent samples is to use each subject as his or her own control; that is, the same individuals are given each experimental treatment. This type of experiment is called a *repeated measures* design or *within-subjects comparison.*

The power of the test using dependent samples is increased through a decrease in the standard deviation of the sampling distribution of mean differences. The standard deviation is called the *standard error of the mean differences* and is symbolized by $\sigma_{\bar{D}}$. $\sigma_{\bar{D}}$ is estimated by $s_{\bar{D}}$, which is called the estimated standard error of the mean differences.

The direct difference method is used to compute a t ratio for dependent or related samples. In the final equation discussed, t is computed by dividing the mean of the differences by the standard error of the mean differences. The computed value of t is then compared with the critical values of t from Table B with $df = N - 1$, where N is the number of pairs of scores.

SYMBOLS

Symbol	Stands For
$\sigma_{\bar{X}_1 - \bar{X}_2}$	standard error of the difference between means
$s_{\bar{X}_1 - \bar{X}_2}$	estimated standard error of the mean differences
$\bar{X}_1 - \bar{X}_2$	score in the sampling distribution of the differences

$\mu_1 - \mu_2$	mean of the sampling distribution of the differences
$z_{\overline{X}_1 - \overline{X}_2}$	z score based on the sampling distribution of the differences
$t_{\overline{X}_1 - \overline{X}_2}$	t score based on the sampling distribution of the differences
s^2_{pooled}	pooled variance; an estimate of the common variance of the parent populations
$\sigma_{\overline{D}}$	standard error of the mean differences
$s_{\overline{D}}$	estimated standard error of the mean differences
$\overline{X}_{\overline{D}}$	mean of the differences
$s_{\overline{X}_D}$	standard error of the differences
$s_{\overline{D}}$	standard deviation of the differences
D	difference between a pair of scores

FORMULAS

Formula 10-3. *Computational formula for the estimated standard error of the mean differences for independent samples*

$$s_{\overline{X}_1 - \overline{X}_2} = \sqrt{\left(\frac{(N_1 - 1)s_1^2 + (N_2 - 1)s_2^2}{N_1 + N_2 - 2}\right)\left(\frac{1}{N_1} + \frac{1}{N_2}\right)}$$

This formula is used to compute the estimated standard error of the mean differences. N_1 and N_2 are the numbers of subjects in the first and second samples, respectively. s_1^2 and s_2^2 are the variances of the two samples.

Formula 10-6. *Equation for the two-sample t test for independent samples*

$$t_{\overline{X}_1 - \overline{X}_2} = \frac{\overline{X}_1 - \overline{X}_2}{s_{\overline{X}_1 - \overline{X}_2}}$$

The t ratio for the two-sample t test for independent samples is the difference in sample means divided by the estimated standard error of the mean differences. When the computational formula for $s_{\overline{X}_1 - \overline{X}_2}$ is substituted in the denominator, the t ratio becomes

Formula 10-7. *Computational equation for the two-sample t test for independent samples*

$$t_{\overline{X}_1 - \overline{X}_2} = \frac{\overline{X}_1 - \overline{X}_2}{\sqrt{\left(\frac{(N_1 - 1)s_1^2 + (N_2 - 1)s_2^2}{N_1 + N_2 - 2}\right)\left(\frac{1}{N_1} + \frac{1}{N_2}\right)}}$$

Formula 10-8. *Computational formulas for the t test for dependent samples*

$$t = \frac{\overline{X}_D}{s_{\overline{X}_D}} \quad \text{or} \quad \frac{\overline{X}_D \sqrt{N}}{s_D}$$

TERMS TO DEFINE AND/OR IDENTIFY

Independent *t* test

Control group

Independent sample

Sampling distribution of the mean differences

Standard error of the difference between means

Estimated standard error of the mean differences

Pooled variance

Two-tailed test

One-tailed test

Homogeneity of variance

Robustness of a test

Matched pairs

Within-subjects comparisons

Repeated measures design

Counterbalancing

Double-blind

FILL-IN-THE-BLANK ITEMS

Introduction

In Chapter 9 we looked at a distribution composed of means of single samples drawn from a population,

whereas in this chapter we considered (1) _____ samples taken simultaneously.

The Sampling Distribution of the Differences Between Sample Means

If the behavior of the members of one sample is not related to the behavior of subjects in the other sample,

the samples are (2) _____. The assumption of independence is often made as long as

subjects are selected at (3) _____ and are (4) _____ assigned to the different treatment conditions.

To construct the sampling distribution of the differences, we first draw (5) _____ of

random samples from the same population. For each sample of the pair, a (6) _____ is

computed and the (7) _____ between the means is found. A frequency (8) _____

based on the differences is then made, and from this a frequency (9) _____ is plotted.

The standard deviation of the sampling distribution of differences is called the (10) _____

_____ of the differences.

Three properties of the sampling distribution of the differences are: the mean of the distribution is equal to (11) _____ ; the larger the size of the samples taken from the population, the more closely the distribution approximates the (12) _____ curve; and the larger the size of the samples, the (13) _____ the standard error of the difference between means.

In the sampling distribution of the differences, a score is symbolized by (14) _____ . The mean is symbolized by (15) _____ , and the standard error is symbolized by (16) _____ . Putting these together, the formula for a z score is (17) _____ = _____ . If we divide by the estimated standard error, we obtain the formula for t, which is usually written as (18) _____ = _____ .

Computing t: Independent Samples

To compute t for independent samples, we need three things: the mean of each sample, the (19) _____ of subjects in each sample, and the (20) _____ of each sample. The null hypothesis is that both samples were drawn from the (21) _____ _____ and that the mean of the sampling distribution is (22) _____ . The degrees of freedom for the test are given by (23) _____ .

One-tailed versus two-tailed tests

A (24) _____ test of significance is one considering both ends of the distribution. To use it, we don't have to make any (25) _____ about the experiment's outcome. The (26) _____ test, on the other hand, looks only at the tail of the distribution predicted by the experimenter before the experiment. However, with a one-tailed test, we must make our prediction (27) _____ doing the study.

The (28) _____ test is a more powerful test if the prediction comes true. A more powerful test is one with which it will be (29) _____ to reject the null hypothesis.

Assumptions of the two-sample t test

The *t* test assumes that the dependent variable is (30) _____ distributed in the population from which the samples are drawn. Another assumption is that the population (31) _____ are homogeneous. If you have reason to suspect that the assumptions will be violated, you should use (32) _____ samples with the same number of subjects in each. Both assumptions can apparently be violated with (33) _____ effect upon the conclusions reached with the *t* test, which means that the *t* test is a (34) _____ test.

Computing *t*: Dependent Samples

In testing H_0, the most desired outcome is (35) _____ of the null hypothesis. One way to increase the (36) _____ of the *t* test is to use dependent samples.

One way to obtain dependent samples is to form (37) _____ _____ of unrelated individuals with one member of a pair assigned to one treatment group and the other member assigned to the other group. In the (38) _____ _____ design, each subject is given both treatments; that is, each subject is his or her own (39) _____. Sometimes, this type of design is called the (40) _____ _____ design. The dependent-samples design increases the power of the test by (41) _____ the standard deviation of the sampling distribution of differences between related samples.

The direct difference method

(42) _____ is a procedure used to control for the effects of the order of presentation of the treatment in experiments. A (43) _____ method of drug presentation is one in which neither the administrator nor the subject knows which drug is being given. With the direct difference method, all calculations are based on the (44) _____ between each pair of scores rather than on the scores themselves. The *t* ratio is the mean of the differences divided by the estimated (45) _____ _____ of the differences. The mean of the differences is defined as the (46) _____ sum of the differences divided by *N,* which is the number of (47) _____ of scores. For the test, $df =$ (48) _____ .

Troubleshooting Your Computations

The (49) _____ used must be appropriate to your data; that is, when the samples are

assumed to be independent of each other, the t test for (50) _____ samples should be

used. If the samples are related or matched in some way, the t test for (51) _____ samples
should be used.

The estimated standard error of the differences should always have a (52) _____

sign. Also, be sure to retain the appropriate (53) _____ when computing the final value

for t. In the t test for dependent samples, all computations are made on the (54) _____
scores rather than on the actual scores themselves. Be careful to add the difference scores

(55) _____—that is, taking the signs into account.

Remember the decision rule for a nondirectional test: If the absolute value of the computed t is equal

to or larger than the critical value of t from Table B, (56) _____ H_0.

PROBLEMS

1. For each of the following, compute $s_{\bar{X}_1 - \bar{X}_2}$ using both the raw-score and the defining formulas. Assume
   that the samples are independent.

   a. $N_1 = N_2 = 12$, $s_1 = 3.6$, $s_2 = 4.3$

   b. $N_1 = 22$, $\Sigma X_1 = 112.2$, $\Sigma X_1^2 = 643.5$; $N_2 = 22$, $\Sigma X_2 = 138.6$, $\Sigma X_2^2 = 1{,}010.68$

   c. $N_1 = N_2 = 25$, $s_1^2 = 2.25$, $s_2^2 = 1.96$

2. In a military training program, the complex reaction-time ability of pilots and navigators is compared. Determine whether there is a significant difference between the groups in the number of errors made (failure to respond) in 100 stimulus presentations.

Pilots	Navigators
$N = 15$	$N = 20$
$\overline{X} = 23.5$	$\overline{X} = 41.3$
$s = 10.5$	$s = 12.7$

3. Experimental evidence indicates that persons with a family history of alcoholism are more likely to become alcoholic than persons with no such history. A large group of adults with and without family histories of alcoholism is selected, and from this large group, eight pairs of participants are matched in terms of race, age, marital status, and drinking history. Each participant is given a drink of alcohol; 30 minutes later, a blood sample is taken, and a metabolite of alcohol is measured. The results are shown here.

Pair Number	Family History (μg/ml)	No Family History (μg/ml)
1	3.1	2.5
2	3.5	2.1
3	3.2	1.8
4	2.8	2.3
5	2.6	2.2
6	3.0	1.9
7	1.9	2.3
8	2.7	2.5

Compare the groups with and without a family history of alcoholism.

4. Thirty-two students are randomly selected from a large introductory class and are randomly and evenly assigned to one of two groups. Each participant is given four 15-second exposures to a list of 15 nouns. After 30 minutes, each participant in one group is given a free recall test, whereas each participant in the other group is given a recognition test. The results in terms of the number of words correctly retained are shown here. Compare the groups.

Recall Test		Recognition Test	
X	f	X	f
4	1	15	6
2	5	14	1
1	7	13	4
0	3	12	2
		10	1
		8	1
		6	1

5. In an attempted replication of the Rosenthal effect (experimenter bias can influence the outcome of an experiment), two groups of 15 randomly selected students each are given some rats to train. One group is told that the rats are retarded, whereas the other group is told that the rats are intelligent. Errors are recorded during training, and the data for each group are shown here.

Group "Stupid"	Group "Intelligent"
$\Sigma X = 379.5$	$\Sigma X = 252$
$\Sigma X^2 = 9,853.5$	$\Sigma X^2 = 4,450.2$
$N = 15$	$N = 15$

a. Before you analyze the data, determine whether there is a rationale for using the one-tailed test of significance. If so, what is it?

b. Compare the groups using the appropriate statistical test.

6. Ten politically active individuals are selected, all of whom label themselves as liberal. Each is attached to a physiograph, and heart rate is recorded while a sequence of 20 slides is projected on a screen at which the participant is looking. Half of the slides are pictures of famous individuals without any expressed political philosophy; the other half are known conservatives. The arrangement of the slides is random. Each participant receives two scores: The first is the average heart rate during exposure to the neutral slides, and the second is the average heart rate during exposure to the conservative slides. The data are shown here. Does reaction to the slides differ?

Participant	Neutral	Conservative
1	65.3	71.8
2	75.7	73.5
3	85.6	99.3
4	73.7	81.7
5	69.5	75.7
6	68.2	73.5
7	70.1	79.8
8	72.5	70.3
9	71.0	85.3
10	83.5	107.1

7. An experiment is performed to compare the performance of students taught statistics by a traditional lecture approach with students taught by group discussion sessions. Fifty students are randomly and equally assigned to one of the two treatment conditions. In each case, the same instructor is present; he lectures to one group and leads the discussion in the other. The final class averages based on scores on standardized, machine-scored tests are presented here. Is there a significant difference between the groups?

Lecture	Discussion
$N = 25$	$N = 25$
$\overline{X} = 81.7$	$\overline{X} = 74.1$
$s = 8.3$	$s = 10.1$

8. The average ACT score for 937 freshmen at State University is 21.4, with a variance of 24.1. For Private University in the same city, the average ACT score for 421 freshmen is 22.1, with a variance of 14.5. Is there a significant difference between the schools in average freshman ACT scores? If so, how can you account for it in terms of factors affecting the power of a test?

9. Ten students are tested for accuracy of distance estimation using either one or both eyes. The test object is 24 inches from the viewer. Is there a significant difference in the amount of error (in inches) between the two conditions?

Student	One Eye	Two Eyes
A	3	2
B	11	8
C	5	7
D	4	2
E	6	4
F	3	1
G	15	10
H	4	5
I	8	7
J	9	7

10. A study is done to see whether children are more likely to have psychic powers than young adults. Thirteen randomly selected 8-year-old children each make one run through a standard PSI deck trying to guess the identity of each target card by "reading" the mind of the tester. There are four different targets, and each child receives a score indicating proportion of "hits." The same procedure is used on 15 randomly selected college students. Compare the groups.

Children	Young Adults
$N = 13$	$N = 15$
$\overline{X} = .28$	$\overline{X} = .24$
$s = .067$	$s = .073$

USING SPSS—EXAMPLES AND EXERCISES

The SPSS procedure for computing *t* tests has options that will compute both the *t* test for independent samples and the *t* test for dependent samples.

Example: First, we will use SPSS to work an exercise for the *t* test for *independent* samples—specifically, Problem 4. The steps are as follows:

1. Start SPSS. Data entry is slightly different for this type of problem. Name the first variable **group** and the second, **words.** Enter the data for the Recall Test group under **words** with a 1 in the **group** column, and enter the data for the Recognition Test group under **words** but with a 2 in the **group** column in front of the data. Part of the Data Editor showing the pattern of data entry follows:

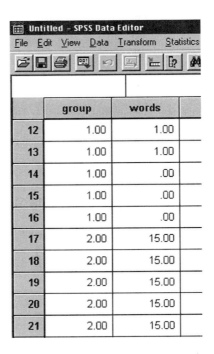

2. Choose Statistics>Compare Means>Independent Samples T Test.
3. Move **words** into the Test Variables box and **group** into the Grouping Variable box.
4. Click on Define Groups and enter the code values for Group 1 and Group 2. The code values will be 1 and 2 because these are the numbers we entered to identify the groups. Click Continue>OK. The results should appear in the output Viewer window.

Notes on Reading the Output

1. The *t* value we will use is the one in the first row labeled "equal variances assumed," because this is one of the assumptions we have made. (Levene's Test is a test of the homogeneity of variances assumption.)
2. "Sig. (2-tailed)" is the exact *p* value for the computed *t*. We reject the null hypothesis if this value is $\leq .05$ and conclude that there is a significant difference between the groups.

```
FORMATS group (F8.2).
FORMATS words (F8.2).
T-TEST
  GROUPS=group(1 2)
  /MISSING=ANALYSIS
  /VARIABLES=words
  /CRITERIA=CIN(.95) .
```

T-Test

Group Statistics

	GROUP	N	Mean	Std. Deviation	Std. Error Mean
WORDS	1.00	15	1.2667	1.0328	.2667
	2.00	16	12.7500	2.6957	.6739

Independent Samples Test

		Levene's Test for Equality of Variances	
		F	Sig.
WORDS	Equal variances assumed	6.193	.019
	Equal variances not assumed		

Independent Samples Test

		t-test for Equality of Means					95% Confidence Interval of the Difference	
		t	df	Sig. (2-tailed)	Mean Difference	Std. Error Difference	Lower	Upper
WORDS	Equal variances assumed	-15.456	29	.000	-11.4833	.7430	-13.0029	-9.9638
	Equal variances not assumed	-15.844	19.551	.000	-11.4833	.7248	-12.9974	-9.9693

Example: Now we will use SPSS to work an example of the *t* test for *dependent* samples—Problem 6. The steps are as follows:

1. Start SPSS, name variables **neutral** and **conserv,** and enter the data.
2. Statistics>Compare Means>Paired-Samples T Test.
3. Move both variables into the Paired Variables box, then click OK. The results should appear in the output Viewer window.

Notes on Reading the Output

1. You should find the results reasonably easy to identify and interpret in this output. The critical results are found in the Paired Samples Test box. The results indicate that $t(9) = -3.389$ and $p = .008$. As before, SPSS labels the *p* value as "Sig. (2-tailed)." Because the obtained *p* value is less than our alpha level of .05, we reject the null hypothesis and conclude that there is a significant difference in the heart rates, which increase when a liberal views the slide of a known conservative.

```
FORMATS neutral (F8.2).
FORMATS conserv (F8.2).
T-TEST
  PAIRS= neutral  WITH conserv (PAIRED)
  /CRITERIA=CIN(.95)
  /MISSING=ANALYSIS.
```

T-Test

Paired Samples Statistics

		Mean	N	Std. Deviation	Std. Error Mean
Pair 1	NEUTRAL	73.5100	10	6.5101	2.0587
	CONSERV	81.8000	10	12.3371	3.9013

Paired Samples Correlations

		N	Correlation	Sig.
Pair 1	NEUTRAL & CONSERV	10	.839	.002

Paired Samples Test

		Paired Differences					t
					95% Confidence Interval of the Difference		
		Mean	Std. Deviation	Std. Error Mean	Lower	Upper	
Pair 1	NEUTRAL - CONSERV	-8.2900	7.7348	2.4460	-13.8232	-2.7568	-3.389

(continued)

Paired Samples Test

		df	Sig. (2-tailed)
Pair 1	NEUTRAL - CONSERV	9	.008

Exercises Using SPSS

1. Use SPSS to work Self-Test Exercise 6, assuming the data are from independent groups; that is, assume that 20 participants were randomly assigned to attend or not to attend a speed reading course. At the conclusion of the course, all participants were given an evaluation to measure their reading speed in words per minute. Was the class effective? (*Hint:* Don't forget the differences in the data input arrangement between the independent and dependent *t* tests.)

2. Use SPSS to work Self-Test Exercise 6 just as stated—as a dependent *t* test problem. You will have to re-enter your data. Compare your results with those from SPSS Exercise 1. Given the same data, which design is more powerful?

CHECKING YOUR PROGRESS: A SELF-TEST

1. What are the properties of the sampling distribution of the mean differences?

2. Describe the research conditions in which a *t* test for independent samples is appropriate.

3. Describe the research conditions in which a *t* test for dependent samples is appropriate.

4. A *t* ratio is another version of which of the following?

   a. standard score
   b. *z* score
   c. two-tailed test
   d. standard error
   e. a and b

5. A social psychologist studied the effect of leadership style on the productivity of workers at an assembly plant for fax machines. Nine teams of workers were supervised by democratic leaders, and 15 teams worked for autocratic leaders. The average number of fax machines assembled in an hour by each team was recorded. The groups working for democratic leaders completed an average of 28.6 machines per hour, with $s^2 = 62.41$. The groups working for autocratic leaders completed an average of 26.2 machines per hour, with $s^2 = 45.32$. Did leadership style affect performance?

6. A group of 10 students completed a class to improve reading speed. Their average reading speed, in words per minute, was measured before and after taking the class. Was the class effective?

Student	Speed Before	Speed After
A	476	519
B	342	460
C	527	499
D	261	450
E	439	610
F	517	547
G	391	519
H	422	662
I	321	456
J	410	420

CHAPTER 11

ONE-WAY ANALYSIS OF VARIANCE WITH POST HOC COMPARISONS

OBJECTIVES

The main objective in Chapter 11 is to present a significance test that can be used to compare three or more levels of one independent variable. As with the t test, there are two versions: one for use with independent samples, called between-subjects analysis of variance, or ANOVA; and one for use with dependent groups, called repeated measures ANOVA. Because these analyses are used with one independent variable, they are termed one-way ANOVA. In addition, two different post hoc tests are discussed for significance testing following a significant ANOVA.

CHAPTER REVIEW

The analysis of variance, or ANOVA, is a widely used test for comparing more than two groups. Two reasons for not using the two-sample t test are that multiple t tests are tedious to compute and that the more tests you do on the same data, the more likely you are to commit a Type I error (reject a true null).

The total variability in some data can be partitioned or divided into the *within-groups variability* and the *between-groups variability*. The variability within each group stems from individual differences and experimental error; the variability between groups comes from individual differences, experimental error, and the treatment effect. The ANOVA test is the ratio of a measure of variability between groups to a measure of the variability within groups. If there is no treatment effect, the computed value of F will be close to 1. However, if there is a treatment effect, the F ratio will be relatively large because of the added source of variability contributing to the between-group differences. One-way between-subjects ANOVA applies to situations in which the data from three or more independent groups are analyzed.

The first step in determining the indices of variability is to compute the sums of squares. The *total sum of squares* is the sum of the squared deviations of each score from the total mean. The *sum of squares within each group* is the sum of the squared deviations of each score in a group from its group mean, with the deviations summed across groups. Finally, the *sum of squares between groups* can be obtained by subtraction: $SS_b = SS_{tot} - SS_w$. Also, SS_b is the square of the deviation between each group mean and the total mean multiplied by the number of subjects in a particular group and summed over groups. It's a good idea to compute SS_b to test the accuracy of your other computations.

After the sums of squares have been determined, an appropriate degrees of freedom is computed for each. For SS_{tot}, or the total sum of squares, $df = N - 1$, where N is the total number of cases sampled. For SS_b, or the sum of squares between groups, $df = K - 1$, where K is the number of groups. df for SS_w, or the sum of squares within groups, is $N - K$.

Both SS_b and SS_w are divided by their respective df to give the average or *mean square*. The ratio of MS_b to MS_w is called the F ratio. A relatively large value of F indicates greater variability between groups than within groups and may indicate sampling from different populations. The computed value of F is compared with values known to cut off deviant portions (5% or 1%) of the distribution of F. If the computed F exceeds critical values from Table C (see Appendix 2), the null hypothesis is rejected, and we conclude that at least one of the samples probably came from a different population. To help summarize the results, as they are computed, values are entered into the analysis of variance summary table shown here.

Summary Table for Between-Subjects ANOVA

Source	SS	df	MS	F
Between groups				
Within groups				
Total				

Two tests are presented for further significance testing following a significant F ratio: the Fisher LSD and the Tukey HSD. Both tests are used to make all pairwise comparisons—comparing all groups by looking at one pair at a time. The LSD test is sometimes called a *protected t test* because it follows a significant F test. In the LSD test, the difference between a pair of means is significant if it is greater than LSD, which is computed with a formula; the same is true for the HSD test; that is, a difference between a pair of means is significant if the difference exceeds the computed value of HSD. A table of differences is used to summarize the results of both tests.

The one-way repeated measures ANOVA applies to situations in which the same (or matched) participants are tested on more than two occasions. The first step is to compute the sums of squares. The total and between-groups sums of square are computed using the same procedures as in one-way between-subjects ANOVA. However, the within-groups sum of squares is divided into two parts: subjects sum of squares (SS_{subj}) and error sum of squares (SS_{error}). SS_{subj} is the deviation between the mean score for each subject and the total mean, multiplied by the number of groups and summed over subjects. SS_{error} is the variability remaining after removing SS_b and SS_{subj} from SS_{tot} and can be obtained by subtraction: $SS_{error} = SS_{tot} - SS_b - SS_{subj}$. Computational formulas were given for each of the sums of squares.

As in one-way between-subjects ANOVA, $df_{tot} = N - 1$, and $df_b = K - 1$. Subjects degrees of freedom (df_{subj}) equal the number of subjects minus 1 ($S - 1$), and error degrees of freedom (df_{error}) equal $(K - 1)(S - 1)$.

Both SS_b and SS_{error} are divided by the appropriate df to give MS_b and MS_{error}, respectively. The F ratio is obtained by dividing MS_b by MS_{error}. If the computed F is greater than or equal to the critical values from

Table C (Appendix 2), the null hypothesis is rejected. With slight modifications, the LSD and HSD tests can be used for post hoc testing following a significant repeated measures ANOVA.

To summarize the results, values are entered in a summary table, as shown here.

Summary Table for One-Way Repeated Measures ANOVA

Source	SS	df	MS	F
Between groups				
Subjects				
Error				
Total				

SYMBOLS

Symbol	Stands For
$\overline{X}_{tot}$	total mean or grand mean (GM)
X_g	score within a group
$\overline{X}_g$	mean of a group
SS_{tot}	total sum of squares
SS_w	within-groups sum of squares
SS_b	between-groups sum of square
SS_{subj}	subjects sum of squares
SS_{error}	error sum of squares
N_g	number of subjects within a group
N	total number of subjects or total number of scores in a repeated measures ANOVA
$\sum_g$	sum over or across groups
MS_b	mean square between groups
MS_w	mean square within groups
df_b	between-groups degrees of freedom
K	number of groups or number of trials in a repeated measures ANOVA
S	number of participants (subjects)
df_w	within-groups degrees of freedom
df_{tot}	total degrees of freedom
df_{subj}	subjects degrees of freedom
df_{error}	error degrees of freedom
F	F ratio, ANOVA test
F_{comp}	your computed F ratio
F_{crit}	the critical value of F from Table C
LSD	least significant difference
HSD	honestly significant difference
q	studentized range statistic
LSD_α, HSD_α	LSD and HSD mean difference values required for significance at a particular α level (.05 or .01, usually)

FORMULAS

Before solving any of the formulas introduced, the following values need to be computed for the data: ΣX_g, ΣX_g^2, N_g, ΣX, ΣX^2, and N. ΣX_g is the sum of the scores within each group; ΣX_g^2 is the sum of the squared scores within each group; N_g is the number of observations within each group; ΣX is the sum of all the scores; ΣX^2 is the sum of all the squared scores; and N is the total number of observations. In addition, for one-way repeated measures ANOVA, ΣX_m, $(\Sigma X_m)^2$, S, and K must be computed. ΣX_m is the sum of scores for each participant; $(\Sigma X_m)^2$ is the square of the sum of the scores for each participant; S is the number of participants; and K is the number of trials or tests.

Formula 11-5. *Computational formula for the total sum of squares*

$$SS_{tot} = \Sigma X^2 - \frac{(\Sigma X)^2}{N}$$

This equation is identical to the numerator of sample variance, which we said in Chapter 6 was sometimes called the sum of squares or *SS*.

Formula 11-6. *Computational formula for the within-group sum of squares*

$$SS_w = \sum_g \left[\Sigma X_g^2 - \frac{(\Sigma X_g)^2}{N_g} \right]$$

This is just the sum of squares equation computed for each group and then summed across groups.

For three groups, the computational formula for SS_w becomes

$$SS_w = \left[\Sigma X_1^2 - \frac{(\Sigma X_1)^2}{N_1} \right] + \left[\Sigma X_2^2 - \frac{(\Sigma X_2)^2}{N_2} \right] + \left[\Sigma X_3^2 - \frac{(\Sigma X_3)^2}{N_3} \right]$$

Formula 11-7. *Computational formula for the between-groups sum of squares*

$$SS_b = \sum_g \left[\frac{(\Sigma X_g)^2}{N_g} \right] - \frac{(\Sigma X)^2}{N}$$

For three groups, the computational formula for SS_b becomes

$$SS_b = \left[\frac{(\Sigma X_1)^2}{N_1} + \frac{(\Sigma X_2)^2}{N_2} + \frac{(\Sigma X_3)^2}{N_3} \right] - \frac{(\Sigma X)^2}{N}$$

Formulas 11-8, 11-9, and 11-10. *Equations for between-groups degrees of freedom, within-groups degrees of freedom, and total degrees of freedom, respectively*

$$df_b = K - 1$$

$$df_w = N - K$$

$$df_{tot} = N - 1$$

Formula 11-11. *Equation for the between-groups mean square*

$$MS_b = \frac{SS_b}{df_b}$$

Formula 11-12. *Equation for the within-groups mean square*

$$MS_w = \frac{SS_w}{df_w}$$

Formula 11-13. *Equation for F ratio in one-way between-subjects ANOVA*

$$F = \frac{MS_b}{MS_w}$$

Formula 11-14. *Least significant difference (LSD) between pairs of means*

$$LSD_\alpha = t_\alpha \sqrt{MS_w \left(\frac{1}{N_1} + \frac{1}{N_2} \right)}$$

Formula 11-15. *Honestly significant difference (HSD) between pairs of means*

$$HSD_\alpha = q_\alpha \sqrt{\frac{MS_w}{N_g}}$$

Formula 11-18. *Computational formula for within-subjects sum of squares in one-way repeated measures ANOVA*

$$SS_{subj} = \sum_s \left[\frac{(\Sigma X_m)^2}{K} \right] - \frac{(\Sigma X)^2}{N}$$

For three subjects, the computational formula for SS_{subj} becomes

$$SS_{subj} = \left[\frac{(\Sigma X_{s_1})^2}{K} + \frac{(\Sigma X_{s_2})^2}{K} + \frac{(\Sigma X_{s_3})^2}{K} \right] - \frac{(\Sigma X)^2}{N}$$

Formula 11-19. *Computational formula for error sum of squares in one-way repeated measures ANOVA*

$$SS_{error} = SS_{tot} - SS_b - SS_{subj}$$

Formula 11-20. *Computational formula for error degrees of freedom*

$$df_{error} = (K - 1)(S - 1)$$

Formula 11-21. *Computational formula for mean square error in one-way repeated measures ANOVA*

$$MS_{error} = \frac{SS_{error}}{df_{error}}$$

Formula 11-22. *Computational formula for F ratio in one-way repeated measures ANOVA*

$$F = \frac{MS_b}{MS_{error}}$$

The degrees of freedom for the *F* ratio are the *df* associated with the numerator ($df_b = K - 1$) and *df* associated with the denominator [$df_{error} = (K - 1)(S - 1)$].

TERMS TO DEFINE AND/OR IDENTIFY

ANOVA

One-way ANOVA

Additivity

Key deviations

Total variability

Within-groups variability

Individual differences

Experimental error

Between-groups variability

Treatment effect

Total sum of squares

Within-groups sum of squares

Between-groups sum of squares

ANOVA summary table

Mean square

F ratio

Post-ANOVA tests

A posteriori test

Post hoc test

A priori test

Fisher LSD test

Protected t test

Pairwise comparisons

Tukey HSD test

Studentized range statistic

Repeated measures ANOVA

FILL-IN-THE-BLANK ITEMS

Introduction

The *t* test in Chapter 10 was used to compare the results from (1) _____ samples in order to see

whether they were drawn from (2) _____ populations. One important technique to

compare the results from two or more groups is the (3) _____ _____ _____.
Two reasons not to apply the *t* test to results from more than two groups are that the computations would be

(4) _____ and the more tests you do on the same data, the greater the likelihood of com-

mitting a Type (5) _____ error, rejecting a (6) _____ null hypothesis.

Between-Subjects ANOVA

Like the *t* test, one-way ANOVA has two versions: a (7) _____ ANOVA, which parallels

the independent *t,* and a (8) _____ _____ ANOVA, which parallels the dependent

t. The *t* score is a measure of the distance between a group mean and a (9) _____ mean,

or another group (10) _____ in standard (11) _____ terms. One of the
reasons that variance can be used to determine whether more than two groups differ is the property of

(12) _____. According to the property of additivity, the variance of the sum of in-

dependent scores is equal to the (13) _____ of the variances of the scores. Because vari-

ance is additive, we can divide the total variability in a set of scores into its (14) _____

_____.

Visualization of ANOVA concepts

The two components of variability in which we're interested are based on within-groups variability and

(15) _____ variability, and the (16) _____ _____ for these

components are $(X_g - \overline{X}_g)$ and $(\overline{X}_g - \overline{X}_{tot})$, respectively. $\overline{X}_{tot}$ is often called the (17) _____

_____. To analyze the variances, we are interested in comparing the (18) _____

variability to the within-groups variability. If the between-groups variability is (19) _____
relative to within-groups variability, we will probably conclude that the treatments had an effect.

Everyday ANOVA. The static on your cellular phone or the distracting noise at a party is analogous to

(20) _____ variability; the message or signal you're trying to detect is analogous to

(21) _____ variability.

Three sources of variability in some data are discussed: (22) _____ variability,

between-groups variability, and (23) _____ variability. The variability within groups

is caused by experimental error and (24) _____ _____. The variability be-

tween groups comes from experimental error, individual differences, and the (25) _____.

The ANOVA test is the ratio of the variability (26) _____ groups to the variability

(27) _____ groups. If there is no treatment effect, the F ratio will be near

(28) _____, whereas a treatment effect will make the statistic relatively (29) _____.

Measuring variability: The sum of squares

The (30) _____ sum of squares is the sum of the squared deviation of each score from

the total mean. The sum of squares (31) _____ groups is the sum of the squared deviations
of each group score from a group mean, with the deviations summed across groups. The sum of squares

(32) _____ groups is based on the deviation between each group mean and the total mean.

Computing the sums of squares

Although computation of the sums of squares can be tedious, the "trick" is to first compute the sum of

the (33) _____ in each group, the sum of the (34) _____ _____

in each group, the (35) _____ sum of scores, the total sum of squared scores, the number

of subjects per group, and the (36) _____ number of subjects. The symbols are ΣX_g,

(37) _____, ΣX, (38) _____, N_g, and N, respectively.
    Remember that variance is additive. In one-way between-subjects ANOVA, once SS_{tot} and one
of its components (either SS_b or SS_w) have been computed, the other component can be found by

(39) _____, although the value should be computed as a check on the accuracy of
your calculations.

The analysis of variance summary table

The ANOVA summary table provides a place for the sums of squares; the (40) _____ for each

of the sums of squares; the (41) _____ squares, which are computed by dividing each

SS by its *df;* and the (42) ____ _____. F is computed by dividing the MS_b by

(43) _____. df_b is equal to $K - 1$, where K is the number of (44) _____.

df_w = (45) _____. If the computed F ratio is larger than the critical F ratio from

Table (46) _____, the null hypothesis is (47) _____. Instead of being symmet-

rical like the *t* distributions, the F distributions are (48) _____ skewed with a

peak around (49) _____. (50) _____ tests are tests that follow a significant F ratio.

Post Hoc Comparisons

There are many post hoc tests available that avoid the problem of inflation of Type I error by

(51) _____ the critical value needed to reject H_0. Because a posteriori or post hoc

tests follow a significant F ratio, they are also called (52) _____ tests. On the other

hand, (53) ____ _____ tests are tests designed to look at specific hypotheses
before the experiment is performed. When the experimenter cannot predict the patterning of

(54) _____ before the research is performed, post hoc tests are appropriate.

The Fisher LSD

As presented in the text, the LSD test does not require equal (55) _____ _____.

Also, the LSD test is a (56) _____ test, which means that we are more likely to be able
to reject the null hypothesis with it than with many other post hoc tests available. The LSD test is some-

times called a (57) _____ *t* test because it follows a significant (58) ____

_____. The significant F ratio tells us that there is at least one (59) _____
comparison, thus protecting the error rate. With the test, the difference between two sample means is

significant if it is greater than (60) _____, which is found with the following formula:

(61) _____. As before (62) _____ is the level of significance, and the value of

t is obtained from Table (63) _____. The results of the Fisher LSD are best summarized in a

(64) _____ _____ _____.

The Tukey HSD

Although the Tukey HSD test can be used for more complex comparisons, we used it for making all

(65) _____ comparisons when the sample sizes are (66) _____ .
Like the Fisher LSD, the difference between two sample means is significant if it is greater than

(67) _____ , which is found with the following formula: (68) _____ . The value

of q comes from the distribution of the (69) _____ _____ _____ ,

whose critical values are found in Table (70) _____ . HSD stands for (71) _____

_____ _____ .

Repeated Measures ANOVA

Repeated measures ANOVA is appropriate in situations in which the (72) _____ partici-

pants are measured on more than (73) _____ occasions. In repeated measures ANOVA,

each participant serves as his or her own (74) _____ . By using a person as his or her own

control, we are able to extract some of the (75) _____ from our scores.

There are two sources of variability that contribute to SS_w: experimental (76) _____

and variability in (77) _____ . Thus, $SS_w = SS_{subj} + (78)$ _____ . SS_{error} is

used as the (79) _____ in computing the F ratio in one-way repeated measures ANOVA.

Because the property of additivity applies, $SS_{tot} = SS_b + SS_{subj} + (80)$ _____ . As compared to one-way between-subjects ANOVA, the additional step in one-way repeated measures ANOVA is

the computation of (81) _____ sum of squares.

The summary table for one-way repeated measures ANOVA is similar to that for one-way between-

subjects ANOVA except that SS_{tot} is divided into (82) _____ _____ instead
of two. For subjects, degrees of freedom are found by subtracting one from the number of

(83) _____ . Degrees of freedom for error are the product of df_b and

(84) _____ or $(K - 1)(S - 1)$.

Normally, an F ratio is not computed for (85) _____ . In one-way repeated measures

ANOVA, F is found by dividing MS_b by (86) _____ .

Troubleshooting Your Computations

Two obvious signs of trouble when computing the sums of squares are a (87) _____ sign

for SS and failure of SS_b and SS_w to sum to (88) _____. The most common error in filling

in the summary table is determining incorrectly the (89) _____ for each SS. Remember that $df_{tot} =$

$df_b + df_w = $ (90) _____ for between-subjects ANOVA, and $df_{tot} = df_b + df_{subj} + df_{error} =$

(91) _____ for repeated measures ANOVA.

The most common computational error made in calculating either LSD or HSD is to use N instead

of (92) _____ in the expression under the radical sign. Another error that is sometimes made is to

use a value from the (93) _____ table rather than the critical (94) _____ in the formula for

LSD or instead of the (95) _____ value in the HSD formula. Also, be sure to subtract to obtain

(96) _____ differences or to use the (97) _____ values or your differences

in the significance tests. Remember, if your computed value is equal to or (98) _____ than
the critical value, then you reject the null hypothesis for that test.

PROBLEMS

1. From a large introductory psychology class, 32 snake-phobic students were selected and randomly assigned to one of four experimental groups. Group 1 received five sessions of relaxation training; Group
   2 received five sessions of imagery training (they were required to imagine each of several feared situations); Group 3 received relaxation training combined with the imagery training; Group 4 participants
   were told that there would be a few weeks' delay in the beginning of therapy. Three weeks from the
   beginning of the experiment, each participant was given a behavioral avoidance test to determine how
   closely he or she would approach a live snake in an aquarium. The response measure is the distance
   from the snake in feet.

Group 1	Group 2	Group 3	Group 4
10	8	1	10
8	8	2	9
8	7	3	9
9	5	5	8
10	4	7	10
7	4	3	7
6	6	4	8
8	3	5	9

Compute the following:

$$\Sigma X_1 = \qquad \Sigma X_2 = \qquad \Sigma X_3 = \qquad \Sigma X_4 = \qquad \Sigma X =$$
$$\Sigma X_1^2 = \qquad \Sigma X_2^2 = \qquad \Sigma X_3^2 = \qquad \Sigma X_4^2 = \qquad \Sigma X^2 =$$
$$N_1 = \qquad N_2 = \qquad N_3 = \qquad N_4 = \qquad N =$$

Find the sums of squares:

$$SS_{tot} =$$

$$SS_w =$$

Find SS_b by subtraction:

$$SS_b = SS_{tot} - SS_w =$$

Compute SS_b:

$$SS_b =$$

Complete the ANOVA summary table:

Source	SS	df	MS	F
Between groups				
Within groups				
Total				

The computed value of F is _____. The df for the numerator is _____,

and the df for the denominator is _____. The table values required for rejection of H_0

are _____ at the 5% level and _____ at the 1% level. What is your decision and what does it mean in the context of the problem?

2. Use the Fisher LSD test to analyze the data in Problem 1 further.

3. Three different commercial sleeping aids and a placebo are given to four groups of randomly selected young adults. After a suitable period of time for the drugs to take effect, each participant is placed in a room with a bed, and his or her EEG is monitored. The response measured is the length of time before onset of sleep as determined by the EEG. The results are as follows: Group Placebo, $N = 9$, $\Sigma X = 29.7$, $\Sigma X^2 = 105.49$; Group Potion 1, $N = 8$, $\Sigma X = 30.4$, $\Sigma X^2 = 120.22$; Group Potion 2, $N = 9$, $\Sigma X = 32$, $\Sigma X^2 = 121.26$; Group Potion 3, $N = 8$, $\Sigma X = 30.1$, $\Sigma X^2 = 131.51$. Compute the sums of squares and fill in the summary table.

$SS_{tot} =$

$SS_w =$

$SS_b =$

ANOVA Summary Table

Source	SS	df	MS	F
Between groups				
Within groups				
Total				

Is the *F* ratio significant, and what does your conclusion mean in the context of the problem?

4. During WWII, the RAF noticed that a large number of fighter pilots were being killed because they were not dark-adapted during night air raids. An experiment was performed to determine whether different levels of preflight illumination might result in significant differences in time to dark adaptation. Twenty-four pilots were randomly and equally assigned to one of three treatment groups. Group A spent 30 minutes in a brightly lighted room; Group B spent 30 minutes in a dimly lighted room; Group C spent 30 minutes in a brightly lighted room wearing red-tinted goggles. The length of time in minutes for complete dark adaptation was recorded for each pilot. Determine whether the groups differed significantly.

Group A	Group B	Group C
$N = 8$	$N = 8$	$N = 8$
$\Sigma X = 260$	$\Sigma X = 78$	$\Sigma X = 36$
$\Sigma X^2 = 8{,}492$	$\Sigma X^2 = 788$	$\Sigma X^2 = 196$

5. Using the Fisher LSD, do all pairwise comparisons of the groups in Problem 4.

6. We hypothesize that the experience of taking a statistics course will reduce mathematics anxiety. To test this hypothesis, we select nine statistics students and assess their mathematics anxiety on four occasions: on the first day of class, after 3 weeks of class, after 6 weeks of class, and after 9 weeks of class. Perform the appropriate overall test of significance.

Student	First Day	3 Weeks	6 Weeks	9 Weeks
A	14	12	9	8
B	8	7	5	3
C	6	7	4	2
D	9	10	8	7
E	15	12	10	9
F	12	10	8	9
G	9	8	7	6
H	7	6	5	3
I	10	9	7	7

7. Use the Fisher LSD test to perform all pairwise comparisons for the data in Problem 6.

8. A manufacturing company is concerned about the effect of fatigue on the speed with which its workers can assemble pocket calculators. For 10 workers, the average time (in seconds) it takes to assemble a pocket calculator is measured at the beginning, in the middle, and at the end of the shift. Does performance change across periods of the workers' shift?

Worker	Beginning	Middle	End
A	20	21	23
B	28	30	31
C	22	23	24
D	19	19	22
E	24	26	28
F	26	27	29
G	19	18	19
H	24	25	27
I	20	21	22
J	19	21	22

9. Use the Tukey HSD to make all pairwise comparisons for the data in Problem 8.

10. In a study of dark adaptation, eight participants seated in an almost totally dark room were asked to determine visually the presence or absence of an object. All participants were given 10 trials after 1 minute of adaptation, after 15 minutes, and after 30 minutes. At each testing, the number of correct detections out of 10 trials was recorded. Perform an overall significance test, and tell what your conclusion means in the context of the problem.

Participant	1 Minute	15 Minutes	30 Minutes
A	2	6	6
B	0	2	4
C	4	7	9
D	3	5	6
E	6	8	10
F	0	2	4
G	2	5	1
H	3	5	8

11. Use the Fisher LSD test to make all pairwise comparisons and summarize your results.

12. A study was done to see whether the source of dietary fat affects visual discrimination. Rats were placed on one of four diets for 2 months: Diet 1 had 5% corn oil; Diet 2 was the same as Diet 1 with the addition of 20% safflower oil; Diet 3 was Diet 1 with 20% added coconut oil; Diet 4 was Diet 1 with 20% added olive oil. All the rats were trained on a simple visual discrimination task, and their errors before achieving a certain criterion were recorded. Test the data to see whether the different diets affected learning of the task.

Diet 1	Diet 2	Diet 3	Diet 4
13	10	7	14
20	20	17	19
31	34	11	27
18	27	23	31
11	7	14	15
11	27	13	21
11	10	26	14
12	12	23	
12	32	4	
12	11		

USING SPSS—EXAMPLES AND EXERCISES

SPSS has several techniques for performing analysis of variance (ANOVA). The ONEWAY procedure is one such method, and it will perform a variety of post hoc tests. For the repeated measures ANOVA, we will need to use the SPSS GLM (General Linear Model)–Repeated Measures procedure to obtain the analysis. The SPSS GLM procedures will perform analyses for many different types of ANOVA designs. Unfortunately—given our desire to keep this as simple as possible—the SPSS GLM procedures are some of the "fancier" SPSS techniques and provide extensive output that is well beyond the level of the textbook.

Example—Independent Groups ANOVA: As an example of an independent groups ANOVA, we will work Problem 1 using SPSS. We will illustrate how to perform the ANOVA, how to do the LSD and HSD post hoc tests, how to graph the means, and how to provide an Error Bar chart of the groups. The steps are as follows:

1. Start SPSS and enter the data. The data entry is an extension of the set-up we used for the two-sample independent-groups *t* test. Name the two variables **group** and **distance**. The group variable will have a 1 entered for each distance score from Group 1, a 2 for each distance score from Group 2, and so on.
2. Select Statistics>Compare Means>One-Way ANOVA.
3. Move **distance** to the Dependent List box because it is the dependent variable. Move **group** to the Factor box.
4. Select the Post Hoc box and choose LSD and Tukey (HSD) in the Post Hoc Multiple Comparisons box. Then select Continue.
5. Select the Options box; click Descriptive and Means plot (this will give you a line graph of the group means), then Continue>OK. The results should appear in the output Viewer window.
6. As an extra illustration for this exercise, we will create an Error Bar chart for the groups, which shows a plot of the confidence intervals for each group. This type of graph is helpful in understanding and emphasizing that there is within-group variability that is not shown in graphs of group means as point estimates.
7. Select Graphs>Error Bar>Simple>Summaries for groups of cases>Define.
8. Move **distance** into the Variable box and move **group** into the Category Axis box. Other settings in this dialog box should indicate a 95% confidence interval for means. Next click OK and the graph should appear in the output Viewer window.

Notes on Reading the Output

1. The ANOVA output box gives the source table. The "Sig." after the *F* value is the exact probability value for the obtained *F* ratio. For example, $p = .000$ means that *p* is 0 when rounded to three decimal places. Because *p* is never exactly 0, it is better to express this probability as $p < .001$.
2. The Multiple Comparisons box is highly redundant. It does not give a test statistic value for each comparison or a minimum difference required for significance between two groups. Instead the box indicates the significant comparisons by an asterisk beside the Mean Difference and the exact *p* value given in the Sig. column. For example, the Tukey HSD results indicate that Group 1 versus Group 4 and Group 2 versus Group 3 are the only comparisons that are not statistically different. The more powerful LSD test indicates that only Groups 1 and 4 are not statistically different.
3. The Means Plots and the Graph showing confidence intervals provide pictures of the results. Because their confidence intervals overlap considerably, we would expect Groups 1 and 4 and Groups 2 and 3 not to be statistically different. Of course, this is what we found with the HSD test.

```
ONEWAY
  distance BY group
  /STATISTICS DESCRIPTIVES
  /PLOT MEANS
  /MISSING ANALYSIS
  /POSTHOC = TUKEY LSD ALPHA(.05).
```

Oneway

Descriptives

DISTANCE

	N	Mean	Std. Deviation	Std. Error	95% Confidence Interval for Mean		Minimum	Maximum
					Lower Bound	Upper Bound		
1.00	8	8.2500	1.3887	.4910	7.0890	9.4110	6.00	10.00
2.00	8	5.6250	1.9226	.6797	4.0177	7.2323	3.00	8.00
3.00	8	3.7500	1.9086	.6748	2.1543	5.3457	1.00	7.00
4.00	8	8.7500	1.0351	.3660	7.8846	9.6154	7.00	10.00
Total	32	6.5938	2.5635	.4532	5.6695	7.5180	1.00	10.00

ANOVA

DISTANCE

	Sum of Squares	df	Mean Square	F	Sig.
Between Groups	131.344	3	43.781	16.938	.000
Within Groups	72.375	28	2.585		
Total	203.719	31			

Post Hoc Tests

Multiple Comparisons

Dependent Variable: DISTANCE

	(I) GROUP	(J) GROUP	Mean Difference (I-J)	Std. Error	Sig.	95% Confidence Interval	
						Lower Bound	Upper Bound
Tukey HSD	1.00	2.00	2.6250*	.804	.014	.4302	4.8198
		3.00	4.5000*	.804	.000	2.3052	6.6948
		4.00	-.5000	.804	.924	-2.6948	1.6948
	2.00	1.00	-2.6250*	.804	.014	-4.8198	-.4302
		3.00	1.8750	.804	.115	-.3198	4.0698
		4.00	-3.1250*	.804	.003	-5.3198	-.9302
	3.00	1.00	-4.5000*	.804	.000	-6.6948	-2.3052
		2.00	-1.8750	.804	.115	-4.0698	.3198
		4.00	-5.0000*	.804	.000	-7.1948	-2.8052
	4.00	1.00	.5000	.804	.924	-1.6948	2.6948
		2.00	3.1250*	.804	.003	.9302	5.3198
		3.00	5.0000*	.804	.000	2.8052	7.1948
LSD	1.00	2.00	2.6250*	.804	.003	.9783	4.2717
		3.00	4.5000*	.804	.000	2.8533	6.1467
		4.00	-.5000	.804	.539	-2.1467	1.1467
	2.00	1.00	-2.6250*	.804	.003	-4.2717	-.9783
		3.00	1.8750*	.804	.027	.2283	3.5217
		4.00	-3.1250*	.804	.001	-4.7717	-1.4783
	3.00	1.00	-4.5000*	.804	.000	-6.1467	-2.8533
		2.00	-1.8750*	.804	.027	-3.5217	-.2283
		4.00	-5.0000*	.804	.000	-6.6467	-3.3533
	4.00	1.00	.5000	.804	.539	-1.1467	2.1467
		2.00	3.1250*	.804	.001	1.4783	4.7717
		3.00	5.0000*	.804	.000	3.3533	6.6467

*. The mean difference is significant at the .05 level.

Homogeneous Subsets

DISTANCE

	GROUP	N	Subset for alpha = .05	
			1	2
Tukey HSD[a]	3.00	8	3.7500	
	2.00	8	5.6250	
	1.00	8		8.2500
	4.00	8		8.7500
	Sig.		.115	.924

Means for groups in homogeneous subsets are displayed.

a. Uses Harmonic Mean Sample Size = 8.000.

Means Plots

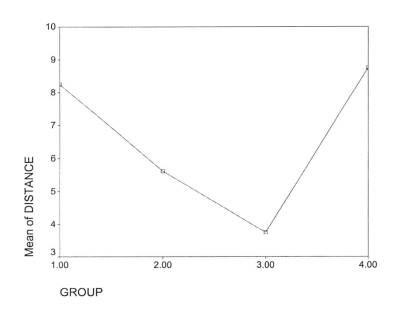

Graph

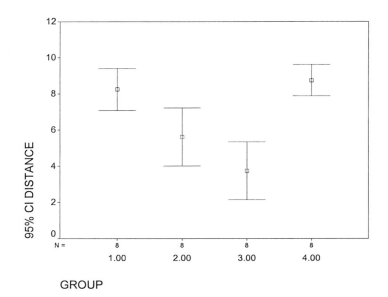

Example—Repeated Measures ANOVA: Our example of the repeated measures ANOVA will use the SPSS GLM–Repeated Measures procedure. This technique will perform the analysis for the one-way repeated measures exercises in the text and in this study guide in addition to analyzing more extensive designs. The procedure does not do post hoc tests for this completely within-subjects design, so we will not be concerned with this part of our computer solution. The supplemental text on using SPSS suggested in Appendix 4 explains how to do such tests. (In short, the post hoc tests are performed by computing sequential pairwise dependent t tests and testing for significance by using the α level obtained by dividing .05 by the number of tests performed.) Alternatively, you can compute the post hoc tests by hand, using information from the output and the procedures described in the text. We will solve Problem 6 as an example. Here are the steps to follow:

1. Start SPSS and name the variables **day1**, **wk3**, **wk6**, and **wk9**. Enter the data for each of these variables. Note that this data entry arrangement is an extension of the arrangement used for the paired-samples t test. Each participant's data are given on one row.
2. Select Statistics>General Linear Model>GLM-Repeated Measures.
3. In the dialog box, enter the number of levels (4 for the four times of measurement), and click Add. The Define Factor(s) dialog box should appear as follows. Then select Define.

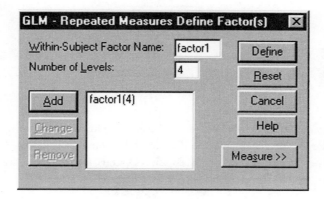

4. In the GLM-Repeated Measures dialog box, highlight each of the variables and move them into the Within-Subjects Variables box in order—that is, **day1** is first and **wk9** is fourth. The dialog box should appear as follows:

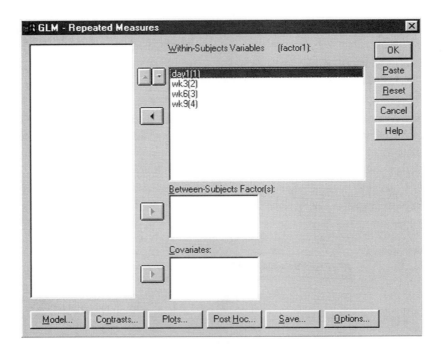

5. Although it is not required for the analysis, we will also get a plot of the means by selecting the Plots box, highlighting "factor 1" and moving it to the Horizontal Axis box, then clicking Add>Continue.
6. We want descriptive statistics for our groups, so select Options, then click on Descriptive Statistics in the Options dialog box, which should appear as follows. Click on Continue.

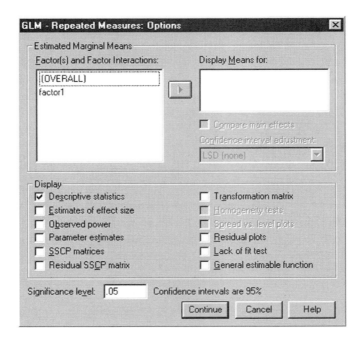

7. You should now be back to the GLM-Repeated Measures dialog box. Click OK, and the results should appear in the output Viewer window.

Notes on Reading the Output

1. As you learn to use statistical software, one skill that you will need to develop is the ability to ignore parts of the output that are superfluous for what you are trying to do. You will also need to learn to focus on the important and necessary parts of the output for your particular problem. In fact, both of these skills are necessary for you to extract the information from the output that you need for solving the present exercise.

2. In the following output, we have included only the portions that are needed for the present exercise. Your task is to ignore other parts of the output that are produced by the process we have described.

3. The Descriptive Statistics box gives exactly that information.

4. Locate the box labeled Tests of Within-Subjects Effects. Also locate the box labeled Tests of Between-Subjects Effects. The following figure shows the information needed from these two boxes to construct the source table needed for this exercise.

Tests of Within-Subjects Effects

Measure: MEASURE_1

Source		Type III Sum of Squares	df	Mean Square	F	Sig.
FACTOR1	Sphericity Assumed	90.000	3	30.000	41.143	.000
	Greenhouse-Geisser	90.000	2.264	39.747	41.143	.000
	Huynh-Feldt	90.000	3.000	30.000	41.143	.000
	Lower-bound	90.000	1.000	90.000	41.143	.000
Error(FACTOR1)	Sphericity Assumed	17.500	24	.729		
	Greenhouse-Geisser	17.500	18.115	.966		
	Huynh-Feldt	17.500	24.000	.729		
	Lower-bound	17.500	8.000	2.187		

Desired Source Table

Source	SS	df	MS	F
Between	90.0	3	30.0	$\frac{30.0}{0.729} = 41.14$
Subjects	186.5	8		
Error	17.5	24	0.729	
Total	294.0	35		

Tests of Between-Subjects Effects

Measure: MEASURE_1

Transformed Variable: Average

Source	Type III Sum of Squares	df	Mean Square	F	Sig.
Intercept	2304.000	1	2304.000	98.831	.000
Error	186.500	8	23.313		

Following is the solutions output for the example based on Problem 6:

```
GLM
  day1 wk3 wk6 wk9
  /WSFACTOR = factor1 4 Polynomial
  /METHOD = SSTYPE(3)
  /PLOT = PROFILE( factor1 )
  /PRINT = DESCRIPTIVE
  /CRITERIA = ALPHA(.05)
  /WSDESIGN = factor1 .
```

General Linear Model

Within-Subjects Factors

Measure: MEASURE_1

FACTOR1	Dependent Variable
1	DAY1
2	WK3
3	WK6
4	WK9

Descriptive Statistics

	Mean	Std. Deviation	N
DAY1	10.0000	3.0822	9
WK3	9.0000	2.1794	9
WK6	7.0000	2.0000	9
WK9	6.0000	2.6926	9

Tests of Within-Subjects Effects

Measure: MEASURE_1

Source		Type III Sum of Squares	df	Mean Square	F	Sig.
FACTOR1	Sphericity Assumed	90.000	3	30.000	41.143	.000
	Greenhouse-Geisser	90.000	2.264	39.747	41.143	.000
	Huynh-Feldt	90.000	3.000	30.000	41.143	.000
	Lower-bound	90.000	1.000	90.000	41.143	.000
Error(FACTOR1)	Sphericity Assumed	17.500	24	.729		
	Greenhouse-Geisser	17.500	18.115	.966		
	Huynh-Feldt	17.500	24.000	.729		
	Lower-bound	17.500	8.000	2.187		

Tests of Between-Subjects Effects

Measure: MEASURE_1
Transformed Variable: Average

Source	Type III Sum of Squares	df	Mean Square	F	Sig.
Intercept	2304.000	1	2304.000	98.831	.000
Error	186.500	8	23.313		

Profile Plots

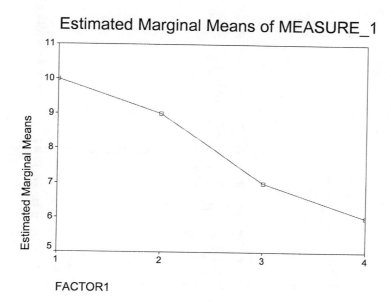

Exercises Using SPSS

1. Work Self-Test Exercise 4 using SPSS. Obtain LSD post hoc test results and an Error Bar graph of the 95% confidence intervals for each group.
2. Work Problem 8 using SPSS with the GLM–Repeated Measures procedure. Obtain a plot of the means and use the output to construct the desired source table.

CHECKING YOUR PROGRESS: A SELF-TEST

1. If there is no treatment effect, the F ratio should be close to which of the following?
   a. 0
   b. 1
   c. 10
   d. ∞
2. True or False: A significant F ratio reveals which of the possible between-group comparisons is significant.

3. Match the following:

_____ df_{error}

_____ df_{tot}

_____ df_{subj}

_____ df_b

_____ df_w

_____ MS_w

_____ F (between subjects)

_____ MS_b

_____ MS_{error}

_____ F (repeated measures)

a. $\dfrac{MS_b}{MS_w}$

b. $N - 1$

c. $\dfrac{SS_w}{df_w}$

d. $\dfrac{SS_b}{df_b}$

e. $\dfrac{SS_b}{df_w}$

f. $K - 1$, where K is the number of groups

g. $K - N$

h. $N - K$

i. $\dfrac{MS_b}{MS_{error}}$

j. $(K - 1)(S - 1)$

k. $\dfrac{SS_{error}}{df_{error}}$

l. $S - 1$

4. At the end of the study described earlier in Problem 12 of this chapter, blood samples from each animal were analyzed for total cholesterol and HDL (high-density lipoprotein) cholesterol. The results are reported below in total cholesterol/HDL ratios; lower ratios are better, according to current health guidelines. Compute the F ratio and test it for significance.

Diet 1	Diet 2	Diet 3	Diet 4
2.7	1.5	2.5	2.2
2.2	1.8	2.4	2.3
2.1	1.7	2.2	1.6
2.0	2.0	1.6	2.6
1.6	1.9	1.7	2.2
2.2	1.5	2.2	2.8
2.8	1.6	2.3	2.7
2.0	1.7	2.0	
2.6	1.7	2.2	
2.6	1.8		

5. A child psychologist is interested in the course of development of object conservation in infants. The psychologist studies seven infants over a 6-month period. The infants are given 20 test trials at the ages of 9 months, 12 months, and 15 months. On each trial, an object is shown to the child and then is covered by a cloth. The child shows conservation if he or she looks for the object or becomes distressed when it is covered. The number of trials, out of 20, on which the child shows conservation is recorded. Perform the appropriate analysis; if significant, do all pairwise comparisons with the Fisher LSD test. Tell what your answers mean in the context of the problem.

Child	9 Months	12 Months	15 Months
A	0	3	17
B	2	4	17
C	3	6	16
D	1	2	14
E	0	1	19
F	4	9	2
G	4	3	20

CHAPTER 12

TWO-WAY
ANALYSIS
OF VARIANCE

OBJECTIVES

The main objective in Chapter 12 is to give a nonquantitative, intuitive look at two-way or two-factor analysis of variance.

CHAPTER REVIEW

The two-way ANOVA is presented in this chapter as a method for analyzing data resulting from the administration of two or more levels of two independent variables. When there is more than one independent variable, the variables are called *factors*.

In a two-factor experiment, the effect of each separate independent variable is called a *main effect*. Thus, a two-factor experiment has two main effects. Also, there is the possibility of *interaction* or the joint effect of two independent variables on behavior. If an interaction effect exists, the effect of one factor depends on the levels of the second factor.

One way to look for interaction or the lack of it is to graph the results of a factorial study. If there is no interaction, the graph will show roughly parallel lines or lines that are approximately equidistant at each data point. Interaction is shown by converging or crossing lines. "Rules" for interpreting graphs of two-factor experiments are as follows:

1. Assuming factor A is shown on the baseline and the levels of factor B are plotted as different lines, if the averages of the points above each level of factor A are unequal, there may be a significant main effect for factor A.

2. If the averages of the points used to plot the lines are unequal, there may be a significant main effect for factor B.

3. If the lines converge, cross, or in some way depart from parallel, there may be a significant interaction.

The main advantage of the two-factor design is that you can test for interaction between the factors. If you manipulated the same variables in two separate one-factor experiments, you would not be able to test for an interaction of the factors. Another advantage of the two-factor design is that it allows a savings in the number of subjects, and probably the time and resources, needed. The two-factor design usually increases the power of the tests on the main effects and permits greater generalizability.

The logic of the tests for two-factor designs is the same as for the one-way ANOVA. Instead of one F test, there are three F tests for the two-way ANOVA: main effects tests for factors A and B, and a test of the interaction between factors A and B. Each F ratio consists of the variance (MS) for each effect divided by the variance within treatments. The same error term, MS_w, is used for each F ratio. The variance between treatments is assumed to be caused by individual differences, experimental error, and a treatment effect; the variance within treatments is caused by individual differences and experimental error. An F ratio close to 1.00 indicates the lack of a treatment effect, and a value much larger than 1.00 signals a valid treatment effect.

Interpretation of the two-way ANOVA depends in large part on whether the interaction is significant. If the interaction is not significant, significant main effects can be analyzed with the post hoc tests discussed in Chapter 11. The first step in interpreting a significant interaction is to plot the group means, with further interpretation requiring individual group comparisons.

TERMS TO DEFINE AND/OR IDENTIFY

Two-way ANOVA

Factors

Factorial design

Main effect

Interaction

FILL-IN-THE-BLANK ITEMS

Introduction

In Chapter 11, we used the (1) _____ _____ to analyze the results of an experi-ment in which two or more levels of an independent variable were manipulated. The (2) _____ _____ is used when another independent variable is added. When more than one independent variable is used, the variables are called (3) _____. An experiment studying the effects of task difficulty and anxiety in which there are three levels of task difficulty and three levels of anxiety is an example of a (4) _____ factorial design.

Main Effects and Effects of Interaction

The effect of each independent variable in a two-factor experiment is called a (5) _____ _____. Also, there is the possibility of the joint effect of the two independent variables on behavior; this effect is called the (6) _____. If an interaction exists, the effect of one factor (7) _____ on the levels of the second factor. If there is no interaction between factors, the graph of the data will show essentially (8) _____ lines or lines that are ap-proximately equidistant at each data point. Thus, interaction is usually revealed by (9) _____ lines or (10) _____ lines. When levels of factor B are plotted as lines above levels of fac-tor A, data can be interpreted from a two-factor experiment with the help of the following "rules":

1. If the averages of the points above each level of factor A are unequal, a significant main effect for factor

   (11) _____ is suggested.

2. If the averages of the points used to plot the (12) _____ are unequal, there may be a significant main effect for factor B.

3. If the lines aren't parallel, there may be a significant (13) _____.

Advantages of the Two-Factor Design

The main advantage of the two-factor design over two one-factor experiments is the test for

(14) _____. A second advantage is economy. The two-factor design allows a reduction in the number of (15) _____ required. Statistical tests on the main effects are usually more

(16) _____ with the two-factor design than with two one-factor designs. Finally, the two-factor design tells about more conditions; that is, it allows for greater (17) _____ .

Logic of the Two-Way ANOVA

The two-factor ANOVA results in (18) _____ F ratios. There are tests of the

(19) _____ _____ of factors A and B and a test of the

(20) _____ of factors A and B. The same error term, symbolized by

(21) _____ is used for each F ratio.

Interpretation of Results

Interpretation of the two-way ANOVA depends mainly on whether the (22) _____ is significant. If it is not significant, a significant main effect can be analyzed with the (23) _____

_____ tests covered in Chapter 11. Plotting the group means is often the first step in interpreting a significant (24) _____ .

PROBLEMS

1. For the problems in this chapter, assume that the within-group variability is small enough that any between-group mean differences will result in a significant F ratio. For each of the following tables, draw a graph and use it to predict the result of each tested main effect and the interaction.

a.

		Factor B	
		B_1	B_2
Factor A	A_1	10	15
	A_2	30	25

b.

		Factor B	
		B_1	B_2
	A_1	15	7
Factor A	A_2	30	22
	A_3	20	12

c.

Factor B

	B_1	B_2	B_3
A_1	10	30	20
Factor A A_2	20	20	20
A_3	30	10	20

2. A pursuit-rotor task is performed by either sinistral or dextral men (left-handed or right-handed, respectively) under three different illumination levels. For each of the hypothetical outcomes, what result would you predict for the F ratios? Cell scores are the average times on target in seconds for a 1-minute test; $N_g = 10$.

a.

Illumination Level

	Low	Medium	High
Sinistrals	25	35	45
Handedness Dextrals	35	45	55

b.

Illumination Level

	Low	Medium	High
Sinistrals	20	40	20
Handedness Dextrals	40	20	40

c.

Illumination Level

	Low	Medium	High
Sinistrals	20	30	40
Handedness Dextrals	40	30	20

3. A study examined the effects of task difficulty and anxiety level on problem-solving ability. There were three levels of task difficulty (easy, moderate, hard) and three levels of anxiety as determined by scores on the Taylor Manifest Anxiety Scale (low, medium, high). The dependent variable was the average time to solve 10 problems in minutes. Using the following table, graph the results and indicate the probable outcome of F tests. Each cell value is a group average in minutes; $N_g = 20$.

		Anxiety Level		
		Low	Medium	High
Task Difficulty	Easy	8.6	6.2	4.3
	Moderate	10.2	8.4	12.5
	Hard	12.7	10.5	21.8

4. A cognitive psychologist studied the effects of mathematics anxiety on the speed of solution of arithmetic problems. Students were tested on the Mathematics Anxiety Rating Scale and separated into high, medium, and low mathematics anxiety groups. Half of each group then solved easy (one-digit) addition problems and the other half solved hard (two-digit) problems. Each cell contains the average number of seconds taken to solve each problem. Graph the means, and predict the outcome of the significance tests.

		Anxiety Level		
		Low	Medium	High
Problem Difficulty	Easy	2	4	4
	Hard	8	12	20

5. A social psychologist is interested in the effects of thrill-seeking tendency and alcohol dose on performance on a simulated driving task. She administers a test that measures thrill-seeking tendency and divides the subject pool into two levels on the basis of subject scores: low and high. Thirty volunteers from each level are given either no alcohol, 1 ounce of alcohol, or 2 ounces of alcohol. After 15 minutes, each participant is tested on the task; the score is the length of time the car stays on the road in a 2-minute test. Each cell value is the average in seconds for 10 participants. Graph the results, and predict the outcome of significance tests.

		Alcohol Level		
		0 oz	1 oz	2 oz
Thrill Seeking	Low	110	105	95
	High	95	75	45

6. Hypothetical F ratios for each part of Problem 2 are shown next. Give the critical value for each F ratio and provide an interpretation for each significant test. For example, a significant F ratio for handedness would mean that time on target was affected by the hand used. Review of the group means would suggest whether left-handed or right-handed participants performed better.

a.

Source	F		p
Between groups			
A (handedness)	6.31	($df = 1, 54$)	
B (illumination)	4.05	($df = 2, 54$)	
A $\times$ B	1.18	($df = 2, 54$)	

b.

Source	F		p
Between groups			
A (handedness)	4.52	($df = 1, 54$)	
B (illumination)	0.67	($df = 2, 54$)	
A $\times$ B	10.91	($df = 2, 54$)	

c.

Source	F		p
Between groups			
A (handedness)	0.75	($df = 1, 54$)	
B (illumination)	1.18	($df = 2, 54$)	
A $\times$ B	9.83	($df = 2, 54$)	

CHECKING YOUR PROGRESS: A SELF-TEST

1. Converging or crossing lines on a graph of the results of a two-factor experiment often signal a significant
   a. main effect for factor A.
   b. main effect for factor B.
   c. interaction.
   d. all of the above

2. Which of the following is *not* an advantage of a two-factor design over two separate one-factor experiments?
   a. a test for interaction
   b. fewer subjects required
   c. greater generalizability
   d. decreased power on the main effects tests

3. An experiment might be done to compare the effects of nicotine and a placebo on hand–eye coordination in smokers and nonsmokers. Different possible outcomes are shown in the following contingency tables. The cell numbers are mean errors on a mirror tracing task. Graph the results, and predict the outcomes of significance tests.

a.

	Placebo	Nicotine
Smoker	15	15
Nonsmoker	8	15

b.

	Placebo	Nicotine
Smoker	15	5
Nonsmoker	5	15

c.

	Placebo	Nicotine
Smoker	15	20
Nonsmoker	5	10

CHAPTER 13

CORRELATION
AND REGRESSION

OBJECTIVES

The main objectives in Chapter 13 are to define correlation and to present techniques to compute the correlation between two variables. The linear regression equation, used for prediction, is introduced.

CHAPTER REVIEW

Correlation is defined as the degree of relationship between two or more variables. Although there are many kinds of correlation, the chapter focuses on *linear* correlation, or the degree to which a straight line best describes the relationship between two variables.

The degree of linear relationship between two variables may assume an infinite range of values, but it is customary to speak of three different classes of correlation. *Zero* correlation is defined as no relationship between variables. *Positive* correlation means there is a direct relationship between the variables, such that as one variable increases, so does the other. An inverse relationship in which low values of one variable are associated with high values of the other is called *negative* correlation.

A *scatterplot* is often used to show the relationship between two variables. Scatterplots are graphs in which pairs of scores are plotted, with the scores on one variable plotted on the X axis and scores on the other variable plotted on the Y axis. On the scatterplot, a pattern of points describing a line sloping upward to the right indicates positive correlation, and points indicating a line sloping downward to the right reveal negative correlation. Zero correlation is shown by a random pattern of points on the scatterplot. High correlation between two variables doesn't necessarily mean that one variable *caused* the other.

When the data are at least interval scale, the *Pearson product-moment correlation coefficient,* or *Pearson r,* is used to compute the degree of relationship between two variables. The Pearson r may be defined as the mean of the z-score products for X and Y pairs, where X stands for one variable and Y stands for the other.

One approach to understanding the Pearson correlation is based on a close relative of variance, the *covariance,* which is the extent to which two variables vary together. Covariance can be used to derive a simple formula for the Pearson correlation, and we can think of the Pearson r as a standardized covariance between X and Y.

The range of r is from -1 to $+1$. Restricting the range of either the X or the Y variable lowers the value of r. The *coefficient of determination,* r^2, tells the amount of variability in one variable explained by variability in the other variable.

After computing the Pearson r, we can test it for significance. First, we assume that our sample was taken from a population in which there is no relationship between the two variables; this is just another version of the null hypothesis. Then, we consult Table E, which contains values of r for different degrees of freedom $(N - 2)$ with probabilities of either .05 or .01. If our computed coefficient, in absolute value, is equal to or greater than the critical value at the 5% level, we reject the null hypothesis and conclude that our sample probably came from a population in which there is a relationship between the variables.

From the definition of correlation as the degree of linear relationship between two variables, we can use the correlation coefficient to compute the equations for the straight lines best describing the relationship between the variables. The equations (one to predict X and one to predict Y) are called *regression equations,* and we can use them to predict a score on one variable if we know a score on the other. The general form of the equation is $Y = bX + a$, where b is the slope of the line and a is where the line intercepts the Y axis. The regression line is also called the *least squares line.*

The *Spearman rank order correlation coefficient,* r_S, is a computationally simple alternative to r that is useful when the measurement level of one or both variables is ordinal scale. Like the Pearson r, the Spearman coefficient can be tested for significance. To test r_S for significance, we compare its value with critical values in Table F for the appropriate sample size; if our computed value is larger in absolute value than the table value at the 5% level, we reject the null hypothesis and conclude that the two variables are related.

Other correlation coefficients briefly considered in the chapter are the point biserial correlation (r_{pbis}) and the phi coefficient (ϕ). The former is useful when one variable is dichotomous (has only two values) and the other variable is continuous or interval level, whereas the latter is used when both variables are dichotomous. All of the inferential statistical methods covered in the text through this chapter can be tied together under the general linear model, which is a general, relationship-oriented multiple predictor approach to inference.

SYMBOLS

Symbol	Stands For
r	Pearson r, Pearson product-moment correlation coefficient
z_X, z_Y	z scores for the X and Y variables, respectively
cov_{XY}	covariance of X and Y
ρ	population correlation coefficient, read "rho"
r_{comp}, r_{crit}	computed value of r and the critical value of r from Table E, respectively
$\hat{Y}$	Y-caret, predicted values for Y based on the regression equation
b	regression coefficient, slope of the regression line
a	Y intercept, value of Y where the regression line crosses the Y axis
s_Y, s_X	standard deviation of the Y variable and the X variable, respectively
r^2	coefficient of determination
r_S	Spearman rank order correlation coefficient
d	difference between the ranks

FORMULAS

Formula 13-2. *Computational formula for the Pearson r*

$$r = \frac{N\Sigma XY - \Sigma X \Sigma Y}{\sqrt{[N\Sigma X^2 - (\Sigma X)^2][N\Sigma Y^2 - (\Sigma Y)^2]}}$$

The values needed to compute the equation are: ΣX, ΣY, ΣX^2, ΣY^2, ΣXY, and N. ΣXY is found by multiplying each X by each Y and summing the result.

Formula 13-3. *Regression equation for predicting Y from X*

$$\hat{Y} = \left(\frac{rs_Y}{s_X}\right)X + \left[\bar{Y} - \left(\frac{rs_Y}{s_X}\right)\bar{X}\right]$$

Formula 13-4. *Equation for determining the proportion of variability in data explained by correlation*

$$\text{coefficient of determination} = \frac{\text{explained variation}}{\text{total variation}} = r^2$$

Formula 13-5. *Equation for the Spearman rank order correlation coefficient*

$$r_S = 1 - \frac{6\Sigma d^2}{N(N^2 - 1)}$$

d is the difference between the *ranks* of individuals on the two variables, and N is the number of pairs of observations.

TERMS TO DEFINE AND/OR IDENTIFY

Correlation

Linear relationship

Positive correlation

Scatterplot

Negative correlation

Zero correlation

Pearson product-moment correlation coefficient

Pearson r

Covariance

Regression equation

Least squares line

Regression coefficient

Multiple regression

Coefficient of determination

Spearman rank order correlation

Point biserial correlation

Phi coefficient

General linear model

FILL-IN-THE-BLANK ITEMS

Linear Correlation

The degree of relationship between two or more variables is called (1) _____ . If

the relationship is best described by means of a straight line, we call this (2) _____

_____ .

Classes of correlation

A direct relationship between two variables, in which a high score is associated with a (3) _____

score and a low score with a (4) _____ score, is called (5) _____ correlation. One

way to study the relationship between the variables is with a (6) _____ or graph on which
scores for one variable are plotted on the X axis and scores for the other variable are plotted on the Y axis.

An inverse relationship between the variables is called (7) _____ correlation and is shown

by a line sloping (8) _____ to the right on a scatterplot. If the relationship between the

variables is very small or nonexistent, the "class" of correlation is called (9) _____ correlation. The

strength of a relationship between two variables is given by the (10) _____ _____
of the correlation coefficient.

Correlation and causation

A high correlation between two variables doesn't automatically mean that one variable

(11) _____ the other. Correlation is necessary but not (12) _____
to determine causality.

The Pearson Product-Moment Correlation Coefficient

The Pearson r is defined as the (13) _____ of the z-score products for X-Y pairs of scores. The range

of r is from (14) _____ to _____ . A (15) _____ value of r indicates a direct rela-

tionship between the variables, and a negative value indicates an (16) _____ relationship.

Values of r close to (17) _____ indicate little or no relationship between the variables.

Correlation, variance, and covariance

We can define the (18) _____ as the extent to which two variables vary together. The variance, then, is a special case of the (19) _____ of X and X—of a variable with itself. Standardizing the covariance gives us a simple formula for the (20) _____ _____.

The effect of range on correlation

Restricting the range of either the X or the Y variable (21) _____ the correlation.

Testing r for significance

To test r for significance, we first assume there is (22) _____ _____ in the population between the variables; that is, we assume that the underlying population correlation coefficient, (23) _____, is (24) _____. Then we look in Table (25) _____ for values of r known to occur 5% or 1% of the time in samples of a given size, converted to (26) _____, from a population with a (27) _____ coefficient. If the absolute value of our sample coefficient exceeds the critical table value, then we (28) _____ the null hypothesis, indicating that there is a significant (29) _____ between the variables in the population sampled.

The linear regression equation

Correlation is defined as the degree of (30) _____ relationship between the variables. Based on this definition, we can use correlation for prediction by first computing the equation for the (31) _____ line that best describes the relationship between the variables. The general equation for the regression equation is (32) _____, where b is the (33) _____ of the line and a is where the line intercepts the (34) _____ _____. The regression line is the line that makes the squared (35) _____ around it as small as possible.

Unless r is (36) _____, we must compute separate equations to predict Y given X and X given Y. The regression formula can be extended to include more than one predictor; this extension is called (37) _____ _____.

The coefficient of determination

The (38) _____ _____ _____, symbolized by (39) _____, tells the amount of variability in one variable explained by variability in the other variable. This gives us a method

to assess how (40) _____ the relationship is between X and Y and is more important than

the (41) _____ level.

The Spearman Rank Order Correlation Coefficient

The Spearman coefficient is useful as an alternative to r because it is easier to (42) _____.

Also, we can use it when the level of measurement on one or both of our variables is (43) _____

scale rather than interval scale as required by the Pearson r. With (44) _____ scale data, the exact length of the intervals between scores cannot be specified.

To compute the Spearman r_S, we first (45) _____ the scores on each of the variables from highest

to lowest and then find the difference between the (46) _____. If two or more subjects are

tied for a particular rank, each subject is given the (47) _____ of the tied ranks.

Other correlation coefficients

The (48) _____ _____ correlation is used when one variable is dichotomous—

has only (49) _____ values—and the other variable is continuous or interval level measurement.

When both variables are dichotomous, the (50) _____ _____ is used.

A Broader View of Inferential Techniques—The *General Linear Model*

The (51) _____ _____ technique is the most general of all the techniques we've

studied. As such, it is called the (52) _____ _____ _____. Basically,

what we are saying is that the most general way of looking at data has to do with (53) _____
between measures. Thus, regression and correlation give us direct information about the statistical signifi-

cance of a relationship and also about the (54) _____ of the relationship. Tests such as the

t test and ANOVA investigate (55) _____ differences, which is the *other* way to study
relationships.

Troubleshooting Your Computations

Any r or r_S computed must fall within the range of values from (56) _____ to _____ . A

common error in computing r_S is forgetting to (57) _____ the scores on the two variables. Remember that the fractional part of the r_S formula is subtracted from (58) _____ .

In computing the regression equation, be particularly careful in handling the last two terms in the equation, (59) _____ . The two numbers are added (60) _____ .

PROBLEMS

1. On the basis of your experience, decide whether the following pairs of variables are positively, negatively, or not correlated.

   a. amount of alcohol consumed and speed of reaction to a suddenly appearing stimulus.

   b. ratings of physical attractiveness of husband–wife pairs

   c. IQ scores and the number of trials to learn a list of nonsense syllables for students in a general psychology class

   d. sales of McDonald's hamburgers per day in a city and the number of people committed per day to a state mental institution

   e. amount of time spent in practice and the average golf score

   f. number of siblings and the likelihood of developing lung cancer

   g. length of depression and the probability of suicide

2. The scores of 10 people on standardized scales of introversion and shyness are shown here (high scores on each scale indicate high introversion and shyness).

Person	Introversion	Shyness
1	17	22
2	6	4
3	12	10
4	13	8
5	19	11
6	20	18
7	9	10
8	4	3
9	8	10
10	21	16

Make a scatterplot of the data. Which class of correlation is revealed in the graph?

Compute r, and test it for significance. How much of the variability is accounted for by r?

3. Using the information in Problem 2, compute the regression equation for $\hat{Y}$.

Use the equation to predict the shyness score of a person with an introversion score of 15.

4. In a physiological psychology class, the first and last exam scores were as follows:

Student	First Score	Last Score
A	60	75
B	88	84
C	99	98
D	62	73
E	86	91
F	92	91
G	99	97
H	78	90
I	92	93
J	62	78
K	61	64
L	75	82
M	92	92
N	86	76
O	58	79
P	32	46
Q	54	67

Compute r, and test it for significance.

Find the regression equation for $\hat{Y}$. Use the equation to predict a last exam score for a student who made a 95 on the first test. Do the same for a student who made a 55 on the first test.

5. Ten female monkeys with male offspring are assigned ratings on a dominance test. The ratings of their male offspring are also determined. Assume the ratings are ordinal level measurement at best. Is there a relationship between the ratings? Test your correlation coefficient for significance.

Female Number	Dominance Ratings	Ratings of Offspring
1	10	8
2	9	10
3	9	8
4	7	6
5	6	6
6	5	6
7	5	4
8	5	5
9	3	4
10	2	1

6. A group of students was asked to estimate the amount of time each spends per day reading the newspaper. Then each student was given a 20-item recognition test of current events. The paired scores are:

Student	Time in Minutes	Score
A	25	12
B	40	13
C	55	18
D	10	8
E	5	5
F	5	3
G	30	10
H	45	15

What is the degree of relationship between the variables? Is it significant? How much of the variability in the data is accounted for by r?

7. Using figures from *Consumer Reports,* a consumer wants to see whether there is any relationship between the weight of a car and the gas mileage it gets in city driving. The following pairs of scores are taken from the annual car buying guide:

Car	Weight in Thousands of Pounds	mpg in Town
1	2.6	17.4
2	2.1	20.8
3	2.2	19.2
4	2.0	19.8
5	3.2	13.9
6	2.7	13.4
7	3.4	11.8
8	3.8	10.3
9	3.9	9.5

Compute the correlation coefficient, and test it for significance.

8. Using the data from Problem 7, find the regression equation for $\hat{Y}$. What gas mileage can the consumer expect from a car weighing 4,300 pounds?

9. In a study of the parents of schizophrenic children, letters have been independently rated by two psychiatrists for the presence of contradictory ideas and feelings. The rating scale assigns numbers from 0 to 7, with higher numbers indicating more contradictions. Assume the ratings are ordinal scale measurement at best. Compute a correlation coefficient, and test it for significance.

Letter	Rater A	Rater B
A	3	7
B	2	4
C	5	3
D	7	6
E	0	5
F	1	4
G	2	4
H	4	2

10. Two experimenters have independently rated the handling characteristics of 12 rats. Compare the correlation between the ratings of Experimenters A and B, assuming that the ratings are ordinal scale measurement at best. Test your coefficient for significance.

Rat	Experimenter A	Experimenter B
1	15	13
2	13	14
3	10	11
4	5	5
5	8	10
6	6	8
7	3	4
8	7	6
9	7	5
10	2	1
11	2	2
12	2	3

11. The following pairs of scores are heart rate values measured by a physiograph for subjects looking at different stimuli. Compute the most appropriate correlation coefficient, and test it for significance.

Subject	Stimulus A	Stimulus B
1	65.3	71.8
2	75.7	73.5
3	85.6	99.3
4	73.7	81.7
5	69.5	75.7
6	68.2	73.5
7	70.1	79.8
8	72.5	70.3
9	71.0	85.3
10	83.5	107.1

USING SPSS—EXAMPLES AND EXERCISES

SPSS provides procedures for both the Pearson and the Spearman correlation coefficients, as well as procedures for simple and multiple regression. We will also show you how to obtain a scatterplot with regression line to assist in visualizing the relationship between two measures and to check the assumption of a *linear* correlation/regression relationship.

Example—Pearson and Spearman Correlation Coefficients: We will use SPSS to work Problem 5. First, let's assume that the dominance ratings are interval level measurement and compute the Pearson correlation. After we complete that process, we will assume that the ratings are pure ranks (ordinal level measurement) and calculate the Spearman correlation. Finally, we will obtain a scatterplot of the data. The steps are as follows:

1. Start SPSS and enter the data into variable columns named **mother** and **son.**
2. Select Statistics>Correlate>Bivariate.
3. Highlight and move both variables into the Variables box and select both the Pearson and Spearman boxes under Correlation Coefficients.
4. Click Options>Means and Standard deviations>Continue>OK, and the results should appear in the output Viewer window.
5. To obtain a scatterplot, select Graph>Scatter>Simple>Define.
6. Highlight and move **mother** to the X-axis box and **son** to the Y-axis box; click OK and the plot should appear in the output Viewer window.

Notes on Reading the Output

1. The Correlations box gives the results for the Pearson correlation as a matrix. The first number in the box is the correlation coefficient, $r = .971$; the next value is the significance of the correlation, $p = .000$ ($p < .001$); and the last value is the sample size, $N = 10$. Thus, the correlation is statistically significant. The Correlations box under the section labeled Nonparametric Correlations gives the Spearman correlation ($r_S = .925$) using the same arrangement.
2. In examining the scatterplot, remember that we never connect the points but look at the plot to confirm the sign and strength of the correlation and to check for a nonlinear pattern, which would be a possible violation of our assumption of a linear relationship. You might want to put an oval around the points to assist you in visualizing the relationship.

```
CORRELATIONS
  /VARIABLES=mother son
  /PRINT=TWOTAIL NOSIG
  /STATISTICS DESCRIPTIVES
  /MISSING=PAIRWISE .
```

Correlations

Descriptive Statistics

	Mean	Std. Deviation	N
MOTHER	6.1000	2.6437	10
SON	5.8000	2.5298	10

Correlations

		MOTHER	SON
MOTHER	Pearson Correlation	1.000	.917**
	Sig. (2-tailed)	.	.000
	N	10	10
SON	Pearson Correlation	.917**	1.000
	Sig. (2-tailed)	.000	.
	N	10	10

**. Correlation is significant at the .01 level (2-tailed).

```
NONPAR CORR
  /VARIABLES=mother son
  /PRINT=SPEARMAN TWOTAIL NOSIG
  /MISSING=PAIRWISE .
```

Nonparametric Correlations

Correlations

			MOTHER	SON
Spearman's rho	MOTHER	Correlation Coefficient	1.000	.925**
		Sig. (2-tailed)	.	.000
		N	10	10
	SON	Correlation Coefficient	.925**	1.000
		Sig. (2-tailed)	.000	.
		N	10	10

**. Correlation is significant at the .01 level (2-tailed).

```
GRAPH
  /SCATTERPLOT(BIVAR)=mother WITH son
  /MISSING=LISTWISE .
```

Graph

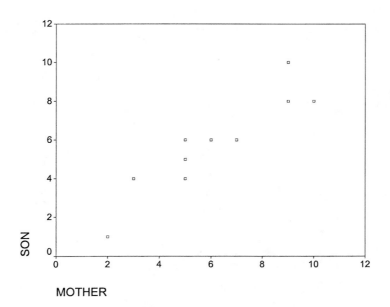

Example—Regression: Let's use SPSS to find the regression equation for Problem 7. Also, we will produce a scatterplot with a regression line. The procedure is as follows:

1. Start SPSS and enter the data under the variable names **weight** and **mpg.**
2. Select Statistics>Regression>Linear.
3. Move **mpg** into the Dependent box and **weight** into the Independent(s) box; click Statistics>Descriptives (Estimates and Model fit should already be checked by default)>Continue>OK. The results should appear in the output Viewer window.
4. To get the scatterplot, switch to the Data Editor window and follow the instructions in the previous example on producing it. Note that in a regression problem, we want the dependent variable—the measure we want to predict—to be plotted on the vertical (*Y*) axis, so **mpg** should appear on the *Y* axis.
5. Once the scatterplot has appeared in the output Viewer window, double-click on the chart and maximize the chart window. In the Menu Bar, click Chart>Options. In the Scatterplot Options box, select Total>OK, and the regression line should appear on the graph. Because we are finished editing the chart, select File>Close to close the chart window. If necessary, switch to the output Viewer window, in which you should find the scatterplot with regression line.

Notes on Reading the Output

1. As with the previous examples, you should find the results relatively easy to identify and interpret in this output. The Coefficients box gives the intercept and slope terms in the column labeled B under the section labeled Unstandardized Coefficients. The term in the row labeled (Constant) is the intercept term, $a = 31.426$, and the term in the row labeled WEIGHT is the slope, $b = -5.678$. Thus, the regression equation could be written as follows:

$$\hat{Y} = 31.426 - 5.678X \text{ or MPG} = 31.426 - 5.678(\text{WEIGHT}).$$

2. The scatterplot with regression line shows a close fit with no indication of nonlinearity.

```
REGRESSION
  /DESCRIPTIVES MEAN STDDEV CORR SIG N
  /MISSING LISTWISE
  /STATISTICS COEFF OUTS R ANOVA
  /CRITERIA=PIN(.05) POUT(.10)
  /NOORIGIN
  /DEPENDENT mpg
  /METHOD=ENTER weight   .
```

Regression

Descriptive Statistics

	Mean	Std. Deviation	N
MPG	15.1222	4.2763	9
WEIGHT	2.8778	.7259	9

Correlations

		MPG	WEIGHT
Pearson Correlation	MPG	1.000	-.964
	WEIGHT	-.964	1.000
Sig. (1-tailed)	MPG	.	.000
	WEIGHT	.000	.
N	MPG	9	9
	WEIGHT	9	9

Variables Entered/Removed[b]

Model	Variables Entered	Variables Removed	Method
1	WEIGHT[a]	.	Enter

a. All requested variables entered.

b. Dependent Variable: MPG

Model Summary

Model	R	R Square	Adjusted R Square	Std. Error of the Estimate
1	.964[a]	.929	.919	1.2184

a. Predictors: (Constant), WEIGHT

ANOVA[b]

Model		Sum of Squares	df	Mean Square	F	Sig.
1	Regression	135.904	1	135.904	91.548	.000[a]
	Residual	10.392	7	1.485		
	Total	146.296	8			

a. Predictors: (Constant), WEIGHT

b. Dependent Variable: MPG

Coefficients[a]

Model		Unstandardized Coefficients		Standardized Coefficients		
		B	Std. Error	Beta	t	Sig.
1	(Constant)	31.462	1.755		17.923	.000
	WEIGHT	-5.678	.593	-.964	-9.568	.000

a. Dependent Variable: MPG

```
GRAPH
  /SCATTERPLOT(BIVAR)=weight WITH mpg
  /MISSING=LISTWISE .
```

Graph

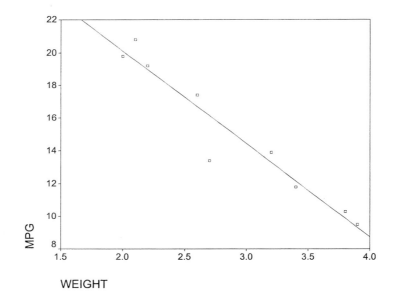

Exercises Using SPSS

1. Use SPSS to work Problem 6.
2. Use SPSS and the data from Problem 6 to compute a regression equation predicting the current events score from time spent reading the newspaper. Give the regression equation and obtain a scatterplot with regression line.
3. Use SPSS to work Problem 9, assuming the data are pure ranks. Obtain a scatterplot.

CHECKING YOUR PROGRESS: A SELF-TEST

1. Match the following:

_____ positive correlation	**a.** a straight line describes the relationship between two variables
_____ negative correlation	**b.** coefficient of determination
_____ zero correlation	**c.** Y intercept of the regression line
_____ ρ	**d.** no relationship between the variables
_____ scatterplot	**e.** direct relationship between the variables
_____ linear correlation	**f.** inverse relationship between the variables
_____ regression equation	**g.** population correlation coefficient
_____ r^2	**h.** used for prediction
_____ b	**i.** graph used to show the relationship between two variables
_____ a	**j.** slope of the regression line

2. The ACT math and science scores for eight students are shown here. Compute r, and test it for significance.

Student	Math ACT	Science ACT
A	26	24
B	22	24
C	13	10
D	30	31
E	12	17
F	15	15
G	19	21
H	20	16

3. Use the data from Problem 2 to compute a regression equation, and use the equation to predict a science ACT score for a student scoring 33 on the math ACT.

4. Without knowing who is married to whom, an observer has rated the attractiveness of 10 couples on a 10-point scale. Compute the appropriate correlation coefficient, and test it for significance. Assume that the ratings are ordinal scale measurement at best.

Couple	Wife's Rating	Husband's Rating
A	7	6
B	6	8
C	5	4
D	8	9
E	3	5
F	1	2
G	5	2
H	9	9
I	10	7
J	7	5

CHAPTER 14

CHI SQUARE

OBJECTIVES

The main objective in Chapter 14 is to present an inferential technique useful in analyzing nominal scale or categorical data. The technique is called chi square.

CHAPTER REVIEW

Previous chapters have detailed the *t* test and the *F* test, both of which are parametric methods. *Parametric* tests examine hypotheses about population parameters such as μ and σ, usually assume at least interval scale measurement, and assume a normal distribution of the measured variable in the population from which samples were drawn. The chi-square test is called a *nonparametric* test because population parameters are not estimated. It is also a *distribution-free* test because no particular population distribution is assumed. The chi-square test is particularly useful with nominal scale or categorical data—data in which there are only frequencies of occurrence.

A chi-square test on a single categorical variable is called a *goodness-of-fit* test. The formula for the goodness-of-fit test is

$$\chi^2 = \sum \frac{(O - E)^2}{E},$$

where O is the *observed* frequency and E is the *expected* frequency. If the expected frequencies are assumed to be equally distributed across the levels of the categorical variable, then the total number of observations (N) is divided by the number of categories to determine E for each category. Expected frequencies may also be determined by assigning the frequencies on the basis of percentages obtained in previous research. The χ^2 computed for the goodness-of-fit test is compared with critical values from Table G (see Appendix 2) with $df = K - 1$, where K is the number of levels of the categorical variable. The chi-square goodness-of-fit test can sometimes be used to confirm the research hypothesis.

The chi-square test for different levels of two categorical variables is called the *chi-square test of independence,* the *two-sample chi square,* or the *chi-square test of significance.* The test assumes that the distribution of frequencies across the levels of one variable is the same for all levels of the other variable; that is, the test assumes that the two categorical variables are independent. The formula for the chi-square test of independence is the same as for the goodness-of-fit test. Expected frequencies may be given by theory or previous research. Most often, however, they must be computed. Expected frequencies for a given cell in a frequency table are computed by dividing the product of the marginal totals for the cell by the total number of observations. The computed χ^2 is compared with critical values from Table G with $df = (R - 1)(C - 1)$, where R is the number of rows and C is the number of columns.

The chi-square test can be used only with frequency data. However, any data can be converted to frequency data by dividing the data into several logical categories and counting the number of observations that occur in each category.

A second restriction on chi square is that the individual observations must be independent of one another. Another restriction is that if you are recording whether an event occurs, you must have in the data both the frequency of occurrence and the frequency of nonoccurrence. Also, no expected frequencies should be less than 5, although the restriction may be relaxed if there are more than four cells and only a few have expected frequencies less than 5. Although there is a statistical alternative to χ^2 with a 2 × 2 table and expected frequencies less than 5, the best approach is to test more subjects to increase the expected frequencies.

SYMBOLS

Symbol	Stands For
χ^2	chi square
O	observed frequency
E	expected frequency
K	number of categories
RT	row total
CT	column total
R	number of rows
C	number of columns

FORMULAS

Formula 14-1. *Equation for chi square (used for both the goodness-of-fit test and the chi-square test of independence [significance])*

$$\chi^2 = \sum \frac{(O - E)^2}{E}$$

O stands for the observed frequencies, and E stands for the expected frequencies.

Formula 14-2. *Equation for finding expected frequencies for the chi-square test of independence if there is no other basis for determining them*

$$E = \frac{(RT)(CT)}{N}$$

RT stands for the row total for a given cell, and CT stands for the column total for the same cell.

Formula 14-3. *Formula for finding degrees of freedom for the chi-square test of independence*

$$df = (R - 1)(C - 1)$$

TERMS TO DEFINE AND/OR IDENTIFY

Parametric tests

Nonparametric tests

Distribution-free tests

Chi-square test

Chi-square goodness-of-fit test

Chi-square test of independence

Contingency table

FILL-IN-THE-BLANK ITEMS

Introduction

The *t* test and the *F* test are examples of (1) _____ tests, or tests designed to test hypotheses about population parameters. Tests that don't test hypotheses about population parameters are called

(2) _____ tests. Also, because the tests don't assume any particular distribution, they are

often called (3) _____ tests.

The (4) _____ scale is used for labeling only; all we can do with it is to record

(5) _____ of occurrence. (6) _____ _____ is an appropriate test with
categorical or nominal scale data.

The Chi-Square Goodness-of-Fit Test

A chi-square test on different levels of a single categorical variable is called a (7) _____
test, because it assesses how well the observed data fit expectations. In the equation for the chi-square test,
for each cell in a frequency table, the difference between the observed and expected frequencies is

(8) _____ and is divided by the expected frequency. If the expected frequencies are as-

sumed to have been (9) _____ _____ across levels of the categorical variable,
then each E can be determined by dividing the total number of observations, N, by the number of levels.

Expected frequencies may also be based on percentages observed in (10) _____

_____.

The results for each cell are (11) _____ for all cells to give the chi-square statistic. The

computed chi square is compared with critical values from Table G with $df = $ (12) _____, where K is

the number of (13) _____ of the categorical variable.

Confirming hypotheses with chi square

Sometimes the chi-square goodness-of-fit test null hypothesis is the (14) _____

_____ that the investigator seeks to confirm. If this is the case, then failure to reject

H_0 may provide some (15) _____ of the theory under investigation. The degree

of confirmation depends on the statistical (16) _____ in the analysis and on whether

(17) _____ leads to the same conclusion.

The Chi-Square Test of Independence

The chi-square test based on (18) _____ categorical variables is called the chi-square test of

(19) _____, the (20) _____ chi square, or the chi-square test of

significance. The test tries to determine whether the two categorical variables are (21) _____.
The frequency table formed from the observations made under each categorical variable is called a

(22) _____ table.

An alternative method for finding expected values

Occasionally, expected frequencies are known because of theory or previous (23) _____.
More often, however, the expected frequencies for a given cell are found by multiplying the

(24) _____ totals for the cell and dividing by (25) _____. Many expected

frequencies can be determined by (26) _____, because the expected frequencies
for a given row or column must sum to the row or column total. *df* for the chi-square test of indepen-

dence equals (27) _____, where R is the number of rows and C is the number of
columns.

Restrictions on Chi Square

Chi square can be used only with (28) _____ data. Also, the events or observations that

make up the data must be (29) _____ of one another. A third restriction on chi square is

that we must have in the data both the frequency of (30) _____ and the frequency of

(31) _____, if we are recording whether an event occurs. No expected frequency should

be less than (32) _____, although this rule may be relaxed if there are more than

(33) _____ cells and only a few have small expected frequencies.

Troubleshooting Your Computations

If you're finding *E* by subtraction, remember that both the (34) _____ frequencies and the
observed frequencies must sum to give you a particular row or column total. Be sure you don't get any

(35) _____ signs for a cell total.

PROBLEMS

1. Determine the expected frequencies for each of the cells in the following contingency tables. For each problem, state how many of the expected values actually had to be computed and how many could be found by subtraction.

a.

14	16
31	4

b.

23	13	15
25	17	10

c.

21	25	27
10	13	17
11	45	13

2. Compute χ^2 for each of the contingency tables from Problem 1, and test it for significance.

a.

14	16
31	4

b.

23	13	15
25	17	10

c.

21	25	27
10	13	17
11	45	13

3. Left- and right-handed individuals with unilateral (on one side) brain damage were compared to see whether brain injury is more likely to produce aphasia (language difficulties) in one group than in the other. Test the observed result for significance, and tell what your result means in the context of the problem.

	Aphasic	Nonaphasic
Left-Handed	10	24
Right-Handed	62	36

4. Research indicates that some alcoholism is inherited. The families of alcoholic and nonalcoholic adults have been studied to determine whether one or both parents were alcoholic. The results are shown here. Test the observed results for significance, and tell what your result means in the context of the problem.

	Alcoholic	Nonalcoholic
No Parental Alcoholism	17	61
One or Both Parents Alcoholic	43	83

5. A rhesus monkey was trained to make same–different judgments about pairs of objects. For 50 trials, the animal was shown pictures of objects; it made correct judgments on 43 of the trials. Use the chi-square test to determine whether the animal had generalized its learned response from objects to pictures of objects. *Note:* The probability of making a correct response on any trial is .5.

6. A survey was conducted of the product preferences of introverts and extraverts. Does introversion or extraversion make a difference in brand preference?

	Brand A	Brand B	Brand C
Introverts	42	18	20
Extraverts	36	16	28

7. A professor teaching introductory psychology gave 25 As, 35 Bs, 60 Cs, 30 Ds, and 20 Fs to 170 students in her class. According to the normal curve, she should have given about 4% As, 14% Bs, 64% Cs, 14% Ds, and 4% Fs. Use the chi-square test to determine whether the actual grade assignment significantly departed from a normal distribution.

8. A test of risk-taking attitudes was given to 60 students, 27 scoring low and 33 scoring high on self-esteem. A score of 10 or higher indicates a positive risk-taking attitude, and a score less than 10 indicates a more cautious approach to life. Determine whether high- and low-self-esteem students differ on this variable.

	Less Than 10	10 or More
High Self-Esteem	14	19
Low Self-Esteem	18	9

9. A professor taught a course in physiological psychology. On the student–teacher evaluation, the professor scored higher than the departmental average on 23 of 28 items. Is this result significantly better than one might expect?

10. In a statistics class, the same professor from Problem 9 scored higher than the departmental average on 10 of 28 items. Is this result significantly different from the expected result?

USING SPSS—EXAMPLES AND EXERCISES

SPSS has procedures for performing the chi-square goodness-of-fit test and the chi-square test of independence between two categorical variables. However, SPSS is designed for use with raw data. The data presented for the exercises in this chapter are in summary form. As a consequence, in order to use SPSS, we must "unsummarize" the data—reconstruct the data as if they came from individual participants. Unfortunately, the process of creating the data file will be somewhat laborious, and you may decide that it's easier to work the problems using a hand calculator than using SPSS. In spite of the difficulties, you will gain experience that will allow you to perform the chi-square-based tests using SPSS on data in the form you would obtain in an actual research setting.

Example—Chi-Square Goodness-of-Fit Test: To illustrate this technique, we will work Problem 7 using SPSS. The steps are as follows:

1. Start SPSS and name the first variable **grade.** We must simulate the grade data for 170 students. Use the code numbers 4 for A, 3 for B, 2 for C, 1 for D, and 0 for F. Because there were 25 As, 35 Bs, 60 Cs, 30 Ds, and 20 Fs, you should enter 4 twenty-five times, 3 thirty-five times, and so on. (*Hint:* Use the editing features of the Windows environment to help. For example, enter 4 five times, copy the block, and paste it below each successive block until you reach 25. Do the same for the other numbers in blocks of 5 or 10 depending on the totals needed.)
2. Select Statistics>Nonparametric Tests>Chi-Square.
3. Move **grade** into the Test Variable List box.
4. We now need to tell SPSS what our expected frequencies ratio is, if it is something other than an equal proportion for each group. In the Expected Values box, select Values and enter 4 (for 4%) in the entry box, then click Add. Repeat this process in order for all five expected value percentages: 4, 14, 64, 14, and 4. The resulting dialog box should appear as follows. Click OK and the results should appear in the output Viewer window.

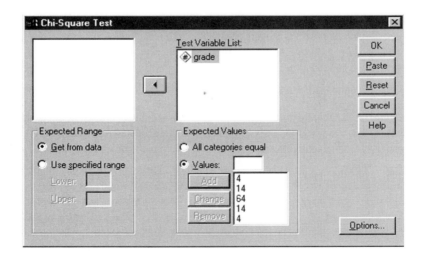

Notes on Reading the Output

1. You should find the output easy to read and understand. The observed frequency, expected frequency, and difference (labeled Residual) are given in the first box and the test statistics in the second box. The results indicate that the actual grade assignment does differ significantly from a normal distribution: $\chi^2 (4, N = 170) = 103.11, p < .001$.

```
NPAR TEST
  /CHISQUARE=grade
  /EXPECTED=4 14 64 14 4
  /MISSING ANALYSIS.
```

NPar Tests

Chi-Square Test

Frequencies

GRADE

	Observed N	Expected N	Residual
.00	20	6.8	13.2
1.00	30	23.8	6.2
2.00	60	108.8	-48.8
3.00	35	23.8	11.2
4.00	25	6.8	18.2
Total	170		

Test Statistics

	GRADE
Chi-Square[a]	103.109
df	4
Asymp. Sig.	.000

a. 0 cells (.0%) have expected frequencies less than 5. The minimum expected cell frequency is 6.8.

Example—Chi-Square Test of Independence: We will use SPSS to work Problem 6. Let's shorten the data entry required for this problem by taking half of the frequency for each condition to result in an $N = 80$ rather than 160. The steps are as follows:

1. Start SPSS and name variables **ie** and **pref.** Use a code value of 1 for introverts and 2 for extraverts; use 1 for Brand A, 2 for Brand B, and 3 for Brand C. You will need 21 entries for introverts preferring Brand A (**ie** = 1 and **pref** = 1), and so on. The data entry window should show a pattern like this: 1, 1 for 21 entries; 2, 1 for 18 entries; 1, 2 for 9 entries; 2, 2 for 8 entries; 1, 3 for 10 entries; and 2, 3 for 14 entries.
2. Select Statistics>Summarize>Crosstabs.
3. In the dialog box, move **ie** into the Rows box and **pref** into the Columns box. Select the Statistics box, then Chi-Square>Continue.
4. Also select the Cells box—in the Counts box, Observed should be checked by default; also check Expected. In the Percentages box, click Total, then Continue and OK. The results should appear in the output Viewer window.

Notes on Reading the Output

1. The IE*PREF Crosstabulation box shows the frequency (count) for each cell. Note that in each cell, the first number is the frequency, the second is the expected frequency, and the third number is the percentage for that cell based on the cell frequency divided by the total sample size. If you look at the percentages across the brand preference groups, you will see that there is not much difference in the pattern between introverts and extraverts. Both prefer Brand A, then Brand C, and Brand B least.

2. Shown in the Chi-Square Tests box, the Pearson Chi-Square value is 0.956, with $p = .62$. Thus, the results indicate that introversion or extraversion does not make a difference in brand preference: $\chi^2 (2, N = 80) = 0.956, p = .62$.

```
CROSSTABS
  /TABLES=ie  BY pref
  /FORMAT= AVALUE TABLES
  /STATISTIC=CHISQ
  /CELLS= COUNT EXPECTED TOTAL .
```

Crosstabs

Case Processing Summary

	Cases					
	Valid		Missing		Total	
	N	Percent	N	Percent	N	Percent
IE * PREF	80	100.0%	0	.0%	80	100.0%

IE * PREF Crosstabulation

			PREF			Total
			1.00	2.00	3.00	
IE	1.00	Count	21	9	10	40
		Expected Count	19.5	8.5	12.0	40.0
		% of Total	26.3%	11.3%	12.5%	50.0%
	2.00	Count	18	8	14	40
		Expected Count	19.5	8.5	12.0	40.0
		% of Total	22.5%	10.0%	17.5%	50.0%
Total		Count	39	17	24	80
		Expected Count	39.0	17.0	24.0	80.0
		% of Total	48.8%	21.3%	30.0%	100.0%

Chi-Square Tests

	Value	df	Asymp. Sig. (2-sided)
Pearson Chi-Square	.956[a]	2	.620
Likelihood Ratio	.960	2	.619
Linear-by-Linear Association	.804	1	.370
N of Valid Cases	80		

a. 0 cells (.0%) have expected count less than 5. The minimum expected count is 8.50.

Exercises Using SPSS

1. Use SPSS to work Problem 9. There should be 28 data entries, with a value of 1 for 23 and 0 for the remaining 5. Chance prediction would be that being above or below the departmental average would be equally likely; thus, the expected frequencies would be equal. This is the default in the Chi-Square Test dialog box. For Expected Values, All Categories Equal already should be checked and is the appropriate setting for this exercise.

2. Use SPSS to perform a chi-square test of independence using the data from Problem 8. Name the variables **esteem** and **risk.** Use a code of 1 for low self-esteem and 2 for high self-esteem; use a code of 1 for low risk takers and 2 for high risk takers. You will need to enter data for 60 participants.

CHECKING YOUR PROGRESS: A SELF-TEST

1. Which of the following statements are true about the chi-square test?
   a. Chi square is a nonparametric test.
   b. Chi square is a parametric test.
   c. Chi square is useful with interval scale data.
   d. Chi square is useful with nominal scale data.
   e. A restriction on chi square is that no expected frequency should be less than 5.
   f. Chi square is based on the normal curve distribution.
   g. The chi-square test on a single categorical variable is called the chi-square test of independence.
   h. Chi square is a distribution-free test.

2. A sample of Republicans and a sample of Democrats in a large city are asked whether they favor increasing spending for entitlement programs for the elderly. The results are shown here. Is there a difference between Republicans and Democrats on this question?

	Favor	Oppose
Republicans	26	78
Democrats	53	44

3. Three groups of 10 rats each are fed diets suspected to affect problem-solving ability. Then they are tested on a series of problems until all subjects have achieved criterion on at least two problems. The total number of problems solved by the rats in each dietary group is as follows: Group A, 33; Group B, 22; Group C, 25. Assuming that problem-solving ability should be evenly distributed across the groups, do the groups differ?

CHAPTER 15

ALTERNATIVES TO t AND F

OBJECTIVES

The main objective in Chapter 15 is to describe the use and computation of alternatives to parametric tests such as t and F when the assumptions of the parametric tests cannot be met. The nonparametric tests presented here are the Mann–Whitney U test (an alternative to the two-sample t test for independent samples), the Wilcoxon test (an alternative to the two-sample t test for dependent samples), and the Kruskal–Wallis one-way ANOVA (an alternative to the F test for independent samples [between-subjects ANOVA]).

CHAPTER REVIEW

Nonparametric alternatives to t and F are useful when the data are ordinal scale, ease of computation is desired, or the samples are small and have unequal Ns. Small samples often have a large amount of variability, which makes resulting t ratios and F ratios relatively small. By avoiding a measure of variability, a nonparametric test may be more powerful than the corresponding parametric test with small sample sizes, and outliers (extreme scores).

   The *Mann–Whitney U test* is a useful alternative to the two-sample t test for independent samples when the measurement level is ordinal and the normality assumption cannot be made. The M–W assumes that the samples are independent, that there is an underlying continuous measurement scale, and that the measurement scale actually used is at least ordinal. The tested hypothesis is that the populations from which the samples are drawn are identical in shape. If the populations are identical, then if we rank the combined observations from two samples, the scores from the two samples should be evenly mixed in the combined ranking. If the scores are not evenly mixed, then they probably come from different populations.

The computed U is a measure of how evenly mixed the scores from the combined samples are, with a low value indicating a lack of mixing. Thus, unlike the previous significance tests, the null hypothesis is rejected if U (or U') is equal to or *less* than values from Table H (see Appendix 2). With samples containing more than 20 observations, U is converted to a z score. The null hypothesis is rejected if the computed score is equal to or *larger* than 1.96 (two-tailed test at the 5% level) or 1.64 (one-tailed test at the 5% level).

The *Wilcoxon matched-pairs signed-ranks test* is a nonparametric alternative to the t test for dependent samples. The test assumes that the subjects are randomly and independently selected, that there is at least ordinal scale measurement, and that it is possible to rank-order the difference scores (difference between a pair of scores). The tested hypothesis is that the distributions of the populations under each condition are identical.

First, the difference between each pair of scores is found, with 0 differences discarded. Next, the absolute values of the difference scores are rank-ordered, but the signs are retained. The ranks with the less frequently occurring sign are summed, and the resulting T is compared with table values in a significance test. If the population distributions are really identical, there will usually be about the same number of positive and negative differences, and the sums of the ranks for the positive and negative differences will not be very different. However, if the distributions are dissimilar, there will be many more differences of one sign than of the other. Thus, the smaller the sum of the less frequently occurring ranks, the more likely that the population distributions are different. If the computed T is equal to or *smaller* than the critical value in Table I (see Appendix 2), the null hypothesis is rejected. For samples larger than 25, the distribution of T is approximately normal, and T is converted to a z score. H_0 is rejected at the 5% level if z is 1.96 or larger in a two-tailed test (1.64 in a one-tailed test).

The *Kruskal–Wallis one-way analysis of variance by ranks* is an extension of the Mann–Whitney test for comparing more than two independent groups. A statistic, H, is computed, and if there are three groups with at least five subjects per group, H is distributed approximately as χ^2. After a significant H, further testing with the M–W test will reveal the between-group differences.

SYMBOLS

Symbol	Stands For
U or M–W U or U'	statistic computed for the Mann–Whitney (M–W) test of significance
N_1, N_2	number of subjects in the first and second groups, respectively
R_1, R_2	sum of the ranks of the scores in the first and second groups, respectively
d	differences between pairs of scores in the Wilcoxon test
T	sum of the ranks of the scores with the less frequent sign (Wilcoxon test)
H or K–W H	statistic computed for the Kruskal–Wallis (K–W) test
N_i	number of observations in a particular sample
R_i	sum of the ranks for a particular sample
K	number of samples

FORMULAS

Formula 15-1. *Computational formula for the Mann–Whitney U test*

$$U = N_1 N_2 + \frac{N_1(N_1 + 1)}{2} - R_1$$

N_1 is the number of observations in the first sample, N_2 is the number of observations in the second sample, and R_1 is the sum of the ranks of the scores in the first sample.

Formula 15-2. *Equation for U'*

$$U' = N_1 N_2 - U$$

The smaller of U and U' is used in the test of significance.

Formula 15-4. *Equation for converting large-sample U to a z score*

$$z = \frac{U - \dfrac{N_1 N_2}{2}}{\sqrt{\dfrac{(N_1)(N_2)(N_1 + N_2 + 1)}{12}}}$$

U or U' is converted to a z score when sample sizes are larger than $N = 20$.

Formula 15-5. *Equation for converting a large-sample T to a z score*

$$z = \frac{T - \dfrac{N(N + 1)}{4}}{\sqrt{\dfrac{N(N + 1)(2N + 1)}{24}}}$$

T is the sum of the ranks with the less frequently occurring sign. With samples of 25 or more, T is converted to a z score.

Formula 15-6. *Computational formula for the Kruskal–Wallis test*

$$H = \frac{12}{N(N + 1)} \sum \frac{R_i^2}{N_i} - 3(N + 1)$$

N_i is the number of observations for a particular sample, N is the total number of observations, and R_i is the sum of the ranks for a particular sample. With sample sizes of at least 5 and at least three samples, H is distributed approximately as χ^2 with $df = K - 1$, where K is the number of samples.

TERMS TO DEFINE AND/OR IDENTIFY

Mann–Whitney test

Wilcoxon test

Kruskal–Wallis test

FILL-IN-THE-BLANK ITEMS

Introduction

A (1) _____ test is one in which population parameters such as μ and σ are not involved; they are also called (2) _____ _____ because no particular distribution is assumed. The tests discussed in this chapter are useful when (3) _____ of the parametric tests are likely to be violated and when the level of measurement is less than (4) _____ scale.

The Mann–Whitney U Test

The M–W test is a useful alternative to the (5) _____ _____ _____ _____ samples.

The assumptions for the M–W are that the samples are (6) _____, that there is an underlying continuous scale of measurement, and that the measurement scale used is at least

(7) _____ scale. The hypothesis tested is that the populations contributing to the samples are (8) _____ in shape.

In the M–W test, the scores from the two samples are (9) _____, and a statistic, the smaller of U or (10) _____, is computed. If the ranks are not evenly mixed, the samples probably come from different (11) _____. For samples with 20 or fewer subjects, the computed U (or U') is compared with critical values in Table (12) _____. If the computed statistic is

(13) _____ than the critical value, H_0 is rejected. For samples larger than 20, U (or U') is converted to a (14) _____, and H_0 is rejected if z is (15) _____ or larger (two-tailed test at 5% level).

The Wilcoxon Matched-Pairs Signed-Ranks Test

The Wilcoxon test is a nonparametric alternative to the t test for (16) _____ samples. The assumptions are that the subjects must be (17) _____ and independently selected, that the measurement scale must be at least (18) _____, and that we must be able to rank-order the difference scores. The null hypothesis is that the population distributions are (19) _____.

Computation begins with finding the (20) _____ between each pair of scores, discarding all (21) _____ differences. The difference scores are (22) _____ ordered on the basis of absolute magnitude, and the (23) _____ of the differences is retained. The sum of the differences with the (24) _____ frequently occurring sign is found and called T. T is compared with critical values in Table I, and if T is equal to or (25) _____ than the critical value, H_0 is rejected. With large samples, $N = 25$ or greater, the distribution of T is approximately (26) _____, and the T score is converted to a (27) _____ .

The Kruskal–Wallis One-Way ANOVA

The K–W test is an extension of the (28) _____ test and is used for comparing more than two groups when the assumptions underlying the (29) _____ cannot be met. At least (30) _____ scale measurement is required.

To perform the test, the combined groups are (31) _____, and the sum of the (32) _____ for each group is found. For three or more samples with at least five subjects each, the computed H is distributed approximately as (33) _____ _____, with $df = $ (34) _____ , where K is the number of groups.

Further Testing After a Significant H

After a significant result is found with the K–W test, the (35) _____ test can be used to make further group comparisons.

Troubleshooting Your Computations

Both the M–W and the K–W tests require (36) _____ the combined scores from lowest to highest. The rank of the highest score should be (37) _____ unless the top scores are tied. The value obtained for either U or H should be a (38) _____ number. In using the M–W test, the smaller of U and (39) _____ is used in the significance test.

With the Wilcoxon test, be sure to discard all (40) _____ differences. The difference scores are ranked in terms of (41) _____ value. Both the computed T and the computed U must be equal to or (42) _____ than the critical table values for H_0 to be rejected.

PROBLEMS

1. For each of the following, tell which significance test would be most appropriate.

    a. two small, independent samples; ordinal scale data

    b. two dependent samples; interval scale data

    c. three or more independent samples; ordinal scale data

    d. two dependent samples; ordinal scale data

    e. two independent samples; frequency data

2. Seven children from families in which there is only one child and six children with at least one sibling are rated for willingness to share toys with another child. Each child is given a rating from 0 (no sharing) to 10 (virtually complete sharing) during a 20-minute observation period. Use the appropriate test to compare the groups, and tell what your decision means in the context of the problem.

Only Child	Child With Sibling(s)
5	10
3	9
2	9
2	7
1	4
0	2
0	

3. Thirty-one randomly selected rats are assigned to one of three different experimental diets. After 30 days on the diets, each animal is given a test of irritability to handling. In the test, the behavior is rated from 0 to 15 with a higher score reflecting greater irritability. The scores are shown here. Do an overall significance test. If a significant result is obtained, do all pairwise comparisons. Tell what each decision means in the context of the problem.

Diet A	Diet B	Diet C
6	14	4
5	12	4
5	12	3
4	11	2
3	9	2
2	7	1
1	7	1
0	5	0
0	4	0
0	1	0
0		

4. A trained speech analyst has received brief taped excerpts of the speech of 18 parents. Ten of the parents have schizophrenic children, and the remaining 8 have nonschizophrenic children. Without knowing whether the parent has a schizophrenic child, the analyst has rated the excerpts from 0 to 20 for defectiveness of speech. The groups do not differ on variables such as IQ, age, education, or social class. Is there evidence for a difference in the speech patterns of the parents of the schizophrenic children?

Parent of Schizophrenic	Parent of Nonschizophrenic
16	12
15	11
13	10
12	9
9	9
7	5
5	4
3	2
3	
2	

5. A self-rating scale was used to measure attitudes toward risk taking before and after alcohol consumption for 12 persons. A high score indicates a positive attitude toward risk taking; a low score indicates greater concern. Compare the before and after ratings.

Person	Rating Before	Rating After
A	14	17
B	14	19
C	13	14
D	12	9
E	11	12
F	9	9
G	9	15
H	8	7
I	5	9
J	4	8
K	2	1
L	2	5

6. Twenty-four students are selected randomly from a large introductory psychology class and assigned randomly to one of two treatment groups. Half are given an alcohol-flavored drink, and the other half receive a drink containing an ounce of alcohol. Ten minutes later, each student fills out a self-rating scale measuring attitudes toward risk taking. Assume the data are ordinal scale at best. The results are shown here. Compare the two groups. As before, a high score indicates a positive attitude toward risk taking.

Alcohol Group	No-Alcohol Group
14	19
14	17
13	15
12	14
11	12
9	9
9	9
8	9
5	8
4	7
2	5
2	1

7. Matched pairs of parents have written letters to a child in a state mental institution. One member of each pair has a schizophrenic child, and the other member has a nonschizophrenic child in the hospital. One letter from each parent has been rated for double-bind statements (incompatible ideas and feelings) on a scale from 1 to 7, with 7 reflecting a high incidence of double-bind statements. Use the appropriate test to compare the groups.

Pair	Parent of Schizophrenic	Parent of Nonschizophrenic
A	7	3
B	5	5
C	3	6
D	2	6
E	6	5
F	1	3
G	2	1
H	4	6
I	3	1
J	7	1
K	3	7
L	1	5

8. An investigator wants to see whether creativity (divergent thinking) can be taught. In one class, the teacher specifically rewards divergent responses during a 1-hour daily art period. In a second class, a 1-hour art period is held, but no effort is made to reward divergent responses. In a third class, a 1-hour study hall is given while the other classes have the art period. At the end of the year, 10 students are randomly selected from each class and given a standard test of creativity on which they receive a score from 1 to 50. A higher score indicates greater creativity. Assume the data are ordinal scale at best. Compare the classes with an overall test. If the result is significant, do all pairwise comparisons, and tell what your conclusions mean in the context of the problem.

Class 1	Class 2	Class 3
48	41	42
46	40	25
43	27	24
40	25	22
39	13	18
38	11	17
35	10	9
28	10	8
27	9	8
15	7	5

USING SPSS—EXAMPLES AND EXERCISES

SPSS provides procedures for computing the Mann–Whitney test, the Wilcoxon test, and the Kruskal–Wallis test, as well as other types of "nonparametric" techniques. Because the M–W, Wilcoxon, and K–W tests involve the median as the preferred measure of central tendency and the ranking of data, SPSS Boxplots provides a useful way to display the results.

Example—Mann–Whitney Test: We will use SPSS to work Problem 6, which is a M–W problem. The steps are as follows:

1. Start SPSS, name variables **group** and **risk,** and enter the data.
2. Select Statistics>Nonparametric Tests>Two-Independent-Samples.
3. Move **risk** into the Test Variable List box, and move **group** into the Grouping Variable box.
4. Define the groups: 1 for Alcohol and 2 for No-Alcohol>Continue.
5. In the Test Type box, be sure the Mann–Whitney U is checked—it should be by default. Then click OK and the output should appear in the Viewer window.
6. For boxplots of the groups, select Graphs>Boxplot>Simple>Summaries of groups of cases>Define. Move **risk** into the Variable box and move **group** into the Category Axis box; then click OK.

Notes on Reading the Output

1. You should find the output easy to read and understand. The U value and p value [Asymp. Sig. (2-tailed)] are given in the Test Statistics box.
2. The results indicate that there is no significant difference between the two alcohol treatment groups in self-rated risk-taking attitude: $U = 58.5, p = .433$.
3. Examination of the boxplots shows that the groups are similar. The heavy line within the box indicates the position of the median, which is virtually identical for the two groups.

```
NPAR TESTS
  /M-W= risk   BY group(1 2)
  /MISSING ANALYSIS.
```

NPar Tests

Mann-Whitney Test

Ranks

	GROUP	N	Mean Rank	Sum of Ranks
RISK	1.00	12	11.38	136.50
	2.00	12	13.63	163.50
	Total	24		

Test Statistics[b]

	RISK
Mann-Whitney U	58.500
Wilcoxon W	136.500
Z	-.784
Asymp. Sig. (2-tailed)	.433
Exact Sig. [2*(1-tailed Sig.)]	.443[a]

a. Not corrected for ties.

b. Grouping Variable: GROUP

```
EXAMINE
  VARIABLES=risk BY group /PLOT=BOXPLOT/STATISTICS=NONE/NOTOTAL
  /MISSING=REPORT.
```

Explore

GROUP

Case Processing Summary

	GROUP	Cases					
		Valid		Missing		Total	
		N	Percent	N	Percent	N	Percent
RISK	1.00	12	100.0%	0	.0%	12	100.0%
	2.00	12	100.0%	0	.0%	12	100.0%

RISK

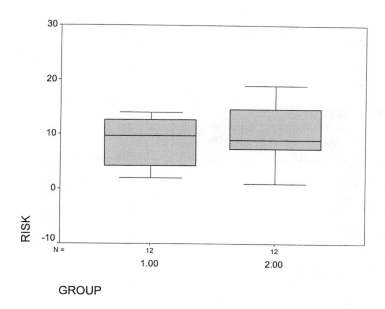

GROUP

Example—Wilcoxon Test: We will use SPSS to work Problem 5. The steps are as follows:

1. Start SPSS and name variables **before** and **after.** Enter the data.
2. Select Statistics>Nonparametric Tests>2 Related Samples.
3. In the dialog box, move the two variables into the Test Pairs List box and check Wilcoxon in the Test Type box, then click OK. The results should appear in the output Viewer window.
4. You can obtain the boxplots in the same manner as for the M–W except click Summaries of separate variables and move both variables into the Boxes Represents box.

Notes on Reading the Output

1. The sum of the ranks with the less frequent sign is 11 ($T = 11$), which is the smaller of the two values in the Ranks box under Sum of Ranks. The Test Statistics box gives T converted to a z score and the p value for z. The results indicate that the null hypothesis of identical population distributions is rejected, $T = 11$, $p = .049$.
2. To determine the direction of the group differences, examine the N and Mean Rank of the AFTER-BEFORE differences given in the Ranks box. There are more positive than negative ranks, which indicates that the After group is greater than the Before group in risk.
3. In this particular example, the boxplot does not clearly show the After group to be greater in risk.

```
RENAME VARIABLES (var00001=before).
RENAME VARIABLES (var00002=after).
NPAR TEST
  /WILCOXON=before  WITH after (PAIRED)
  /MISSING ANALYSIS.
```

NPar Tests

Wilcoxon Signed Ranks Test

Ranks

		N	Mean Rank	Sum of Ranks
AFTER - BEFORE	Negative Ranks	3[a]	3.67	11.00
	Positive Ranks	8[b]	6.88	55.00
	Ties	1[c]		
	Total	12		

a. AFTER < BEFORE

b. AFTER > BEFORE

c. BEFORE = AFTER

Test Statistics[b]

	AFTER - BEFORE
Z	-1.971[a]
Asymp. Sig. (2-tailed)	.049

a. Based on negative ranks.

b. Wilcoxon Signed Ranks Test

```
EXAMINE
  VARIABLES=before after /COMPARE VARIABLE/PLOT=BOXPLOT/STATISTICS=NONE/NOTOTAL
  /MISSING=LISTWISE .
```

Explore

Case Processing Summary

	Cases					
	Valid		Missing		Total	
	N	Percent	N	Percent	N	Percent
BEFORE	12	100.0%	0	.0%	12	100.0%
AFTER	12	100.0%	0	.0%	12	100.0%

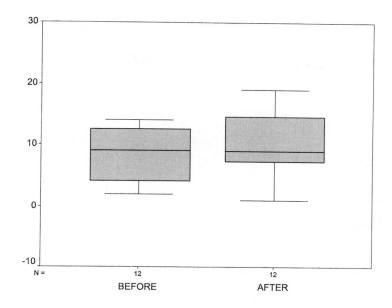

N =   12   12
        BEFORE   AFTER

Example—Kruskal–Wallis Test: We will use SPSS to work Problem 3, a K–W example. The steps are as follows:

1. Start SPSS and name variables **group** and **irritate.** Enter the data, coding the groups 1, 2, and 3 for the diet groups A, B, and C, respectively.
2. Select Statistics>Nonparametric Tests>K Independent Samples.
3. In the dialog box, move **irritate** into the Test Variable List box and move **group** into the Grouping Variable box. Click Define Range, indicate the minimum (1) and maximum (3) range for the grouping variable, then click Continue.
4. Be sure Kruskal–Wallis H is checked in the Test Type box (it should be by default), then OK, and the results should appear in the output Viewer window.
5. Obtain the boxplot of groups by adapting the instructions given in the M–W example to this problem.
6. Looking ahead, we see that the test is significant, so we will need to perform pairwise M–W tests to determine the group differences. Follow the steps in the M–W example and compare groups 1 and 2, 1 and 3, and 2 and 3.

Notes on Reading the Output

1. The output provides the mean ranks for each group in the Ranks box. In the Test Statistics box, SPSS does not provide the exact H value; instead, a chi-square equivalent is given with a p value.
2. The results indicate that the null hypothesis is rejected, and the samples come from different populations. We conclude that the diet groups are significantly different in terms of irritability by the K–W test, $\chi^2 (2, N = 31) = 13.657, p = .001$. The mean ranks in ascending order are as follows: Diet C = 10.95, Diet A = 12.77, and Diet B = 24.6.
3. The boxplot indicates that Group 2 (Diet B) is higher than either of the other two groups, which do not appear to differ. Further testing is needed to confirm this observation.
4. Pairwise group comparisons: Comparison 1 versus 2 (Diet A vs. Diet B) indicates that Diet B animals have higher irritability than Diet A animals, $U = 12, p = .002$. Comparison 1 versus 3 (Diet A vs. Diet

C) showed no significant difference in irritability, $U = 47.5$, $p = .59$. Comparison 2 versus 3 (Diet B vs. Diet C) indicated that Diet B rats had higher irritability than Diet C rats, $U = 7.0$, $p = .001$. These results can be summarized in terms of irritability as follows: Diet C = Diet A < Diet B.

```
FORMATS group (F8.2).
FORMATS irritate (F8.2).
NPAR TESTS
  /K-W=irritate   BY group(1 3)
  /MISSING ANALYSIS.
```

NPar Tests

Kruskal-Wallis Test

Ranks

	GROUP	N	Mean Rank
IRRITATE	1.00	11	12.77
	2.00	10	24.60
	3.00	10	10.95
	Total	31	

Test Statistics[a,b]

	IRRITATE
Chi-Square	13.657
df	2
Asymp. Sig.	.001

a. Kruskal Wallis Test

b. Grouping Variable: GROUP

```
EXAMINE
  VARIABLES=irritate BY group /PLOT=BOXPLOT/STATISTICS=NONE/NOTOTAL
  /MISSING=REPORT.
```

Explore

GROUP

Case Processing Summary

		Cases					
		Valid		Missing		Total	
	GROUP	N	Percent	N	Percent	N	Percent
IRRITATE	1.00	11	100.0%	0	.0%	11	100.0%
	2.00	10	100.0%	0	.0%	10	100.0%
	3.00	10	100.0%	0	.0%	10	100.0%

IRRITATE

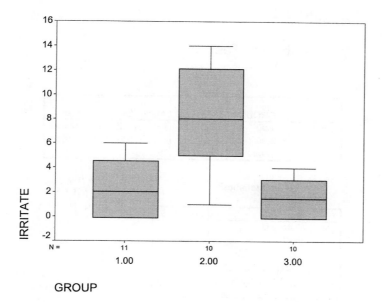

```
NPAR TESTS
  /M-W= irritate   BY group(1 2)
  /MISSING ANALYSIS.
```

NPar Tests

Mann-Whitney Test

Ranks

	GROUP	N	Mean Rank	Sum of Ranks
IRRITATE	1.00	11	7.09	78.00
	2.00	10	15.30	153.00
	Total	21		

Test Statistics[b]

	IRRITATE
Mann-Whitney U	12.000
Wilcoxon W	78.000
Z	-3.046
Asymp. Sig. (2-tailed)	.002
Exact Sig. [2*(1-tailed Sig.)]	.002[a]

a. Not corrected for ties.

b. Grouping Variable: GROUP

```
NPAR TESTS
 /M-W= irritate   BY group(1 3)
 /MISSING ANALYSIS.
```

NPar Tests

Mann-Whitney Test

Ranks

	GROUP	N	Mean Rank	Sum of Ranks
IRRITATE	1.00	11	11.68	128.50
	3.00	10	10.25	102.50
	Total	21		

Test Statistics[b]

	IRRITATE
Mann-Whitney U	47.500
Wilcoxon W	102.500
Z	-.541
Asymp. Sig. (2-tailed)	.589
Exact Sig. [2*(1-tailed Sig.)]	.605[a]

a. Not corrected for ties.

b. Grouping Variable: GROUP

```
NPAR TESTS
 /M-W= irritate   BY group(2 3)
 /MISSING ANALYSIS.
```

NPar Tests

Mann-Whitney Test

Ranks

	GROUP	N	Mean Rank	Sum of Ranks
IRRITATE	2.00	10	14.80	148.00
	3.00	10	6.20	62.00
	Total	20		

Test Statistics[b]

	IRRITATE
Mann-Whitney U	7.000
Wilcoxon W	62.000
Z	-3.269
Asymp. Sig. (2-tailed)	.001
Exact Sig. [2*(1-tailed Sig.)]	.000[a]

a. Not corrected for ties.

b. Grouping Variable: GROUP

Exercises Using SPSS

1. Work Problem 2, using SPSS to perform the Mann–Whitney test. Also provide boxplots of the data.
2. Use SPSS to perform the Wilcoxon test on the data in Problem 7. Also provide boxplots of the data.
3. Use SPSS to perform the K–W test on the data in Problem 8. Also provide boxplots of the data. If overall differences are obtained, do all pairwise comparisons using the M–W test; interpret the results in the context of the problem.

CHECKING YOUR PROGRESS: A SELF-TEST

1. Match the nonparametric test with its parametric alternative.

   _____ Mann–Whitney   **a.** one-way between-subjects ANOVA

   _____ Kruskal–Wallis   **b.** t test for dependent samples

   _____ Wilcoxon   **c.** t test for independent samples

2. Three groups of rats are fed different diets for 4 weeks. Each animal's latency (rounded to the nearest whole second) to leave a lighted platform is recorded, and the results are shown here. Because of the unequal and small sample sizes and the large amount of within-group variability, the one-way ANOVA may not be appropriate. Use the nonparametric alternative to perform an overall test. If the overall test is significant, do all pairwise comparisons, and tell what your conclusions mean in the context of the problem.

Group 1	Group 2	Group 3
30	43	13
25	33	12
23	30	10
16	28	8
12	25	7
10	15	6
8	14	5
5	10	

3. Fifteen students, rated as extreme introverts on the Myers–Briggs Type Indicator, are given 5 hours of assertiveness training. The MBTI is again administered. Did assertiveness training affect the introversion score on the MBTI?

Student	Score Before Training	Score After Training
1	27	27
2	33	27
3	35	27
4	45	35
5	47	43
6	31	35
7	35	37
8	31	25
9	29	15
10	27	11
11	35	31
12	43	45
13	39	27
14	35	37
15	31	25

APPENDIX 1

BRIEF MATH–ALGEBRA REVIEW

Let's face it: There's a lot of variability in the mathematical sophistication undergraduates bring to their first statistics courses. From our experience, preparation ranges from avoidance of any college math to completion of an advanced college calculus course. If your background qualifies you for the calculus end of the range, read no further; this appendix is not for you. On the other hand, if you've avoided college math before this, read on. The material in this appendix is designed to refresh your memory of topics long forgotten and to prepare you for the very basic mathematics presented elsewhere in this text.

SYMBOLS

Symbol	Read	Example
$=$	equals	$7 = 7$
$\neq$	is not equal to	$6 \neq 37$
$>$	greater than	$5 > 2$
$<$	less than	$2 < 5$
$\geq$	greater than or equal to	$p \geq .05$
$\leq$	less than or equal to	$p \leq .01$
$+$	plus	$3 + 3 = 6$
$-$	minus	$3 - 3 = 0$
$\times$ or $(\ )(\ )$ or $\cdot$	times	$3 \times 3 = 9$
		$(3)(3) = 9$
		$3 \cdot 3 = 9$

Symbol	Read	Example
$\div$ or $/$	divided by	$6 \div 3 = 2$
		$6/3 = 2$
$(\ )^2$	square	$(2)^2 = 2^2 = 4$
$\sqrt{\ }$	square root	$\sqrt{4} = 2$
$|\ \ |$	absolute value of (the number without	$|-5| = 5$
	regard to sign)	$|5| = 5$
$\pm$	plus or minus	6 ± 5 is
		$6 + 5 = 11$ and
		$6 - 5 = 1$

ARITHMETIC OPERATIONS

Addition

Numbers may be added in any order or combination.

Example:

$$8 + 4 + 3 = 3 + 4 + 8 = (3 + 4) + 8 = 15$$

Addition of Negative Numbers

Add as though the numbers were positive; then put a negative sign before the result.

Example:

$$(-1) + (-3) + (-5) + (-7) = -(1 + 3 + 5 + 7) = -16$$

Subtraction

Subtraction is equivalent to the addition of a negative number.

Example:

$$12 - 3 = 12 + (-3) = 9$$

As with addition, numbers may be subtracted in any order or combination.

Example:

$$27 - 4 - 12 = 27 + (-4) + (-12) = 27 + [(-4) + (-12)] = -4 + (-12) + 27 = 11$$

Adding a Combination of Positive and Negative Numbers

Sum the positive and negative numbers separately, take the difference between the sums, then put the sign of the larger sum on the result.

Examples:

$$(+5) + (+3) + (+6) + (-2) + (-5) + (-15) = +14 + (-22) = -8$$

(The difference between 22 and 14 is 8, and the sign of the larger difference is −.)

$$(+5) + (+10) + (-3) + (-5) = +15 + (-8) = 7$$

Subtracting Negative Numbers

Change the sign of the negative number to be subtracted and add.

Examples:

$$10 - (-5) = 10 + 5 = 15$$
$$-15 - (-6) = -15 + 6 = -9$$

Multiplication and Division

In multiplication and division, the result is positive if all of the terms are positive or if there is an even number of negative terms. The result is negative if there is an odd number of negative terms.

Examples:

$$(6)(3) = +18$$
$$(-6)(-3) = +18$$
$$(-6)(3) = -18 \quad \text{or} \quad (6)(-3) = -18$$
$$\frac{-6}{-3} = +2$$
$$\frac{6}{3} = +2$$
$$\frac{6}{-3} = -2$$
$$\frac{-6}{3} = -2$$

As with addition and subtraction, order of computation makes no difference.

Example:

$$(6)(-3)(-4) = (-4)(-3)(6) = 72$$

ORDER OF OPERATIONS

Work from the inside out; that is, do everything inside parentheses or brackets first. Within an expression, follow the order of operations summarized in the mnemonic "Follow My Dear Aunt Sally."

1. Follow = Functional operations such as square or square root
2. My Dear = Multiplication and Division
3. Aunt Sally = Addition and Subtraction

Example 1

$$6(5 - 2^2) + \frac{13\sqrt{25}}{8} = 6(5 - 4) + \frac{(13)(5)}{8} = 6(1) + \frac{65}{8} = 6 + 8.13 = 14.13$$

Example 2

$$\left[\frac{(.9)(5)}{4}\right]X + \left[20 - \left(\frac{(.9)(5)}{4}\right)(12)\right]$$

Do everything inside parentheses or brackets first. Multiply, then divide:

$$\left(\frac{4.5}{4}\right)X + \left[20 - \left(\frac{4.5}{4}\right)(12)\right]$$

$$1.13X + [20 - (1.13)(12)]$$

Multiply before adding:

$$1.13X + (20 - 13.56) = 1.13X + 6.44$$

WORKING WITH FRACTIONS

In these days of the pocket calculator, the simplest way to work with fractions is to convert them to decimals and carry out the operations specified by the equation. To convert a fraction to a decimal, divide the numerator (top part of the fraction) by the denominator (bottom part of the fraction).

Examples:

$$\frac{1}{15} + \frac{1}{17} = 0.07 + 0.06 = 0.13$$

$$\left(\frac{3}{19}\right)\left(\frac{7}{16}\right) = (0.16)(0.44) = 0.07$$

Nevertheless, there are times at which it is more convenient or it is necessary (such as when your calculator breaks) to work with fractions. In these situations, there are several rules, specific to fractions, that must be followed.

Addition or Subtraction of Fractions

In adding or subtracting fractions, first express each fraction in terms of the least common denominator. Then add (or subtract) the numerators and place the result over the common denominator.

Examples:

$$\frac{1}{8} + \frac{1}{2} + \frac{1}{4} = \frac{1}{8} + \frac{4}{8} + \frac{2}{8} = \frac{7}{8}$$

$$\frac{11}{12} - \frac{1}{6} - \frac{1}{3} = \frac{11}{12} - \frac{2}{12} - \frac{4}{12} = \frac{5}{12}$$

Multiplication of Fractions

In multiplying fractions, find the product of the numerators and divide by the product of the denominators.

Examples:

$$\frac{2}{3} \times \frac{3}{5} = \frac{2 \times 3}{3 \times 5} = \frac{6}{15}$$

$$\frac{1}{2} \times \frac{3}{7} \times \frac{3}{5} = \frac{1 \times 3 \times 3}{2 \times 7 \times 5} = \frac{9}{70}$$

Multiplying a Whole Number by a Fraction

In multiplying fractions and whole numbers, multiply the numerator of the fraction(s) by the whole number(s) and divide by the denominator.

Examples:

$$\left(\frac{1}{9}\right)(5) = \frac{(1)(5)}{9} = \frac{5}{9}$$

$$\left(\frac{1}{7}\right)(4)(3) = \frac{(1)(4)(3)}{7} = \frac{12}{7}$$

$$\left(\frac{4}{5}\right)\left(\frac{1}{3}\right)(7) = \frac{(4)(1)(7)}{(5)(3)} = \frac{28}{15}$$

SOLVING EQUATIONS WITH ONE UNKNOWN

You frequently will be required to solve equations with one unknown. These are quite simple and usually involve performing arithmetic steps to isolate the unknown on one side of the equation and then simplifying the other side of the equation. The specific steps required are different for each problem. The principle to remember is that whatever you do on one side of the equation must also be done on the other side of the equation. Examples of the basic types of problems you may encounter will illustrate the procedures involved.

Solving for X by addition:

$$X - 7 = 4$$
$$X - 7 + 7 = 4 + 7 \quad \text{(add 7 to both sides)}$$
$$X = 11$$

Solving for X by subtraction:

$$X + 6 = 10$$
$$X + 6 - 6 = 10 - 6 \qquad \text{(subtract 6 from both sides)}$$
$$X = 4$$

Solving for X by division:

$$3X = 15$$
$$\frac{3X}{3} = \frac{15}{3} \qquad \text{(divide both sides by 3)}$$
$$X = 5$$

Solving for X by multiplication:

$$\frac{X}{7} = 4$$
$$(7)\frac{X}{7} = (7)4 \qquad \text{(multiply both sides by 7)}$$
$$X = 28$$

Solving for X by a combination of procedures:

$$4X + 2 = 18$$
$$4X + 2 - 2 = 18 - 2 \qquad \text{(subtract 2 from both sides)}$$
$$4X = 16$$
$$\frac{4X}{4} = \frac{16}{4} \qquad \text{(divide both sides by 4)}$$
$$X = 4$$

$$\frac{X - 10}{3} = 2$$
$$(3)\left(\frac{X - 10}{3}\right) = (3)2 \qquad \text{(multiply both sides by 3)}$$
$$X - 10 = 6$$
$$X - 10 + 10 = 6 + 10 \qquad \text{(add 10 to both sides)}$$
$$X = 16$$

EXERCISES

1. $\dfrac{3 + (13 - 3^2)}{(4)(6 - 3)(5 + 2^2)} = ?$

2. $\dfrac{1}{10} + \dfrac{5}{17} + \left(\dfrac{6}{23}\right)\left(\dfrac{5}{11}\right) = ?$

3. $\left(\dfrac{15}{27}\right)\left(\dfrac{3^2}{13^2}\right) = ?$

4. $13 + (-7) + 14 + (-3^2) = ?$

5. $15 - (-10) = ?$

6. $|-27| = ?$

7. $(-11)^2 = ?$

8. $(-10)(13) = ?$

9. $\dfrac{10\sqrt{5}}{\sqrt{\dfrac{275}{12} - 4^2}} = ?$

10. $\dfrac{(8)(7^2) + 1/3(7 + 6^2)}{(10 + 11 - 2)(6 - 3)} = ?$

11. $\dfrac{17}{10 - 15} = ?$

12. $\dfrac{3X + 14}{5} = 10 \qquad X = ?$

13. $\dfrac{2}{3}X - 3 = 11 \qquad X = ?$

14. $\dfrac{3(X + 2)}{7} = 6 \qquad X = ?$

15. $7X - 15 = -1 \qquad X = ?$

APPENDIX 2

TABLES FOR INFERENTIAL TESTS

TABLE A. Areas under the right half (positive z scores) of the standard normal curve ($\mu = 0$, $\sigma = 1$)

(A)	(B)	(C)	(A)	(B)	(C)	(A)	(B)	(C)
z	area between mean and z	area beyond z	z	area between mean and z	area beyond z	z	area between mean and z	area beyond z
0.00	00.00	50.00	0.55	20.88	29.12	1.10	36.43	13.57
0.01	00.40	49.60	0.56	21.23	28.77	1.11	36.65	13.35
0.02	00.80	49.20	0.57	21.57	28.43	1.12	36.86	13.14
0.03	01.20	48.80	0.58	21.90	28.10	1.13	37.08	12.92
0.04	01.60	48.40	0.59	22.24	27.76	1.14	37.29	12.71
0.05	01.99	48.01	0.60	22.57	27.43	1.15	37.49	12.51
0.06	02.39	47.61	0.61	22.91	27.09	1.16	37.70	12.30
0.07	02.79	47.21	0.62	23.24	26.76	1.17	37.90	12.10
0.08	03.19	46.81	0.63	23.57	26.43	1.18	38.10	11.90
0.09	03.59	46.41	0.64	23.89	26.11	1.19	38.30	11.70
0.10	03.98	46.02	0.65	24.22	25.78	1.20	38.49	11.51
0.11	04.38	45.62	0.66	24.54	25.46	1.21	38.69	11.31
0.12	04.78	45.22	0.67	24.86	25.14	1.22	38.88	11.12
0.13	05.17	44.83	0.68	25.17	24.83	1.23	39.07	10.93
0.14	05.57	44.43	0.69	25.49	24.51	1.24	39.25	10.75
0.15	05.96	44.04	0.70	25.80	24.20	1.25	39.44	10.56
0.16	06.36	43.64	0.71	26.11	23.89	1.26	39.62	10.38
0.17	06.75	43.25	0.72	26.42	23.58	1.27	39.80	10.20
0.18	07.14	42.86	0.73	26.73	23.27	1.28	39.97	10.03
0.19	07.53	42.47	0.74	27.04	22.96	1.29	40.15	09.85
0.20	07.93	42.07	0.75	27.34	22.66	1.30	40.32	09.68
0.21	08.32	41.68	0.76	27.64	22.36	1.31	40.49	09.51
0.22	08.71	41.29	0.77	27.94	22.06	1.32	40.66	09.34
0.23	09.10	40.90	0.78	28.23	21.77	1.33	40.82	09.18
0.24	09.48	40.52	0.79	28.52	21.48	1.34	40.99	09.01
0.25	09.87	40.13	0.80	28.81	21.19	1.35	41.15	08.85
0.26	10.26	39.74	0.81	29.10	20.90	1.36	41.31	08.69
0.27	10.64	39.36	0.82	29.39	20.61	1.37	41.47	08.53
0.28	11.03	38.97	0.83	29.67	20.33	1.38	41.62	08.38
0.29	11.41	38.59	0.84	29.95	20.05	1.39	41.77	08.23
0.30	11.79	38.21	0.85	30.23	19.77	1.40	41.92	08.08
0.31	12.17	37.83	0.86	30.51	19.49	1.41	42.07	07.93
0.32	12.55	37.45	0.87	30.78	19.22	1.42	42.22	07.78
0.33	12.93	37.07	0.88	31.06	18.94	1.43	42.36	07.64
0.34	13.31	36.69	0.89	31.33	18.67	1.44	42.51	07.49
0.35	13.68	36.32	0.90	31.59	18.41	1.45	42.65	07.35
0.36	14.06	35.94	0.91	31.86	18.14	1.46	42.79	07.21
0.37	14.43	35.57	0.92	32.12	17.88	1.47	42.92	07.08
0.38	14.80	35.20	0.93	32.38	17.62	1.48	43.06	06.94
0.39	15.17	34.83	0.94	32.64	17.36	1.49	43.19	06.81
0.40	15.54	34.46	0.95	32.89	17.11	1.50	43.32	06.68
0.41	15.91	34.09	0.96	33.15	16.85	1.51	43.45	06.55
0.42	16.28	33.72	0.97	33.40	16.60	1.52	43.57	06.43
0.43	16.64	33.36	0.98	33.65	16.35	1.53	43.70	06.30
0.44	17.00	33.00	0.99	33.89	16.11	1.54	43.82	06.18
0.45	17.36	32.64	1.00	34.13	15.87	1.55	43.94	06.06
0.46	17.72	32.28	1.01	34.38	15.62	1.56	44.06	05.94
0.47	18.08	31.92	1.02	34.61	15.39	1.57	44.18	05.82
0.48	18.44	31.56	1.03	34.85	15.15	1.58	44.29	05.71
0.49	18.79	31.21	1.04	35.08	14.92	1.59	44.41	05.59
0.50	19.15	30.85	1.05	35.31	14.69	1.60	44.52	05.48
0.51	19.50	30.50	1.06	35.54	14.46	1.61	44.63	05.37
0.52	19.85	30.15	1.07	35.77	14.23	1.62	44.74	05.26
0.53	20.19	29.81	1.08	35.99	14.01	1.63	44.84	05.16
0.54	20.54	29.46	1.09	36.21	13.79	1.64	44.95	05.05

Source: This table is from *Fundamentals of Behavioral Statistics* (Third Edition), by R. P. Runyon and A. Haber, 1976, Addison-Wesley, pp. 377–379. Copyright © 1976 by Addison-Wesley. Reprinted with permission of The McGraw-Hill Companies.

TABLE A. continued

(A)	(B)	(C)	(A)	(B)	(C)	(A)	(B)	(C)
z	area between mean and z	area beyond z	z	area between mean and z	area beyond z	z	area between mean and z	area beyond z
1.65	45.05	04.95	2.22	48.68	01.32	2.79	49.74	00.26
1.66	45.15	04.85	2.23	48.71	01.29	2.80	49.74	00.26
1.67	45.25	04.75	2.24	48.75	01.25	2.81	49.75	00.25
1.68	45.35	04.65	2.25	48.78	01.22	2.82	49.76	00.24
1.69	45.45	04.55	2.26	48.81	01.19	2.83	49.77	00.23
1.70	45.54	04.46	2.27	48.84	01.16	2.84	49.77	00.23
1.71	45.64	04.36	2.28	48.87	01.13	2.85	49.78	00.22
1.72	45.73	04.27	2.29	48.90	01.10	2.86	49.79	00.21
1.73	45.82	04.18	2.30	48.93	01.07	2.87	49.79	00.21
1.74	45.91	04.09	2.31	48.96	01.04	2.88	49.80	00.20
1.75	45.99	04.01	2.32	48.98	01.02	2.89	49.81	00.19
1.76	46.08	03.92	2.33	49.01	00.99	2.90	49.81	00.19
1.77	46.16	03.84	2.34	49.04	00.96	2.91	49.82	00.18
1.78	46.25	03.75	2.35	49.06	00.94	2.92	49.82	00.18
1.79	46.33	03.67	2.36	49.09	00.91	2.93	49.83	00.17
1.80	46.41	03.59	2.37	49.11	00.89	2.94	49.84	00.16
1.81	46.49	03.51	2.38	49.13	00.87	2.95	49.84	00.16
1.82	46.56	03.44	2.39	49.16	00.84	2.96	49.85	00.15
1.83	46.64	03.36	2.40	49.18	00.82	2.97	49.85	00.15
1.84	46.71	03.29	2.41	49.20	00.80	2.98	49.86	00.14
1.85	46.78	03.22	2.42	49.22	00.78	2.99	49.86	00.14
1.86	46.86	03.14	2.43	49.25	00.75	3.00	49.87	00.13
1.87	46.93	03.07	2.44	49.27	00.73	3.01	49.87	00.13
1.88	46.99	03.01	2.45	49.29	00.71	3.02	49.87	00.13
1.89	47.06	02.94	2.46	49.31	00.69	3.03	49.88	00.12
1.90	47.13	02.87	2.47	49.32	00.68	3.04	49.88	00.12
1.91	47.19	02.81	2.48	49.34	00.66	3.05	49.89	00.11
1.92	47.26	02.74	2.49	49.36	00.64	3.06	49.89	00.11
1.93	47.32	02.68	2.50	49.38	00.62	3.07	49.89	00.11
1.94	47.38	02.62	2.51	49.40	00.60	3.08	49.90	00.10
1.95	47.44	02.56	2.52	49.41	00.59	3.09	49.90	00.10
1.96	47.50	02.50	2.53	49.43	00.57	3.10	49.90	00.10
1.97	47.56	02.44	2.54	49.45	00.55	3.11	49.91	00.09
1.98	47.61	02.39	2.55	49.46	00.54	3.12	49.91	00.09
1.99	47.67	02.33	2.56	49.48	00.52	3.13	49.91	00.09
2.00	47.72	02.28	2.57	49.49	00.51	3.14	49.92	00.08
2.01	47.78	02.22	2.58	49.51	00.49	3.15	49.92	00.08
2.02	47.83	02.17	2.59	49.52	00.48	3.16	49.92	00.08
2.03	47.88	02.12	2.60	49.53	00.47	3.17	49.92	00.08
2.04	47.93	02.07	2.61	49.55	00.45	3.18	49.93	00.07
2.05	47.98	02.02	2.62	49.56	00.44	3.19	49.93	00.07
2.06	48.03	01.97	2.63	49.57	00.43	3.20	49.93	00.07
2.07	48.08	01.92	2.64	49.59	00.41	3.21	49.93	00.07
2.08	48.12	01.88	2.65	49.60	00.40	3.22	49.94	00.06
2.09	48.17	01.83	2.66	49.61	00.39	3.23	49.94	00.06
2.10	48.21	01.79	2.67	49.62	00.38	3.24	49.94	00.06
2.11	48.26	01.74	2.68	49.63	00.37	3.25	49.94	00.06
2.12	48.30	01.70	2.69	49.64	00.36	3.30	49.95	00.05
2.13	48.34	01.66	2.70	49.65	00.35	3.35	49.96	00.04
2.14	48.38	01.62	2.71	49.66	00.34	3.40	49.97	00.03
2.15	48.42	01.58	2.72	49.67	00.33	3.45	49.97	00.03
2.16	48.46	01.54	2.73	49.68	00.32	3.50	49.98	00.02
2.17	48.50	01.50	2.74	49.69	00.31	3.60	49.98	00.02
2.18	48.54	01.46	2.75	49.70	00.30	3.70	49.99	00.01
2.19	48.57	01.43	2.76	49.71	00.29	3.80	49.99	00.01
2.20	48.61	01.39	2.77	49.72	00.28	3.90	49.995	00.005
2.21	48.64	01.36	2.78	49.73	00.27	4.00	49.997	00.003

Table B. Critical Values of *t*

$df = N - 1$ for one-sample *t* test, confidence intervals, and for the *t* test for dependent samples

$df = N_1 + N_2 - 2$ for two-sample *t* test

	Level of Significance for Two-Tailed Test (For One-Tailed Test, Halve the Following Percentages)			
df	10% (*p* = .10)	5% (*p* = .05)	2% (*p* = .02)	1% (*p* = .01)
1	6.3138	12.7062	31.8207	63.6574
2	2.9200	4.3027	6.9646	9.9248
3	2.3534	3.1824	4.5407	5.8409
4	2.1318	2.7764	3.7469	4.6041
5	2.0150	2.5706	3.3649	4.0322
6	1.9432	2.4469	3.1427	3.7074
7	1.8946	2.3646	2.9980	3.4995
8	1.8595	2.3060	2.8965	3.3554
9	1.8331	2.2622	2.8214	3.2498
10	1.8125	2.2281	2.7638	3.1693
11	1.7959	2.2010	2.7181	3.1058
12	1.7823	2.1788	2.6810	3.0545
13	1.7709	2.1604	2.6503	3.0123
14	1.7613	2.1448	2.6245	2.9768
15	1.7531	2.1315	2.6025	2.9467
16	1.7459	2.1199	2.5835	2.9208
17	1.7396	2.1098	2.5669	2.8982
18	1.7341	2.1009	2.5524	2.8784
19	1.7291	2.0930	2.5395	2.8609
20	1.7247	2.0860	2.5280	2.8453
21	1.7207	2.0796	2.5177	2.8314
22	1.7171	2.0739	2.5083	2.8188
23	1.7139	2.0687	2.4999	2.8073
24	1.7109	2.0639	2.4922	2.7969
25	1.7081	2.0595	2.4851	2.7874
26	1.7056	2.0555	2.4786	2.7787
27	1.7033	2.0518	2.4727	2.7707
28	1.7011	2.0484	2.4671	2.7633
29	1.6991	2.0452	2.4620	2.7564
30	1.6973	2.0423	2.4573	2.7500
35	1.6869	2.0301	2.4377	2.7238
40	1.6839	2.0211	2.4233	2.7045
45	1.6794	2.0141	2.4121	2.6896
50	1.6759	2.0086	2.4033	2.6778
60	1.6706	2.0003	2.3901	2.6603
70	1.6669	1.9944	2.3808	2.6479
80	1.6641	1.9901	2.3739	2.6387
90	1.6620	1.9867	2.3685	2.6316
100	1.6602	1.9840	2.3642	2.6259
110	1.6588	1.9818	2.3607	2.6213
120	1.6577	1.9799	2.3598	2.6174
∞	1.6449	1.9600	2.3263	2.5758

Source: This table is from *Handbook of Statistical Tables* by D. B. Owen, 1962, Addison-Wesley, pp. 28–30. Copyright © 1962 by Addison-Wesley Publishing Company, Inc. Reprinted with permission of Addison Wesley Longman.

Table C. Critical Values of F

df associated with the denominator df_w		df associated with the numerator (df_b)								
		1	2	3	4	5	6	7	8	9
1	5%	161	200	216	225	230	234	237	239	241
	1%	4052	5000	5403	5625	5764	5859	5928	5982	6022
2	5%	18.5	19.0	19.2	19.2	19.3	19.3	19.4	19.4	19.4
	1%	98.5	99.0	99.2	99.2	99.3	99.3	99.4	99.4	99.4
3	5%	10.1	9.55	9.28	9.12	9.01	8.94	8.89	8.85	8.81
	1%	34.1	30.8	29.5	28.7	28.2	27.9	27.7	27.5	27.3
4	5%	7.71	6.94	6.59	6.39	6.26	6.16	6.09	6.04	6.00
	1%	21.2	18.0	16.7	16.0	15.5	15.2	15.0	14.8	14.7
5	5%	6.61	5.79	5.41	5.19	5.05	4.95	4.88	4.82	4.77
	1%	16.3	13.3	12.1	11.4	11.0	10.7	10.5	10.3	10.2
6	5%	5.99	5.14	4.76	4.53	4.39	4.28	4.21	4.15	4.10
	1%	13.7	10.9	9.78	9.15	8.75	8.47	8.26	8.10	7.98
7	5%	5.59	4.74	4.35	4.12	3.97	3.87	3.79	3.73	3.68
	1%	12.2	9.55	8.45	7.85	7.46	7.19	6.99	6.84	6.72
8	5%	5.32	4.46	4.07	3.84	3.69	3.58	3.50	3.44	3.39
	1%	11.3	8.65	7.59	7.01	6.63	6.37	6.18	6.03	5.91
9	5%	5.12	4.26	3.86	3.63	3.48	3.37	3.29	3.23	3.18
	1%	10.6	8.02	6.99	6.42	6.06	5.80	5.61	5.47	5.35
10	5%	4.96	4.10	3.71	3.48	3.33	3.22	3.14	3.07	3.02
	1%	10.0	7.56	6.55	5.99	5.64	5.39	5.20	5.06	4.94
11	5%	4.84	3.98	3.59	3.36	3.20	3.09	3.01	2.95	2.90
	1%	9.65	7.21	6.22	5.67	5.32	5.07	4.89	4.74	4.63
12	5%	4.75	3.89	3.49	3.26	3.11	3.00	2.91	2.85	2.80
	1%	9.33	6.93	5.95	5.41	5.06	4.82	4.64	4.50	4.39
13	5%	4.67	3.81	3.41	3.18	3.03	2.92	2.83	2.77	2.71
	1%	9.07	6.70	5.74	5.21	4.86	4.62	4.44	4.30	4.19
14	5%	4.60	3.74	3.34	3.11	2.96	2.85	2.76	2.70	2.65
	1%	8.86	6.51	5.56	5.04	4.70	4.46	4.28	4.14	4.03
15	5%	4.54	3.68	3.29	3.06	2.90	2.79	2.71	2.64	2.59
	1%	8.68	6.36	5.42	4.89	4.56	4.32	4.14	4.00	3.89
16	5%	4.49	3.63	3.24	3.01	2.85	2.74	2.66	2.59	2.54
	1%	8.53	6.23	5.29	4.77	4.44	4.20	4.03	3.89	3.78
17	5%	4.45	3.59	3.20	2.96	2.81	2.70	2.61	2.55	2.49
	1%	8.40	6.11	5.18	4.67	4.34	4.10	3.93	3.79	3.68

Source: This table is adapted from "Tables of percentage points of the inverted beta (F) distribution," by M. Merrington and C. M. Thompson, 1943, *Biometrika, 33,* pp. 73–88, with permission of the Biometrika Trustees.

Table C. continued

df associated with the denominator df_w		df associated with the numerator (df_b)								
		1	2	3	4	5	6	7	8	9
18	5%	4.41	3.55	3.16	2.93	2.77	2.66	2.58	2.51	2.46
	1%	8.29	6.01	5.09	4.58	4.25	4.01	3.84	3.71	3.60
19	5%	4.38	3.52	3.13	2.90	2.74	2.63	2.54	2.48	2.42
	1%	8.18	5.93	5.01	4.50	4.17	3.94	3.77	3.63	3.52
20	5%	4.35	3.49	3.10	2.87	2.71	2.60	2.51	2.45	2.39
	1%	8.10	5.85	4.94	4.43	4.10	3.87	3.70	3.56	3.46
21	5%	4.32	3.47	3.07	2.84	2.68	2.57	2.49	2.42	2.37
	1%	8.02	5.78	4.87	4.37	4.04	3.81	3.64	3.51	3.40
22	5%	4.30	3.44	3.05	2.82	2.66	2.55	2.46	2.40	2.34
	1%	7.95	5.72	4.82	4.31	3.99	3.76	3.59	3.45	3.35
23	5%	4.28	3.42	3.03	2.80	2.64	2.53	2.44	2.37	2.32
	1%	7.88	5.66	4.76	4.26	3.94	3.71	3.54	3.41	3.30
24	5%	4.26	3.40	3.01	2.78	2.62	2.51	2.42	2.36	2.30
	1%	7.82	5.61	4.72	4.22	3.90	3.67	3.50	3.36	3.26
25	5%	4.24	3.39	2.29	2.76	2.60	2.49	2.40	2.34	2.28
	1%	7.77	5.57	4.68	4.18	3.86	3.63	3.46	3.32	3.22
26	5%	4.23	3.37	2.98	2.74	2.59	2.47	2.39	2.32	2.27
	1%	7.72	5.53	4.64	4.14	3.82	3.59	3.42	3.29	3.18
27	5%	4.21	3.35	2.96	2.73	2.57	2.46	2.37	2.31	2.25
	1%	7.68	5.49	4.60	4.11	3.78	3.56	3.39	3.26	3.15
28	5%	4.20	3.34	2.95	2.71	2.56	2.45	2.36	2.29	2.24
	1%	7.64	5.45	4.57	4.07	3.75	3.53	3.36	3.23	3.12
29	5%	4.18	3.33	2.93	2.70	2.55	2.43	2.35	2.28	2.22
	1%	7.60	5.42	4.54	4.04	3.73	3.50	3.33	3.20	3.09
30	5%	4.17	3.32	2.92	2.69	2.53	2.42	2.33	2.27	2.21
	1%	7.56	5.39	4.51	4.02	3.70	3.47	3.30	3.17	3.07
40	5%	4.08	3.23	2.84	2.61	2.45	2.34	2.25	2.18	2.12
	1%	7.31	5.18	4.31	3.83	3.51	3.29	3.12	2.99	2.89
60	5%	4.00	3.15	2.76	2.53	2.37	2.25	2.17	2.10	2.04
	1%	7.08	4.98	4.13	3.65	3.34	3.12	2.95	2.82	2.72
120	5%	3.92	3.07	2.68	2.45	2.29	2.18	2.09	2.02	1.96
	1%	6.85	4.79	3.95	3.48	3.17	2.96	2.79	2.66	2.56

Table D. Critical Values of q_α

df_w	α	2	3	4	5	6	7	8	9	10
		\multicolumn{9}{c}{K = Number of Groups (Means)}								
1	.05	17.97	26.98	32.82	37.08	40.41	43.12	45.40	47.36	49.07
	.01	90.03	135.00	164.30	185.60	202.20	215.80	227.20	237.00	245.60
2	.05	6.08	8.33	9.80	10.88	11.74	12.44	13.03	13.54	13.99
	.01	14.04	19.02	22.29	24.72	26.63	28.20	29.53	30.68	31.69
3	.05	4.50	5.91	6.82	7.50	8.04	8.48	8.85	9.18	9.46
	.01	8.26	10.62	12.17	13.33	14.24	15.00	15.64	16.20	16.69
4	.05	3.93	5.04	5.76	6.29	6.71	7.05	7.35	7.60	7.83
	.01	6.51	8.12	9.17	9.96	10.58	11.10	11.55	11.93	12.27
5	.05	3.64	4.60	5.22	5.67	6.03	6.33	6.58	6.80	6.99
	.01	5.70	6.98	7.80	8.42	8.91	9.32	9.67	9.97	10.24
6	.05	3.46	4.34	4.90	5.30	5.63	5.90	6.12	6.32	6.49
	.01	5.24	6.33	7.03	7.56	7.97	8.32	8.61	8.87	9.10
7	.05	3.34	4.16	4.68	5.06	5.36	5.61	5.82	6.00	6.16
	.01	4.95	5.92	6.54	7.01	7.37	7.68	7.94	8.17	8.37
8	.05	3.26	4.04	4.53	4.89	5.17	5.40	5.60	5.77	5.92
	.01	4.75	5.64	6.20	6.62	6.96	7.24	7.47	7.68	7.86
9	.05	3.20	3.95	4.41	4.76	5.02	5.24	5.43	5.59	5.74
	.01	4.60	5.43	5.96	6.35	6.66	6.91	7.13	7.33	7.49
10	.05	3.15	3.88	4.33	4.65	4.91	5.12	5.30	5.46	5.60
	.01	4.48	5.27	5.77	6.14	6.43	6.67	6.87	7.05	7.21
11	.05	3.11	3.82	4.26	4.57	4.82	5.03	5.20	5.35	5.49
	.01	4.39	5.15	5.62	5.97	6.25	6.48	6.67	6.84	6.99
12	.05	3.08	3.77	4.20	4.51	4.75	4.95	5.12	5.27	5.39
	.01	4.32	5.05	5.50	5.84	6.10	6.32	6.51	6.67	6.81
13	.05	3.06	3.73	4.15	4.45	4.69	4.88	5.05	5.19	5.32
	.01	4.26	4.96	5.40	5.73	5.98	6.19	6.37	6.53	6.67
14	.05	3.03	3.70	4.11	4.41	4.64	4.83	4.99	5.13	5.25
	.01	4.21	4.89	5.32	5.63	5.88	6.08	6.26	6.41	6.54
15	.05	3.01	3.67	4.08	4.37	4.59	4.78	4.94	5.08	5.20
	.01	4.17	4.84	5.25	5.56	5.80	5.99	6.16	6.31	6.44
16	.05	3.00	3.65	4.05	4.33	4.56	4.74	4.90	5.03	5.15
	.01	4.13	4.79	5.19	5.49	5.72	5.92	6.08	6.22	6.35
17	.05	2.98	3.63	4.02	4.30	4.52	4.70	4.86	4.99	5.11
	.01	4.10	4.74	5.14	5.43	5.66	5.85	6.01	6.15	6.27
18	.05	2.97	3.61	4.00	4.28	4.49	4.67	4.82	4.96	5.07
	.01	4.07	4.70	5.09	5.38	5.60	5.79	5.94	6.08	6.20
19	.05	2.96	3.59	3.98	4.25	4.47	4.65	4.79	4.92	5.04
	.01	4.05	4.67	5.05	5.33	5.55	5.73	5.89	6.02	6.14
20	.05	2.95	3.58	3.96	4.23	4.45	4.62	4.77	4.90	5.01
	.01	4.02	4.64	5.02	5.29	5.51	5.69	5.84	5.97	6.09
24	.05	2.92	3.53	3.90	4.17	4.37	4.54	4.68	4.81	4.92
	.01	3.96	4.55	4.91	5.17	5.37	5.54	5.69	5.81	5.92
30	.05	2.89	3.49	3.85	4.10	4.30	4.46	4.60	4.72	4.82
	.01	3.89	4.45	4.80	5.05	5.24	5.40	5.54	5.65	5.76
40	.05	2.86	3.44	3.79	4.04	4.23	4.39	4.52	4.63	4.73
	.01	3.82	4.37	4.70	4.93	5.11	5.26	5.39	5.50	5.60
60	.05	2.83	3.40	3.74	3.98	4.16	4.31	4.44	4.55	4.65
	.01	3.76	4.28	4.59	4.82	4.99	5.13	5.25	5.36	5.45
120	.05	2.80	3.36	3.68	3.92	4.10	4.24	4.36	4.47	4.56
	.01	3.70	4.20	4.50	4.71	4.87	5.01	5.12	5.21	5.30
∞	.05	2.77	3.31	3.63	3.86	4.03	4.17	4.29	4.39	4.47
	.01	3.64	4.12	4.40	4.60	4.76	4.88	4.99	5.08	5.16

Source: This table is from Table 29 of E. S. Pearson and H. O. Hartley (Eds.), *Biometrika Tables for Statisticians,* Vol. 1, 3rd ed., Cambridge University Press. Reprinted with permission of the Biometrika Trustees.

Table E. Critical Values of r

$df = N - 2$, where N is the number of pairs of scores.

Degrees of Freedom (df)	5%	1%	Degrees of Freedom (df)	5%	1%
1	.997	1.000	24	.388	.496
2	.950	.990	25	.381	.487
3	.878	.959	26	.374	.478
4	.811	.917	27	.367	.470
5	.754	.874	28	.361	.463
6	.707	.834	29	.355	.456
7	.666	.798	30	.349	.449
8	.632	.765	35	.325	.418
9	.602	.735	40	.304	.393
10	.576	.708	45	.288	.372
11	.553	.684	50	.273	.354
12	.532	.661	60	.250	.325
13	.514	.641	70	.232	.302
14	.497	.623	80	.217	.283
15	.482	.606	90	.205	.267
16	.468	.590	100	.195	.254
17	.456	.575	125	.174	.228
18	.444	.561	150	.159	.208
19	.433	.549	200	.138	.181
20	.423	.537	300	.113	.148
21	.413	.526	400	.098	.128
22	.404	.515	500	.088	.115
23	.396	.505	1000	.062	.081

Source: This table is adapted from Table VII of Fisher and Yates, *Statistical Tables for Biological, Agricultural and Medical Research,* published by Longman Group Ltd., London (previously published by Oliver and Boyd, Edinburgh), and by permission of Pearson Education Limited.

Table F. Critical Values of r_s

N	5%	1%
5	1.000	—
6	.886	1.000
7	.786	.929
8	.738	.881
9	.683	.833
10	.648	.794
12	.591	.777
14	.544	.714
16	.506	.665
18	.475	.625
20	.450	.591
22	.428	.562
24	.409	.537
26	.392	.515
28	.377	.496
30	.364	.478

Source: This table is adapted from "Distribution of Sums of Squares of Rank Differences for Small Samples," by E. G. Olds, 1938, *Annals of Mathematical Statistics, 9,* pp. 133–148, and "The 5% Significance Levels for Sums of Squares of Rank Differences and a Correction," 1949, *Annals of Mathematical Statistics, 20,* pp. 117–118, with permission of the editor.

Table G. Critical Values of χ^2

$df = K - 1$ for the chi-square goodness-of-fit test. K is the number of categories.

$df = (R - 1)(C - 1)$ for the chi-square test of independence. R is the number of rows; C is the number of columns.

Degrees of Freedom (df)	5%	1%
1	3.84	6.64
2	5.99	9.21
3	7.82	11.34
4	9.49	13.28
5	11.07	15.09
6	12.59	16.81
7	14.07	18.48
8	15.51	20.09
9	16.92	21.67
10	18.31	23.21
11	19.68	24.72
12	21.03	26.22
13	22.36	27.69
14	23.68	29.14
15	25.00	30.58
16	26.30	32.00
17	27.59	33.41
18	28.87	34.80
19	30.14	36.19
20	31.41	37.57
21	32.67	38.93
22	33.92	40.29
23	35.17	41.64
24	36.42	42.98
25	37.65	44.31
26	38.88	45.64
27	40.11	46.96
28	41.34	48.28
29	42.56	49.59
30	43.77	50.89

Source: This table is from Table IV of Fisher and Yates, *Statistical Tables for Biological, Agricultural and Medical Research,* published by Longman Group Ltd., London (previously published by Oliver and Boyd, Edinburgh). Reprinted by permission of Pearson Education Limited.

Table H. Critical Values for the Mann–Whitney U

For a two-tailed test at the 10% level (roman type, $\alpha = .10$) and at the 5% level (boldface type, $\alpha = .05$). For a one-tailed test, halve the probabilities.

Dashes in the body of the table mean that no decision is possible at the given α.

$N_2 \backslash N_1$	1	2	3	4	5	6	7	8	9	10	11	12	13	14	15	16	17	18	19	20
1	—	—	—	—	—	—	—	—	—	—	—	—	—	—	—	—	—	—	0	0
																			—	—
2	—	—	—	—	0	0	0	1	1	1	1	2	2	2	3	3	3	4	4	4
					—	—	—	**0**	**0**	**0**	**0**	**1**	**1**	**1**	**1**	**1**	**2**	**2**	**2**	**2**
3	—	—	0	0	1	2	2	3	3	4	5	5	6	7	7	8	9	9	10	11
	—	—	—	—	**0**	**1**	**1**	**2**	**2**	**3**	**3**	**4**	**4**	**5**	**5**	**6**	**6**	**7**	**7**	**8**
4	—	—	0	1	2	3	4	5	6	7	8	9	10	11	12	14	15	16	17	18
	—	—	—	**0**	**1**	**2**	**3**	**4**	**4**	**5**	**6**	**7**	**8**	**9**	**10**	**11**	**11**	**12**	**13**	**13**
5	—	0	1	2	4	5	6	8	9	11	12	13	15	16	18	19	20	22	23	25
	—	—	**0**	**1**	**2**	**3**	**5**	**6**	**7**	**8**	**9**	**11**	**12**	**13**	**14**	**15**	**17**	**18**	**19**	**20**
6	—	0	2	3	5	7	8	10	12	14	16	17	19	21	23	25	26	28	30	32
	—	—	**1**	**2**	**3**	**5**	**6**	**8**	**10**	**11**	**13**	**14**	**16**	**17**	**19**	**21**	**22**	**24**	**25**	**27**
7	—	0	2	4	6	8	11	13	15	17	19	21	24	26	28	30	33	35	37	39
	—	—	**1**	**3**	**5**	**6**	**8**	**10**	**12**	**14**	**16**	**18**	**20**	**22**	**24**	**26**	**28**	**30**	**32**	**34**
8	—	1	3	5	8	10	13	15	18	20	23	26	28	31	33	36	39	41	44	47
	—	**0**	**2**	**4**	**6**	**8**	**10**	**13**	**15**	**17**	**19**	**22**	**24**	**26**	**29**	**31**	**34**	**36**	**38**	**41**
9	—	1	3	6	9	12	15	18	21	24	27	30	33	36	39	42	45	48	51	54
	—	**0**	**2**	**4**	**7**	**10**	**12**	**15**	**17**	**20**	**23**	**26**	**28**	**31**	**34**	**37**	**39**	**42**	**45**	**48**
10	—	1	4	7	11	14	17	20	24	27	31	34	37	41	44	48	51	55	58	62
	—	**0**	**3**	**5**	**8**	**11**	**14**	**17**	**20**	**23**	**26**	**29**	**33**	**36**	**39**	**42**	**45**	**48**	**52**	**55**
11	—	1	5	8	12	16	19	23	27	31	34	38	42	46	50	54	57	61	65	69
	—	**0**	**3**	**6**	**9**	**13**	**16**	**19**	**23**	**26**	**30**	**33**	**37**	**40**	**44**	**47**	**51**	**55**	**58**	**62**
12	—	2	5	9	13	17	21	26	30	34	38	42	47	51	55	60	64	68	72	77
	—	**1**	**4**	**7**	**11**	**14**	**18**	**22**	**26**	**29**	**33**	**37**	**41**	**45**	**49**	**53**	**57**	**61**	**65**	**69**
13	—	2	6	10	15	19	24	28	33	37	42	47	51	56	61	65	70	75	80	84
	—	**1**	**4**	**8**	**12**	**16**	**20**	**24**	**28**	**33**	**37**	**41**	**45**	**50**	**54**	**59**	**63**	**67**	**72**	**76**
14	—	2	7	11	16	21	26	31	36	41	46	51	56	61	66	71	77	82	87	92
	—	**1**	**5**	**9**	**13**	**17**	**22**	**26**	**31**	**36**	**40**	**45**	**50**	**55**	**59**	**64**	**67**	**74**	**78**	**83**
15	—	3	7	12	18	23	28	33	39	44	50	55	61	66	72	77	83	88	94	100
	—	**1**	**5**	**10**	**14**	**19**	**24**	**29**	**34**	**39**	**44**	**49**	**54**	**59**	**64**	**70**	**75**	**80**	**85**	**90**
16	—	3	8	14	19	25	30	36	42	48	54	60	65	71	77	83	89	95	101	107
	—	**1**	**6**	**11**	**15**	**21**	**26**	**31**	**37**	**42**	**47**	**53**	**59**	**64**	**70**	**75**	**81**	**86**	**92**	**98**
17	—	3	9	15	20	26	33	39	45	51	57	64	70	77	83	89	96	102	109	115
	—	**2**	**6**	**11**	**17**	**22**	**28**	**34**	**39**	**45**	**51**	**57**	**63**	**67**	**75**	**81**	**87**	**93**	**99**	**105**
18	—	4	9	16	22	28	35	41	48	55	61	68	75	82	88	95	102	109	116	123
	—	**2**	**7**	**12**	**18**	**24**	**30**	**36**	**42**	**48**	**55**	**61**	**67**	**74**	**80**	**86**	**93**	**99**	**106**	**112**
19	0	4	10	17	23	30	37	44	51	58	65	72	80	87	94	101	109	116	123	130
	2	**7**	**13**	**19**	**25**	**32**	**38**	**45**	**52**	**58**	**65**	**72**	**78**	**85**	**92**	**99**	**106**	**113**	**119**
20	0	4	11	18	25	32	39	47	54	62	69	77	84	92	100	107	115	123	130	138
	2	**8**	**13**	**20**	**27**	**34**	**41**	**48**	**55**	**62**	**69**	**76**	**83**	**90**	**98**	**105**	**112**	**119**	**127**

Source: This table is from *Elementary Statistics* (2nd Edition) by Roger E. Kirk, Copyright © 1984, 1978 by Roger E. Kirk. Adapted by permission of the author.

Table H. continued

For a two-tailed test at the 2% level (roman type, $\alpha = .02$) and at the 1% level (boldface type, $\alpha = .01$). For a one-tailed test, halve the probabilities.

Dashes in the body of the table mean that no decision is possible at the given α.

N_2 \ N_1	1	2	3	4	5	6	7	8	9	10	11	12	13	14	15	16	17	18	19	20
1	—	—	—	—	—	—	—	—	—	—	—	—	—	—	—	—	—	—	—	—
2	—	—	—	—	—	—	—	—	—	—	—	—	0	0	0	0	0	0	1	1
													—	—	—	—	—	—	**0**	**0**
3	—	—	—	—	—	—	—	0	0	1	1	1	2	2	2	3	3	4	4	4	5
							—	—	**0**	**0**	**0**	**1**	**1**	**1**	**2**	**2**	**2**	**2**	**3**	**3**
4	—	—	—	—	0	1	1	2	3	3	4	5	5	6	7	7	8	9	9	10
				—	**0**	**0**	**1**	**1**	**2**	**2**	**3**	**3**	**4**	**5**	**5**	**6**	**6**	**7**	**8**
5	—	—	—	0	1	2	3	4	5	6	7	8	9	10	11	12	13	14	15	16
			—	**0**	**1**	**1**	**2**	**3**	**4**	**5**	**6**	**7**	**7**	**8**	**9**	**10**	**11**	**12**	**13**
6	—	—	—	1	2	3	4	6	7	8	9	11	12	13	15	16	18	19	20	22
			0	**1**	**2**	**3**	**4**	**5**	**6**	**7**	**9**	**10**	**11**	**12**	**13**	**15**	**16**	**17**	**18**
7	—	—	0	1	3	4	6	7	9	11	12	14	16	17	19	21	23	24	26	28
		—	**0**	**1**	**3**	**4**	**6**	**7**	**9**	**10**	**12**	**13**	**15**	**16**	**18**	**19**	**21**	**22**	**24**
8	—	—	0	2	4	6	7	9	11	13	15	17	20	22	24	26	28	30	32	34
		—	**1**	**2**	**4**	**6**	**7**	**9**	**11**	**13**	**15**	**17**	**18**	**20**	**22**	**24**	**26**	**28**	**30**
9	—	—	1	3	5	7	9	11	14	16	18	21	23	26	28	31	33	36	38	40
		0	**1**	**3**	**5**	**7**	**9**	**11**	**13**	**16**	**18**	**20**	**22**	**24**	**27**	**29**	**31**	**33**	**36**
10	—	—	1	3	6	8	11	13	16	19	22	24	27	30	33	36	38	41	44	47
		0	**2**	**4**	**6**	**9**	**11**	**13**	**16**	**18**	**21**	**24**	**26**	**29**	**31**	**34**	**37**	**39**	**42**
11	—	—	1	4	7	9	12	15	18	22	25	28	31	34	37	41	44	47	50	53
		0	**2**	**5**	**7**	**10**	**13**	**16**	**18**	**21**	**24**	**27**	**30**	**33**	**36**	**39**	**42**	**45**	**48**
12	—	—	2	5	8	11	14	17	21	24	28	31	35	38	42	46	49	53	56	60
		1	**3**	**6**	**9**	**12**	**15**	**18**	**21**	**24**	**27**	**31**	**34**	**37**	**41**	**44**	**47**	**51**	**54**
13	—	0	2	5	9	12	16	20	23	27	31	35	39	43	47	51	55	59	63	67
	—	**1**	**3**	**7**	**10**	**13**	**17**	**20**	**24**	**27**	**31**	**34**	**38**	**42**	**45**	**49**	**53**	**56**	**60**
14	—	0	2	6	10	13	17	22	26	30	34	38	43	47	51	56	60	65	69	73
	—	**1**	**4**	**7**	**11**	**15**	**18**	**22**	**26**	**30**	**34**	**38**	**42**	**46**	**50**	**54**	**58**	**63**	**67**
15	—	0	3	7	11	15	19	24	28	33	37	42	47	51	56	61	66	70	75	80
	—	**2**	**5**	**8**	**12**	**16**	**20**	**24**	**29**	**33**	**37**	**42**	**46**	**51**	**55**	**60**	**64**	**69**	**73**
16	—	0	3	7	12	16	21	26	31	36	41	46	51	56	61	66	71	76	82	87
	—	**2**	**5**	**9**	**13**	**18**	**22**	**27**	**31**	**36**	**41**	**45**	**50**	**55**	**60**	**65**	**70**	**74**	**79**
17	—	0	4	8	13	18	23	28	33	38	44	49	55	60	66	71	77	82	88	93
	—	**2**	**6**	**10**	**15**	**19**	**24**	**29**	**34**	**39**	**44**	**49**	**54**	**60**	**65**	**70**	**75**	**81**	**86**
18	—	0	4	9	14	19	24	30	36	41	47	53	59	65	70	76	82	88	94	100
	—	**2**	**6**	**11**	**16**	**21**	**26**	**31**	**37**	**42**	**47**	**53**	**58**	**64**	**70**	**75**	**81**	**87**	**92**
19	—	1	4	9	15	20	26	32	38	44	50	56	63	69	75	82	88	94	101	107
	0	**3**	**7**	**12**	**17**	**22**	**28**	**33**	**39**	**45**	**51**	**56**	**63**	**69**	**74**	**81**	**87**	**93**	**99**
20	—	1	5	10	16	22	28	34	40	47	53	60	67	73	80	87	93	100	107	114
	0	**3**	**8**	**13**	**18**	**24**	**30**	**36**	**42**	**48**	**54**	**60**	**67**	**73**	**79**	**86**	**92**	**99**	**105**

Table I. Critical Values of T

N	Level of Significance for Two-Tailed Test (For One-Tailed Test, Halve the Probabilities)			N			
	.05	.02	.01		.05	.02	.01
6	0	—	—	16	30	24	20
7	2	0	—	17	35	28	23
8	4	2	0	18	40	33	28
9	6	3	2	19	46	38	32
10	8	5	3	20	52	43	38
11	11	7	5	21	59	49	43
12	14	10	7	22	66	56	49
13	17	13	10	23	73	62	55
14	21	16	13	24	81	69	61
15	25	20	16	25	89	77	68

Source: This table is from Table 1 of F. Wilcoxon, 1949, *Some Rapid Approximate Statistical Procedures,* American Cyanamid Company, p. 13.

APPENDIX 3

ANSWERS TO EXERCISES AND PROBLEMS

Note: We have provided answers to SPSS problems using the format and terminology employed by SPSS. We have noted differences in format and presentation in comparison to the conventions in your textbook.

On the fill-in-the-blank items, it is possible that more than one answer may be correct. We have listed the answer we intended, but if your answer is synonymous with ours, then it is also correct. *Slight* differences in answers to the problems are probably the result of rounding differences and should be ignored.

CHAPTER 1

Fill-in-the-blanks

(1) statistics
(2) statistics
(3) statistics
(4) consumer
(5) behavior
(6) variable
(7) vocabulary
(8) consumer
(9) literature
(10) tools
(11) language
(12) practice
(13) vocabulary
(14) anxiety
(15) uncertainty
(16) practice
(17) pencils
(18) calculator
(19) class attendance

Problems

2. a. 344

   b. 46.4

   c. 2.31

   d. 14

   e. 142

   f. 120.14

CHAPTER 2

Fill-in-the-blanks

(1) variable

(2) independent

(3) dependent

(4) independent

(5) dependent

(6) population

(7) sample

(8) parameter

(9) statistic

(10) biased

(11) random

(12) replacement

(13) stratified

(14) scales

(15) measurement

(16) frequency

(17) nominal

(18) ordinal

(19) interval

(20) ratio

(21) ratio

(22) interval

(23) Descriptive

(24) inferential

(25) descriptive

Problems

1. a. independent, kind of drug; dependent, score on IQ test

   b. independent, presence (or absence) of others; dependent, performance

   c. independent, odd versus even answer; dependent, seconds to solution

   d. independent, illumination level; dependent, time to identify the stimulus

2. a. ratio

   b. nominal

   c. ordinal

   d. nominal

   e. ratio

   f. ordinal

   g. ordinal

   h. interval

3. a. parameter, characteristic of the population of all left-handed boys at Fairlawn High School

   b. statistic, 15 randomly selected students constitutes a sample

   c. parameter, characteristic of the population of all inmates

   d. statistic, characteristic of the sample consisting of every 100th name

4. a. descriptive

   b. inferential

   c. inferential

   d. descriptive

   e. inferential

   f. descriptive

CHAPTER 3

Fill-in-the-blanks

(1) highest
(2) lowest
(3) scores
(4) *X*
(5) frequency distribution
(6) frequency
(7) *f*

(8) omitted
(9) continuous
(10) discrete
(11) apparent
(12) half
(13) half
(14) real

(15) percentage
(16) *N*
(17) sum
(18) size
(19) accumulate
(20) lower or previous
(21) Cum *f*

Problems

1.

X	f	Cum f	Cum %age
15	5	15	100.00
14	1	10	66.67
13	4	9	60.00
12	2	5	33.33
10	1	3	20.00
8	1	2	13.33
6	1	1	6.67
	N = 15		

2.

X	f
4	1
3	1
2	4
1	6
0	3
	N = 15

The sample sizes are equivalent.

3. a.

X	f	X	f
37	1	22	1
33	1	21	4
31	1	20	3
30	1	19	3
29	1	18	3
28	1	17	5
27	1	16	4
26	2	15	5
25	6	14	1
24	2	12	1
23	3		N = 50

b.

X	Real Limits	f	%age f
37	36.5–37.5	1	2
33	32.5–33.5	1	2
31	30.5–31.5	1	2
30	29.5–30.5	1	2
29	28.5–29.5	1	2
28	27.5–28.5	1	2
27	26.5–27.5	1	2
26	25.5–26.5	2	4
25	24.5–25.5	6	12
24	23.5–24.5	2	4
23	22.5–23.5	3	6
22	21.5–22.5	1	2
21	20.5–21.5	4	8
20	19.5–20.5	3	6
19	18.5–19.5	3	6
18	17.5–18.5	3	6
17	16.5–17.5	5	10
16	15.5–16.5	4	8
15	14.5–15.5	5	10
14	13.5–14.5	1	2
12	11.5–12.5	1	2
		$N = 50$	

4.

	Apparent Limit	Real Limits
a.	25	24.5–25.5
b.	11.7	11.65–11.75
c.	12.55	12.545–12.555
d.	7.853	7.8525–7.8535

5.

X	f	Cum f	%age f
45	1	20	5
42	1	19	5
39	1	18	5
37	1	17	5
36	1	16	5
35	2	15	10
34	2	13	10
33	1	11	5
32	3	10	15
31	1	7	5
30	2	6	10
28	1	4	5
26	2	3	10
25	1	1	5
$N = 20$			

6.

Distribution A			Distribution B		
X	f	%age f	X	f	%age f
79	1	1.18	79	1	3.13
77	1	1.18	78	2	6.25
76	1	1.18	77	2	6.25
74	2	2.35	76	2	6.25
65	2	2.35	75	3	9.38
64	3	3.53	74	2	6.25
62	2	2.35	73	2	6.25
60	2	2.35	71	1	3.13
57	5	5.88	70	2	6.25
56	4	4.71	69	3	9.38
54	6	7.06	68	4	12.50
53	7	8.24	65	1	3.13
52	6	7.06	60	1	3.13
51	7	8.24	58	2	6.25
50	10	11.76	55	1	3.13
49	7	8.24	50	1	3.13
48	6	7.06	44	1	3.13
47	4	4.71	39	1	3.13
45	2	2.35		$N = 32$	
44	1	1.18			
42	3	3.53			
40	2	2.35			
39	1	1.18			
	$N = 85$				

7.

X	Real Limits	f	Cum f	Cum %age
49	48.5–49.5	1	169	100.00
48	47.5–48.5	6	168	99.41
47	46.5–47.5	6	162	95.86
46	45.5–46.5	11	156	92.31
45	44.5–45.5	13	145	85.80
44	43.5–44.5	16	132	78.11
43	42.5–43.5	8	116	68.64
42	41.5–42.5	15	108	63.91
41	40.5–41.5	16	93	55.03
40	39.5–40.5	13	77	45.56
39	38.5–39.5	9	64	37.87
38	37.5–38.5	5	55	32.54
37	36.5–37.5	3	50	29.59
36	35.5–36.5	7	47	27.81
35	34.5–35.5	8	40	23.67
34	33.5–34.5	3	32	18.93

X	Real Limits	f	Cum f	Cum %age
33	32.5–33.5	1	29	17.16
32	31.5–32.5	7	28	16.57
31	30.5–31.5	3	21	12.43
30	29.5–30.5	4	18	10.65
29	28.5–29.5	3	14	8.28
28	27.5–28.5	4	11	6.51
27	26.5–27.5	1	7	4.14
26	25.5–26.5	3	6	3.55
25	24.5–25.5	2	3	1.78
23	22.5–23.5	1	1	0.59
		$N = 169$		

EXERCISE USING SPSS

Follow these steps:

1. Enter data and name variable **test.**
2. Statistics>Summarize>Frequencies
3. Highlight and move **test** into the Variable(s) box.
4. Format>Descending values>Continue
5. OK

```
FREQUENCIES
  VARIABLES=test
 /FORMAT=DVALUE
 /ORDER  ANALYSIS .
```

Frequencies

Statistics

TEST

N	Valid	40
	Missing	0

TEST

		Frequency	Percent	Valid Percent	Cumulative Percent
Valid	35.00	8	20.0	20.0	20.0
	34.00	3	7.5	7.5	27.5
	33.00	1	2.5	2.5	30.0
	32.00	7	17.5	17.5	47.5
	31.00	3	7.5	7.5	55.0
	30.00	4	10.0	10.0	65.0
	29.00	3	7.5	7.5	72.5
	28.00	4	10.0	10.0	82.5
	27.00	1	2.5	2.5	85.0
	26.00	3	7.5	7.5	92.5
	25.00	2	5.0	5.0	97.5
	23.00	1	2.5	2.5	100.0
	Total	40	100.0	100.0	

SELF-TEST

1. c, j, h, a, i, b, e

2.

X	Real Limits	f	Cum f	Cum %age
93	92.5–93.5	1	42	100.00
81	80.5–81.5	1	41	97.62
75	74.5–75.5	1	40	95.24
71	70.5–71.5	1	39	92.86
65	64.5–65.5	2	38	90.48
61	60.5–61.5	1	36	85.71
52	51.5–52.5	1	35	83.33
37	36.5–37.5	1	34	80.95
32	31.5–32.5	1	33	78.57
22	21.5–22.5	1	32	76.19
21	20.5–21.5	1	31	73.81
17	16.5–17.5	1	30	71.43
15	14.5–15.5	2	29	69.05
13	12.5–13.5	1	27	64.29
12	11.5–12.5	3	26	61.90
10	9.5–10.5	5	23	54.76
9	8.5–9.5	2	18	42.86
8	7.5–8.5	4	16	38.10
7	6.5–7.5	1	12	28.57
6	5.5–6.5	2	11	26.19
5	4.5–5.5	3	9	21.43
3	2.5–3.5	3	6	14.29
2	1.5–2.5	1	3	7.14
0	−0.5–0.5	2	2	4.76
		$N = \overline{42}$		

$$\text{Cum \%age} = \frac{\text{Cum } f}{N}(100)$$

$$\text{Cum \%age of Cum } f \text{ of } 2 = \frac{2}{42}(100) = \frac{200}{42} = 4.76$$

CHAPTER 4

Fill-in-the-blanks

(1) 1,000

(2) graphs

(3) cumulative

(4) histogram

(5) line

(6) *Y*

(7) three-fourths

(8) three-quarters

(9) 0

(10) deviations

(11) scores

(12) frequencies

(13) Score

(14) Frequency

(15) caption

(16) percentages

(17) relative

(18) normal

(19) skewed	(27) frequency	(35) 13
(20) positively skewed	(28) halfway	(36) 3
(21) negatively skewed	(29) nominal	(37) vertical
(22) scores	(30) arbitrary	(38) leaves
(23) vertical	(31) stem	(39) scores
(24) horizontal	(32) leaf	(40) histogram
(25) horizontal	(33) stem	(41) independent
(26) bar	(34) leaf	(42) continuous

Problems

1. a.

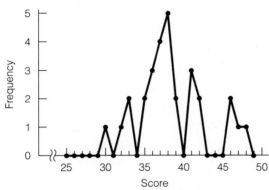

Frequency polygon showing test scores from introductory class.

b.

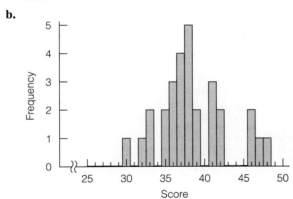

Frequency histogram of introductory class test scores.

c.

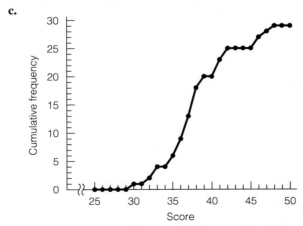

Cumulative frequency polygon of introductory class scores.

d.

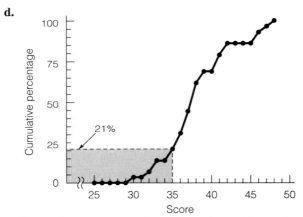

Cumulative percentage polygon of introductory class test scores. Approximately 21% of students made scores of 35 or less.

2.

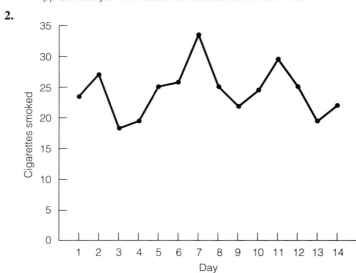

Line graph showing number of cigarettes smoked per day over a 2-week period.

3.

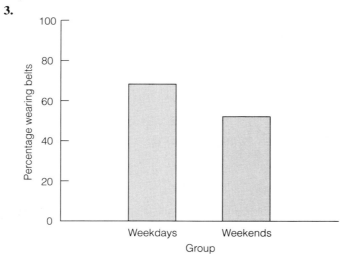

Bar graph showing percentage of people wearing seatbelts stopped for traffic violations on weekdays and weekends.

4.

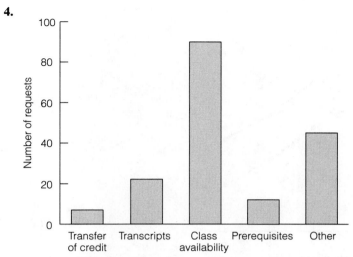

Bar graph showing number of requests for information at the registration office.

5.

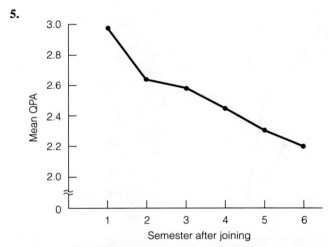

Line graph showing mean QPA by semester after joining a campus organization.

6.

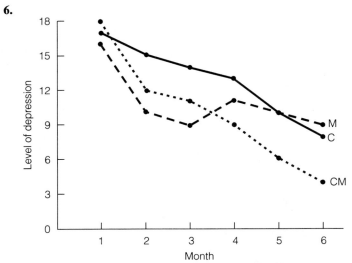

Line graphs showing depression by month of treatment. C = counseling group; M = medication group; CM = counseling and medication group.

7. a.

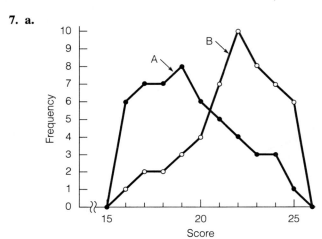

Frequency polygons showing the shapes of Distributions A (positively skewed) and B (negatively skewed).

b.

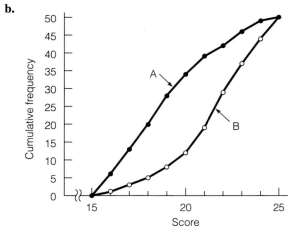

Cumulative frequency polygons for Distributions A and B.

8.

Stems	Leaves
15	9
16	6 8 9 7
17	7 5 7 2
18	3 8 5 5 5 8 8 8 9
19	9 7 9 7 2 5 2 9 3 5 8
20	3 7 1 5 4
21	0

```
                              8
                              5
                      9       3
                      8       9
                      8       2
Leaves                8       5
                      5   2   4
              7   2   5   7   5
              9   7   5   9   1
              8   5   8   3   7
          9   6   7   3   9   3   0
        ─────────────────────────────
Stems    15  16  17  18  19  20  21
```

EXERCISES USING SPSS

1.

```
RENAME VARIABLES (fcig=freqcig).
GRAPH
   /LINE(SIMPLE)=VALUE( freqcig ) BY day .
```

Graph

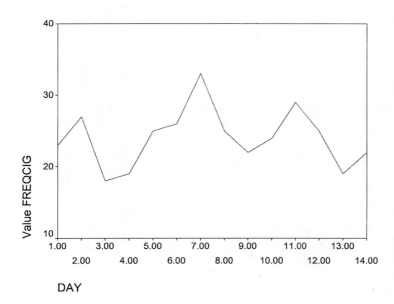

2.
```
EXAMINE
    VARIABLES=speeds
    /PLOT STEMLEAF
    /COMPARE GROUP
    /STATISTICS NONE
    /CINTERVAL 95
    /MISSING LISTWISE
    /NOTOTAL.
```

Explore

Case Processing Summary

	Cases					
	Valid		Missing		Total	
	N	Percent	N	Percent	N	Percent
SPEEDS	35	100.0%	0	.0%	35	100.0%

SPEEDS

```
SPEEDS Stem-and-Leaf Plot

Frequency     Stem &   Leaf

     1.00      15 .   9
     4.00      16 .   6789
     4.00      17 .   2577
     9.00      18 .   355588889
    11.00      19 .   22335578999
     5.00      20 .   13457
     1.00      21 .   0

Stem width:     10.00
Each leaf:       1 case(s)
```

Note that SPSS arranges the leaves in ascending order rather than placing them as they appear in the data set.

SELF-TEST

1. b

2. True

3. c

4.

Stems	Leaves
2	9
3	
4	
5	5 4
6	6 5 9
7	6 4 6
8	6 0 6 8 9 9 8 0 4
9	3 1 0 2 2 5

5.

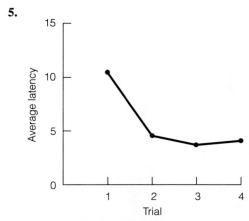

Line graph showing average latency over trials for rats to leave a platform.

6.

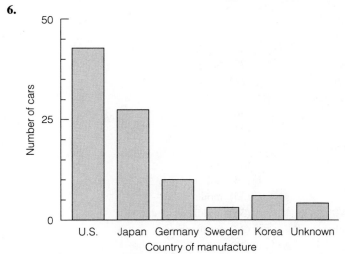

Bar graph showing number of cars made in a particular country passing through an intersection.

7. a.

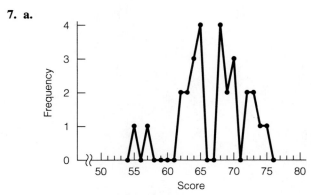

Frequency polygon of typing test scores.

b.

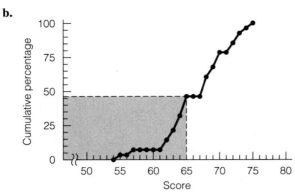

Cumulative percentage polygon of typing test scores. Approximately 46% of students typed 65 or fewerwords per minute.

CHAPTER 5

Fill-in-the-blanks

(1) middle
(2) mean
(3) median
(4) mode
(5) mode
(6) *Mo*
(7) least
(8) bimodal
(9) 50th
(10) percentile
(11) $(N/2)$th
(12) $(N/2)$th $+ 1$
(13) $(N + 1)/2$th

(14) scores
(15) number
(16) frequencies
(17) $\overline{X}$
(18) μ
(19) hundredths
(20) final
(21) three
(22) drop
(23) up
(24) balancing
(25) 0
(26) mode

(27) median
(28) missing
(29) statistical
(30) stable
(31) unbiased
(32) same
(33) mean
(34) tail
(35) mode
(36) middle or center
(37) frequencies
(38) twice

Problems

1. a. $\overline{X} = 10$
 b. $\overline{X} = 8$
 c. $\overline{X} = 3$
 d. $\overline{X} = 16$

2.

X	f	$X - \overline{X}$	$f(X - \overline{X})$
10	1	4	4
9	2	3	6
8	1	2	2
7	4	1	4
6	6	0	0
5	5	-1	-5
4	2	-2	-4
3	1	-3	-3
2	2	-4	-4
	$N = 23$		$\Sigma f(X - \overline{X}) = 0$

$Mo = 6$

$\overline{X} = 6$

Md(counting method) $= 6$

3. $Mo = 6, Md = 6, \overline{X} = 5.8$

4. $Mo = 2, Md = 3, \overline{X} = 2.8$

5. $Mo = 15, Md = 14, \overline{X} = 12.6$

6. $Mo = 27, Md = 27.5, \overline{X} = 27.85$

7. with nonresponders: $Md = 35$

omitting nonresponders: $Mo = 33, Md = 33, \overline{X} = 33.15$

8. a. 1.45. If the number in the thousandths place is less than 5, drop it and all the following numbers.

b. 1.56. If the number in the thousandths place is 5 or more, round the preceding digit up.

c. 3.67; same as b

d. 23.33; same as a

e. 7.83; same as b

EXERCISE USING SPSS

1.
```
FREQUENCIES
   VARIABLES=neurot
   /STATISTICS=MEAN MEDIAN MODE
   /ORDER  ANALYSIS .
```

Frequencies

Statistics

NEUROT

N	Valid	50
	Missing	0
Mean		5.8000
Median		6.0000
Mode		6.00

NEUROT

		Frequency	Percent	Valid Percent	Cumulative Percent
Valid	1.00	2	4.0	4.0	4.0
	2.00	4	8.0	8.0	12.0
	3.00	4	8.0	8.0	20.0
	4.00	5	10.0	10.0	30.0
	5.00	7	14.0	14.0	44.0
	6.00	8	16.0	16.0	60.0
	7.00	7	14.0	14.0	74.0
	8.00	5	10.0	10.0	84.0
	9.00	4	8.0	8.0	92.0
	10.00	4	8.0	8.0	100.0
	Total	50	100.0	100.0	

SELF-TEST

1. a, a, c, a, b, b, c, c
2. $Mo = -1, Md = -0.5, \overline{X} = -1.28$
3. $Mo = 122, Md = 127, \overline{X} = 125.46$

CHAPTER 6

Fill-in-the-blanks

(1) spread or dispersion
(2) variance
(3) standard deviation
(4) range
(5) *AD*
(6) variance
(7) absolute value
(8) variance
(9) standard deviation
(10) biased
(11) underestimate

(12) $N - 1$
(13) square root
(14) computational
(15) computations
(16) baseline
(17) range
(18) 4
(19) sum of squares
(20) mean
(21) *SS*

(22) standard
(23) *z*
(24) *z* score
(25) sign
(26) negative
(27) mean
(28) feel
(29) one-sixth
(30) positive
(31) square root

Problems

1. $AD = 1.45$, so Karl is correct; $R = 7$; $s_{approx} = 1.75$; $s^2 = 3.61$; $s = 1.90$
2. a. $R = 8$, $s_{approx} = 2$, $s^2 = 3.64$, $s = 1.91$

b.

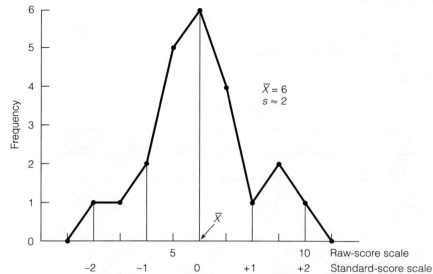

Frequency polygon of correctly solved analogy problems showing both the raw-score scale and the standard-score scale.

3. $R = 65$, $s_{approx} = 16.25$, $s^2 = 264.75$, $s = 16.27$, $z_{96} = 0.91$. The score 2 standard deviation units below $\overline{X}$ is 48.6.

4. $R = 4$, $s_{approx} = 1$, $s^2 = 1.62$, $s = 1.27$

5. $s_A = 0.16$, $s_B = 0.11$. Applicant B gets the job.

6. $\overline{X} = 74.33$, $s = 13.64$. All employees scoring less than $74.33 - 13.64 = 60.69$ are required to take another week of training. Five employees scored less than 60.69.

7. $\overline{X} = 24.35$, $s^2 = 3.71$, $s = 1.93$

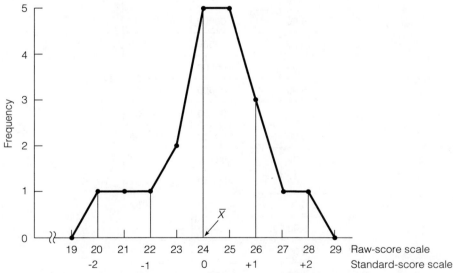

Frequency polygon showing both the raw-score scale and the standard-score scale.

8. a. $z_{3.75} = 1.42$
   b. $z_{2.10} = -0.57$
   c. A score of 1.3 is 1.53 standard deviation units below the mean.
   d. $X = 4.02$
   e. $X = 0.77$

EXERCISES USING SPSS

1. ```
DESCRIPTIVES
  VARIABLES=correct /SAVE
  /STATISTICS=MEAN STDDEV VARIANCE RANGE MIN MAX .
```

## Descriptives

**Descriptive Statistics**

|  | N | Range | Minimum | Maximum | Mean | Std. Deviation | Variance |
|---|---|---|---|---|---|---|---|
| CORRECT | 23 | 8.00 | 2.00 | 10.00 | 6.0000 | 1.9069 | 3.636 |
| Valid N (listwise) | 23 | | | | | | |

**2.** ```
COMPUTE correctz = (correct-6.0)/1.9069 .
EXECUTE .
```

	correct	zcorrect	correctz
1	10.00	2.09762	2.10
2	9.00	1.57321	1.57
3	9.00	1.57321	1.57
4	8.00	1.04881	1.05
5	7.00	.52440	.52
6	7.00	.52440	.52
7	7.00	.52440	.52
8	7.00	.52440	.52
9	6.00	.00000	.00
10	6.00	.00000	.00
11	6.00	.00000	.00
12	6.00	.00000	.00
13	6.00	.00000	.00
14	6.00	.00000	.00
15	5.00	-.52440	-.52
16	5.00	-.52440	-.52
17	5.00	-.52440	-.52
18	5.00	-.52440	-.52
19	5.00	-.52440	-.52
20	4.00	-1.04881	-1.05

SELF-TEST

1. c, g, f, d, b, e, h
2. The size of z tells how far the score is from the mean in standard deviation units.
3. The sign of a z score indicates whether the score is above ($+$) or below ($-$) the mean.
4. **a.** $s^2 = 3.27$, $s = 1.81$

   b. $z_6 = 0.92$, $z_3 = 0.73$

   c. 7.05, 0.71

CHAPTER 7

Fill-in-the-blanks

(1) Statistical hypotheses
(2) probability
(3) statistics
(4) population
(5) gambler's fallacy
(6) probability
(7) any
(8) patterns or tendencies
(9) guarantees
(10) Theoretical
(11) empirical
(12) relative frequency
(13) personal
(14) subjective
(15) Bayesian
(16) inference
(17) Bayesian
(18) wrong or distorted
(19) conclusions
(20) sum
(21) addition
(22) $p(A) + p(B)$
(23) multiplication
(24) $p(A, B) = p(A) \times p(B)$
(25) independent
(26) Conditional probability
(27) $p(B \mid A)$
(28) $p(A) \times p(B \mid A)$
(29) Conditional
(30) A
(31) B
(32) probability
(33) controversial
(34) two
(35) symmetrical
(36) normal probability distribution

Problems

1. There's no change in the probability of getting another head on the 10th flip: $p = .5$.
2. **a.** $p = .019$

   b. $p = .077$

   c. $p = .308$

   d. $p = .25$

   e. $p = .75$

3. **a.** $p = .20$

   b. $p = .40$

   c. $p = .00$

   d. $p = .87$

   e. $p = .40$

   f. $p = .33$

4. **a.** $p = .50$

   b. $p = .50$

5. **a.** $p = .25$

   b. $p = .75$

   c. True−false is easier.

6. **a.** $p = .001$

   b. $p = .003$

c. $p = .006$

d. $p = .01$

7. **a.** $p = .028$

  b. $p = .25$

  c. $p = .11$

  d. $p = .083$

  e. $p = .17$

  f. $p = .33$

8. **a.** $p = .00$

  b. $p = .13$

  c. $p = .20$

  d. $p = .40$

9. **a.** $p = .00667$

  b. $p = .0134$

  c. $p = .0267$

  d. $p = .0535$

  e. $p = .000268$

10. $p(3 \text{ heads in 5 flips}) = .346$

  $p(4 \text{ heads in 5 flips}) = .259$

11. **a.** $p = .38$

  b. $p = .538$

  c. Yes, added information about personality type increases the probability of holding office.

  d. Extraversion and holding office are related, not independent. Knowing personality type changes the probability of holding office.

SELF-TEST

1. a
2. d
3. **a.** $1/3 = .33$

  b. $1/3 \times 1/3 \times 1/3 = .04$

4. **a.** $(1/6)^3 = .0046$

  b. $2/6 \times 2/6 \times 3/6 = .056$

  c. $(.056)(3) \doteq .168$

5. **a.** $1/6 \times 2/5 \times 3/4 = .05$

  b. $2/6 \times 1/5 \times 3/4 = .05$

  c. $3/6 \times 2/5 \times 1/4 = .05$

6. **a.** $p(\text{held office}) = .38$

  b. $p(\text{held office} \mid \text{intuition}) = .38$

  c. No, the added information about personality does not change the probability of holding office.

  d. Intuition-sensing personality type and holding office *are* independent. Knowing the personality type does not change the probability of holding office. $p(A \mid B) = p(A)$ indicates that events A and B are independent.

CHAPTER 8

Fill-in-the-blanks

(1) Rosetta
(2) Gauss
(3) De Moivre
(4) empirical
(5) Empirical
(6) limiting
(7) means
(8) probability
(9) probability
(10) z scores
(11) A
(12) area
(13) symmetrical
(14) central
(15) tails
(16) standard
(17) 6
(18) z score
(19) below
(20) above
(21) B
(22) C
(23) Percentile rank
(24) draw
(25) z score
(26) raw score
(27) A
(28) A
(29) how many
(30) z scores
(31) added
(32) 100
(33) 1
(34) z score
(35) both
(36) half
(37) percentage area
(38) 100
(39) normal curve
(40) reasonable
(41) form

Problems

1. **a.** $z_{89.6} = 1.21$
  b. $z_{61.5} = -0.72$
  c. 48.8
  d. 95.2
  e. 50.25 or less, 93.75 or more

2. **a.** 21.57%
  b. 21.57%
  c. $z = 1.75$; yes
  d. $z = 1.28$
  e. 7.53%
  f. 2.50%
  g. 99.02%
  h. 10.03%

3. **a.** 92.22
  b. 6.68
  c. 12
  d. 73.69
  e. 40.70
  f. 8
  g. 35.77 or less, 71.23 or more
  h. 21.74 or less, 85.26 or more

4. **a.** 9
  b. .1949
  c. 62
  d. 15.28% (*Note:* 47.6 is as deviant from 78.8 as is 110.)
  e. 36.09 or less, 121.51 or more

5. **a.** 79.02 mph
  b. 637.87 or 638 automobiles

c. 5.82%

d. 83.89%

e. 435.4 or 435 automobiles

f. 51.99 mph or less, 82.61 mph or more

SELF-TEST

1. The standard normal curve has a mean of 0 and a standard deviation of 1.

2. False; areas are always positive, whereas z scores below the mean are negative.

3. a. 9.98 or 10 applicants

   b. 85.02 or 85 applicants

   c. 31.21%

   d. .0721

   e. 58.5

   f. 28.89 or below, 67.11 or above

CHAPTER 9

Fill-in-the-blanks

(1) estimates

(2) population

(3) estimation

(4) estimates

(5) unbiased

(6) N

(7) means

(8) frequency

(9) sampling distribution of means

(10) μ

(11) normal

(12) central limit theorem

(13) standard deviation

(14) standard error

(15) $\sigma_{\bar{X}}$

(16) $z = \dfrac{\bar{X} - \mu}{\sigma_{\bar{X}}}$

(17) raw score

(18) sample

(19) $\bar{X}$

(20) s

(21) $N - 1$

(22) underestimate

(23) degrees of freedom

(24) values

(25) restrictions

(26) z score

(27) t

(28) Gosset

(29) Student

(30) confidence interval

(31) 99%

(32) z scores

(33) t scores

(34) B

(35) $N - 1$

(36) sample size

(37) interval

(38) null hypothesis

(39) H_0

(40) μ

(41) μ

(42) H_1

(43) nondirectional

(44) directional

(45) null

(46) alpha or α

(47) .05

(48) rejection

(49) test

(50) decision

(51) conclusion

(52) context

(53) same

(54) less

(55) one tail

(56) more

(57) direction

(58) making a decision

(59) I

(60) α

(61) α

(62) decrease

(63) II

(64) β

(65) decreases

(66) power

(67) power = $1 - \beta$

(68) α

(69) size

(70) less

(71) larger

(72) greater

(73) effect size

(74) meta-analysis
(75) effect size
(76) abandon
(77) error rate
(78) power

(79) II or β
(80) power
(81) reasonable
(82) mean
(83) *df*

(84) sign
(85) negative
(86) rejecting

Problems

1. a. $s_{\bar{X}} = 0.87$

   b. $s_{\bar{X}} = 0.79$

   c. $s_{\bar{X}} = 0.40$

   d. $s_{\bar{X}} = 2.68$

   e. $s_{\bar{X}} = 2.15$

2. a. $t = \pm 2.2622$

   b. $t = \pm 2.5758.$ ± 2.58 are the *t* scores cutting off the deviant 1% of the normal curve.
$t = \pm 1.9600.$ ± 1.96 are the *t* scores cutting off the deviant 5% of the normal curve.

   c. $t = \pm 2.0141$, approximately
$t = \pm 2.6896$, approximately

   d. The sampling distribution of means becomes more compact with larger sample sizes. Thus, deviant scores are closer to the mean as sample size (and *df*) increases.

   e. Use the values for the *df* closest to the observed *df*.

3. a. With $df = 120$, 95% CI $= 20 \pm 0.49 = 19.51$ to 20.49;
99% CI $= 20 \pm 0.65 = 19.35$ to 20.65

   b. 95% CI $= 10 \pm 0.80 = 9.20$ to 10.80
99% CI $= 10 \pm 1.09 = 8.91$ to 11.09

   c. 95% CI $= 10.5 \pm 0.83 = 9.67$ to 11.33
99% CI $= 10.5 \pm 1.11 = 9.39$ to 11.61

4. a. $t(53) = 2.01, p < .05$. Applicants demonstrate significantly higher Conscientiousness scores than the general population.

   b. 95% CI $= 54.2 \pm 4.40 = 49.80$ to 58.60

   c. 99% CI $= 54.2 \pm 5.86 = 48.34$ to 60.06

5. a. 95% CI $= 29.6 \pm 2.09 = 27.51$ to 31.69

   b. 99% CI $= 29.6 \pm 2.78 = 26.82$ to 32.38

6. a. $\sigma_{\bar{X}} = 2.10$

   b. $s_{\bar{X}} = 1.70$

   c. $t(24) = 0.82, p > .05$

   d. If you made an error, it was a Type II error (failure to reject a false null hypothesis).

7. $t(25) = -2.55, p < .05$. Significantly fewer calculators were assembled in the last hour of the shift.

8. a. $s_{\bar{X}} = 2.43$

   b. 95% CI $= 77.6 \pm 5.35 = 72.25$ to 82.95. No, 71.1 is not in the interval.

   c. $t(11) = 2.67, p < .05$

   d. Working with the psychologist significantly improved free-throw shooting.

9. a. $s_{\bar{X}} = 1.28$

   b. $\sigma_{\bar{X}} = 1.30$. This is very similar to $s_{\bar{X}}$.

   c. $t(9) = -1.40, p > .05$. The sample probably came from the population with $\mu = 22.5$.

   d. 95% CI $= 20.85 \pm 2.67 = 18.18$ to 23.52

EXERCISE USING SPSS

```
T-TEST
  /TESTVAL=9
  /MISSING=ANALYSIS
  /VARIABLES=ncorrect
  /CRITERIA=CIN (.95) .
```

T-Test

One-Sample Statistics

	N	Mean	Std. Deviation	Std. Error Mean
NCORRECT	20	10.6500	3.0826	.6893

One-Sample Test

	Test Value = 9					
			Sig. (2-tailed)	Mean Difference	95% Confidence Interval of the Difference	
	t	df			Lower	Upper
NCORRECT	2.394	19	.027	1.6500	.2073	3.0927

```
T-TEST
  /TESTVAL=0
  /MISSING=ANALYSIS
  /VARIABLES=ncorrect
  /CRITERIA=CIN (.95) .
```

T-Test

One-Sample Statistics

	N	Mean	Std. Deviation	Std. Error Mean
NCORRECT	20	10.6500	3.0826	.6893

Only the 95% CI is correct in the following output.

One-Sample Test

	Test Value = 0					
			Sig. (2-tailed)	Mean Difference	95% Confidence Interval of the Difference	
	t	df			Lower	Upper
NCORRECT	15.451	19	.000	10.6500	9.2073	12.0927

SELF-TEST

1. b
2. b
3. c

4. Its mean is equal to μ; the larger the sample sizes, the more nearly the distribution approximates the normal curve; the larger the sample sizes, the smaller the standard error of the mean.

5. a. $t(216) = 1.38, p > .05$. The program has not improved reading significantly.

  b. 95% CI = $28.2 \pm 1.15 = 27.05$ to 29.35

6. a. $t(12) = -4.50, p < .01$. Couples experiencing marital difficulty engaged in significantly fewer nods.

  b. 99% CI = $22.6 \pm 6.44 = 16.16$ to 29.04

7. a. $\overline{X} = 58.42$

  b. $s^2 = 173.36$

  c. $s = 13.17$

  d. $s_{\overline{X}} = 3.80$

  e. 95% CI = $58.42 \pm 8.36 = 50.06$ to 66.78

  f. $t(11) = 2.43, p < .05$. Students seeking counseling exhibit more hypochondriasis than would be expected from test norms.

CHAPTER 10

Fill-in-the-blanks

(1) two
(2) independent
(3) random
(4) randomly
(5) pairs
(6) mean
(7) difference
(8) distribution
(9) polygon
(10) standard error
(11) 0
(12) normal
(13) smaller
(14) $\overline{X}_1 - \overline{X}_2$
(15) $\mu_1 - \mu_2$
(16) $\sigma_{\overline{X}_1 - \overline{X}_2}$
(17) $z_{\overline{X}_1 - \overline{X}_2} = \dfrac{(\overline{X}_1 - \overline{X}_2) - (\mu_1 - \mu_2)}{\sigma_{\overline{X}_1 - \overline{X}_2}}$
(18) $t_{\overline{X}_1 - \overline{X}_2} = \dfrac{\overline{X}_1 - \overline{X}_2}{s_{\overline{X}_1 - \overline{X}_2}}$
(19) number

(20) variance
(21) same population
(22) 0
(23) $N_1 + N_2 - 2$
(24) two-tailed
(25) predictions
(26) one-tailed
(27) before
(28) one-tailed
(29) easier
(30) normally
(31) variances
(32) large
(33) little
(34) robust
(35) rejection
(36) power
(37) matched pairs
(38) repeated measures
(39) control
(40) within-subjects

(41) reducing
(42) Counterbalancing
(43) double-blind
(44) differences
(45) standard error
(46) algebraic
(47) pairs
(48) $N - 1$
(49) t ratio
(50) independent
(51) dependent
(52) positive
(53) sign
(54) difference
(55) algebraically
(56) reject

Problems

1. a. $s_{\overline{X}_1 - \overline{X}_2} = 1.62$

  b. $s_{\overline{X}_1 - \overline{X}_2} = 0.67$

  c. $s_{\overline{X}_1 - \overline{X}_2} = 0.41$

2. $t(33) = -4.41, p < .01$. Pilots made fewer errors (failure to respond) than navigators.

3. $t(7) = 2.95, p < .05$. The adults with a family history of alcoholism had a higher level of the metabolite of alcohol in their blood 30 minutes after drinking alcohol.

4. $t(30) = -15.89, p < .01$. Performance was better on the recognition test; more nouns were recognized than were recalled.

5. a. Yes, this is an attempted replication of an effect in which "stupid" rats perform worse than "intelligent" rats. Group "Stupid" should have a larger mean number of errors than Group "Intelligent."

    b. $t(28) = 5.70, p < .005$, one-tailed test. Group "Stupid" rats made more errors.

6. $t(9) = -3.39, p < .01$. The average heart rate increased following exposure to the slides of known conservatives.

7. $t(48) = 2.91, p < .01$. The final averages were higher in the lecture group.

8. $t(1,356) = -2.59, p < .01$. The average freshman ACT score at Private University is higher than at State University. Even though there is little difference in the means, the large sample sizes result in a small standard error and a more powerful test.

9. $t(9) = 2.42, p < .05$. There was less error in distance estimation when the student used both eyes.

10. $t(26) = 1.50, p > .05$. Children and young adults did not differ in ESP ability.

EXERCISES USING SPSS

1.
```
FORMATS group (F8.2).
FORMATS wpm (F8.2).
T-TEST
  GROUPS=group(1 2)
  /MISSING=ANALYSIS
  /VARIABLES=wpm
  /CRITERIA=CIN(.95) .
```

T-Test

Group Statistics

	GROUP	N	Mean	Std. Deviation	Std. Error Mean
WPM	1.00	10	410.6000	85.3635	26.9943
	2.00	10	514.2000	75.7889	23.9666

Independent Samples Test

		Levene's Test for Equality of Variances	
		F	Sig.
WPM	Equal variances assumed	.153	.700
	Equal variances not assumed		

Independent Samples Test

		t-test for Equality of Means			
		t	df	Sig. (2-tailed)	Mean Difference
WPM	Equal variances assumed	-2.870	18	.010	-103.6000
	Equal variances not assumed	-2.870	17.751	.010	-103.6000

Independent Samples Test

		t-test for Equality of Means		
			95% Confidence Interval of the Difference	
		Std. Error Difference	Lower	Upper
WPM	Equal variances assumed	36.0983	-179.4398	-27.7602
	Equal variances not assumed	36.0983	-179.5161	-27.6839

2. `T-TEST`
`    PAIRS= noclass  WITH class (PAIRED)`
`    /CRITERIA=CIN(.95)`
`    /MISSING=ANALYSIS.`

T-Test

Paired Samples Statistics

		Mean	N	Std. Deviation	Std. Error Mean
Pair 1	NOCLASS	410.6000	10	85.3635	26.9943
	CLASS	514.2000	10	75.7889	23.9666

Paired Samples Correlations

		N	Correlation	Sig.
Pair 1	NOCLASS & CLASS	10	.428	.217

Paired Samples Test

		Paired Differences					
					95% Confidence Interval of the Difference		
		Mean	Std. Deviation	Std. Error Mean	Lower	Upper	t
Pair 1	NOCLASS - CLASS	-103.6000	86.5373	27.3655	-165.5051	-41.6949	-3.786

Paired Samples Test

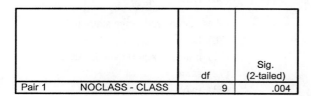

		df	Sig. (2-tailed)
Pair 1	NOCLASS - CLASS	9	.004

For the between-groups design used in Exercise 1, $t = -2.87$, $p = .010$. For the dependent-groups design used in Exercise 2, $t = -3.79$, $p = .004$. The dependent-groups or paired-samples design is more powerful.

SELF-TEST

1. Properties of the sampling distribution of the mean differences:
   a. Its mean is equal to 0.
   b. The larger the sample sizes, the more closely the distribution approximates the normal curve.
   c. The larger the sample sizes, the smaller the standard error of the mean differences.
2. A t test for independent samples is used when data are gathered from unrelated (independent) groups, such as when a control group is compared to a separate experimental group.
3. A t test for dependent samples is used when data are gathered from the same, related, or matched samples on two occasions (repeated measures), such as when participants are pretested, receive a treatment, and then are posttested.
4. e (a and b are correct)
5. $t(22) = 0.79, p > .05$. Leadership style did not significantly influence worker productivity.
6. $t(9) = -3.79, p < .01$. The course significantly improved reading speed.

CHAPTER 11

Fill-in-the-blanks

(1) two	(28) 1.00	(55) sample sizes
(2) different	(29) large	(56) powerful
(3) analysis of variance	(30) total	(57) protected
(4) tedious	(31) within	(58) F ratio
(5) I	(32) between	(59) significant
(6) true	(33) scores	(60) LSD
(7) between-subjects	(34) squared scores	(61) $LSD_\alpha = t_\alpha \sqrt{MS_w \left(\dfrac{1}{N_1} + \dfrac{1}{N_2} \right)}$
(8) repeated measures	(35) total	
(9) population	(36) total	(62) α
(10) mean	(37) ΣX_g^2	(63) β
(11) score	(38) ΣX^2	(64) Table of Differences
(12) additivity	(39) subtraction	(65) pairwise
(13) sum	(40) df	(66) equal
(14) component parts	(41) mean	(67) HSD
(15) between-groups	(42) F ratio	(68) $HSD_\alpha = q_\alpha \sqrt{\dfrac{MS_w}{N_g}}$
(16) key deviations	(43) MS_w	
(17) grand mean	(44) groups	(69) studentized range statistic
(18) between-groups	(45) $N - K$	(70) D
(19) large	(46) C	(71) honestly significant difference
(20) within-groups	(47) rejected	(72) same
(21) between-groups	(48) positively	(73) two
(22) total	(49) 1.00	(74) control
(23) within-groups	(50) Post-ANOVA	(75) variance
(24) individual differences	(51) increasing	(76) error
(25) treatment effect	(52) post-ANOVA	(77) subjects
(26) between	(53) a priori	(78) SS_{error}
(27) within	(54) means	(79) denominator

(80) SS_{error}
(81) subjects
(82) three parts
(83) subjects
(84) df_{subj}
(85) subjects
(86) MS_{error}

(87) negative
(88) SS_{tot}
(89) df
(90) $N - 1$
(91) $N - 1$
(92) N_g

(93) F
(94) t
(95) q
(96) positive
(97) absolute
(98) larger

Problems

1. $\Sigma X_1 = 66, \Sigma X_2 = 45, \Sigma X_3 = 30, \Sigma X_4 = 70, \Sigma X = 211$
   $\Sigma X_1^2 = 558, \Sigma X_2^2 = 279, \Sigma X_3^2 = 138, \Sigma X_4^2 = 620, \Sigma X^2 = 1,595$
   $N_1 = 8, N_2 = 8, N_3 = 8, N_4 = 8, N = 32$
   $SS_{tot} = 203.72$
   $SS_w = 72.38$
   $SS_b = 131.34$

ANOVA Summary Table

Source	SS	df	MS	F
Between groups	131.34	3	43.78	16.94
Within groups	72.38	28	2.585	
Total	203.72	31		

The computed value of F is 16.94. The df for the numerator is 3 and the df for the denominator is 28. The table values required for rejection of H_0 are 2.95 at the 5% level and 4.57 at the 1% level. What is your decision? Reject H_0 at the 1% level and conclude that the groups differ significantly. The treatments had an effect on how closely a phobic student would approach a live snake.

2. $LSD_{.05} = 1.65$; $LSD_{.01} = 2.22$.

Table of Differences

	Group 3 3.750	Group 2 5.625	Group 1 8.250	Group 4 8.750
Group 3 3.750		1.875*	4.500**	5.000**
Group 2 5.625			2.625**	3.125**
Group 1 8.250				0.500
Group 4 8.750				

Note. *$p < .05$; **$p < .01$.

Conclusion: Group 3, which got both relaxation training and imagery training, had significantly lower behavioral avoidance scores (displayed less fear) than any of the other groups. Group 2 participants, who had imagery training, were significantly less fearful than Groups 1 and 4 participants, who did not differ from each other.

3. $SS_{tot} = 39.28$, $SS_w = 37.92$, $SS_b = 1.36$

ANOVA Summary Table

Source	SS	df	MS	F
Between groups	1.36	3	0.453	$F = 0.36$
Within groups	37.92	30	1.264	$F_{crit}(3, 30) = 2.92$ ($p = .05$)
Total	39.28	33		

Thus, $F(3, 30) = 0.36$, $p > .05$. There's no evidence that the sleeping aids affected the speed of sleep onset.

4. $F(2, 21) = 359.54$, $p < .01$. Different levels of preflight illumination had an effect on time to complete dark adaptation.

5. $LSD_{.05} = 2.31$; $LSD_{.01} = 3.14$.

Table of Differences

		Group C 4.50	Group B 9.75	Group A 32.50
Group C	4.50		5.25**	28.00**
Group B	9.75			22.75**
Group A	32.50			

Note. *$p < .05$; **$p < .01$.

Conclusion: All comparisons were significant, with Group C pilots who spent 30 minutes wearing red-tinted goggles having the shortest times to dark adaptation, followed by Group B pilots (30 minutes in a dimly lighted room), and Group A pilots (30 minutes in a bright room).

6. $F(3, 24) = 41.15$, $p < .01$. Mathematics anxiety varied over time in the course.

7. $LSD_{.05} = 0.83$; $LSD_{.01} = 1.12$.

Table of Differences

		9 Weeks 6	6 Weeks 7	3 Weeks 9	First Day 10
9 Weeks	6		1*	3**	4**
6 Weeks	7			2**	3**
3 Weeks	9				1*
First Day	10				

Note. *$p < .05$; **$p < .01$.

Conclusion: All pairwise comparisons were significant, with students showing progressively less math anxiety with passage of time in the course.

8. $F(2, 18) = 40.95$, $p < .01$. Fatigue affected time to assemble pocket calculators.

9. $HSD_{.05} = 0.74$; $HSD_{.01} = 0.96$.

Table of Differences

		Beginning 22.1	Middle 23.1	End 24.7
Beginning	22.1		1.0**	2.6**
Middle	23.1			1.6**
End	24.7			

*Note. *$p < .05$; **$p < .01$.*

Conclusion: All pairwise comparisons were significant. The average time to assemble pocket calculators got progressively longer as the shift progressed.

10. $F(2, 14) = 17.06$, $p < .01$. The amount of dark adaptation affected the number of object detections.

11. $LSD_{.05} = 1.32$; $LSD_{.01} = 1.84$.

Table of Differences

		1 Minute 2.5	15 Minutes 5.0	30 Minutes 6.0
1 Minute	2.5		2.5**	3.5**
15 Minutes	5.0			1.0
30 Minutes	6.0			

*Note. *$p < .05$; **$p < .01$.*

Conclusion: Object identification was significantly better after 15 minutes and after 30 minutes in the dark than after 1 minute. There was no significant difference in identification between 15 and 30 minutes in the dark.

12. $F(3, 32) = 0.88$, $p > .05$. The different diets had no effect on errors to learn the visual discrimination task.

EXERCISES USING SPSS

1.
```
FORMATS colratio (F8.2).
ONEWAY
   colratio BY diet
   /STATISTICS DESCRIPTIVES
   /MISSING ANALYSIS
   /POSTHOC = LSD ALPHA(.05).
```

Oneway

Descriptives

COLRATIO

	N	Mean	Std. Deviation	Std. Error	95% Confidence Interval for Mean		Minimum	Maximum
					Lower Bound	Upper Bound		
1.00	10	2.2800	.3824	.1209	2.0065	2.5535	1.60	2.80
2.00	10	1.7200	.1619	5.121E-02	1.6042	1.8358	1.50	2.00
3.00	9	2.1222	.3032	.1011	1.8891	2.3553	1.60	2.50
4.00	7	2.3429	.4077	.1541	1.9658	2.7199	1.60	2.80
Total	36	2.0972	.3953	6.589E-02	1.9635	2.2310	1.50	2.80

ANOVA

COLRATIO

	Sum of Squares	df	Mean Square	F	Sig.
Between Groups	2.185	3	.728	7.096	.001
Within Groups	3.285	32	.103		
Total	5.470	35			

Post Hoc Tests

Multiple Comparisons

Dependent Variable: COLRATIO

LSD

(I) DIET	(J) DIET	Mean Difference (I-J)	Std. Error	Sig.	95% Confidence Interval	
					Lower Bound	Upper Bound
1.00	2.00	.5600*	.143	.000	.2681	.8519
	3.00	.1578	.147	.292	-.1421	.4576
	4.00	-6.2857E-02	.158	.693	-.3845	.2587
2.00	1.00	-.5600*	.143	.000	-.8519	-.2681
	3.00	-.4022*	.147	.010	-.7021	-.1024
	4.00	-.6229*	.158	.000	-.9445	-.3013
3.00	1.00	-.1578	.147	.292	-.4576	.1421
	2.00	.4022*	.147	.010	.1024	.7021
	4.00	-.2206	.161	.181	-.5495	.1082
4.00	1.00	6.286E-02	.158	.693	-.2587	.3845
	2.00	.6229*	.158	.000	.3013	.9445
	3.00	.2206	.161	.181	-.1082	.5495

*. The mean difference is significant at the .05 level.

Means Plots

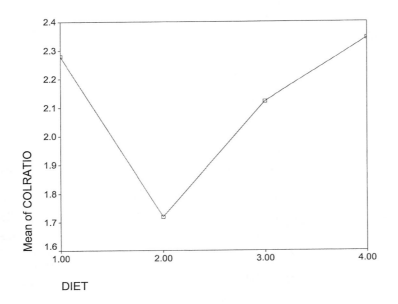

```
GRAPH
  /ERRORBAR( CI 95 )=colratio BY diet
  /MISSING=REPORT.
```

Graph

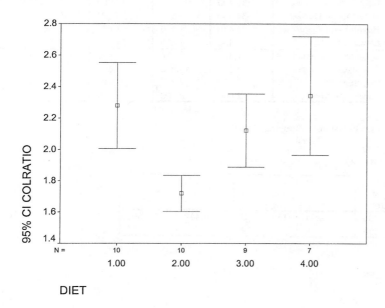

DIET

2. *Note.* Only the necessary portions of the output are given. Your solution will generate additional output that should be ignored.

```
GLM
    begin middle end
  /WSFACTOR = factor1 3 Polynomial
  /METHOD = SSTYPE(3)
  /PLOT = PROFILE( factor1 )
  /PRINT = DESCRIPTIVE
  /CRITERIA = ALPHA(.05)
  /WSDESIGN = factor1 .
```

General Linear Model

Within-Subjects Factors

Measure: MEASURE_1

FACTOR1	Dependent Variable
1	BEGIN
2	MIDDLE
3	END

Descriptive Statistics

	Mean	Std. Deviation	N
BEGIN	22.1000	3.2472	10
MIDDLE	23.1000	3.8137	10
END	24.7000	3.8312	10

Tests of Within-Subjects Effects

Measure: MEASURE_1

Source		Type III Sum of Squares	df	Mean Square	F	Sig.
FACTOR1	Sphericity Assumed	34.400	2	17.200	40.737	.000
	Greenhouse-Geisser	34.400	1.652	20.821	40.737	.000
	Huynh-Feldt	34.400	1.976	17.406	40.737	.000
	Lower-bound	34.400	1.000	34.400	40.737	.000
Error(FACTOR1)	Sphericity Assumed	7.600	18	.422		
	Greenhouse-Geisser	7.600	14.870	.511		
	Huynh-Feldt	7.600	17.787	.427		
	Lower-bound	7.600	9.000	.844		

Tests of Between-Subjects Effects

Measure: MEASURE_1
Transformed Variable: Average

Source	Type III Sum of Squares	df	Mean Square	F	Sig.
Intercept	16286.700	1	16286.700	418.442	.000
Error	350.300	9	38.922		

Profile Plots

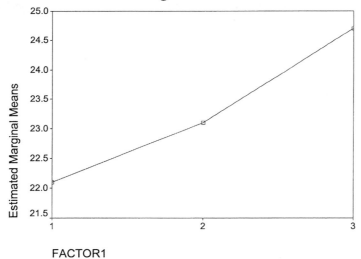

Estimated Marginal Means of MEASURE

SELF-TEST

1. b

2. False. Further testing is necessary to determine which groups differ significantly.

3. j, b, l, f, h, c, a, d, k, i

4. $F(3, 32) = 7.12$, $p < .01$. The total cholesterol/HDL ratios were significantly affected by the diets.

5. $F(2, 12) = 16.78$, $p < .01$. There's a significant change in object conservation ability as the children get older.

$LSD_{.05} = 5.27$; $LSD_{.01} = 7.38$.

Table of Differences

		9 Months 2	12 Months 4	15 Months 15
9 Months	2		2	13**
12 Months	4			11**
15 Months	15			

*Note. *$p < .05$; **$p < .01$.*

Conclusion: There was significantly greater object conservation at 15 months than at either 9 months or 12 months and no difference in ability at the earlier ages.

CHAPTER 12

Fill-in-the-blanks

(1) one-way ANOVA

(2) two-way ANOVA

(3) factors

(4) 3×3

(5) main effect

(6) interaction

(7) depends

(8) parallel

(9) converging

(10) crossing

(11) A

(12) lines

(13) interaction

(14) interaction

(15) subjects

(16) powerful

(17) generalization

(18) three

(19) main effects

(20) interaction

(21) MS_w

(22) interaction

(23) post hoc

(24) interaction

Problems

1. a. factor A, significant; factor B, nonsignificant; interaction, significant

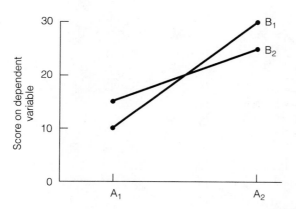

b. factor A, significant; factor B, significant; interaction, nonsignificant

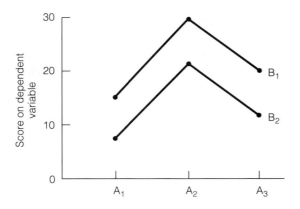

c. factor A, nonsignificant; factor B, nonsignificant; interaction, significant

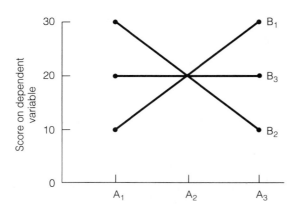

2. a. handedness main effect, significant; illumination main effect, significant; interaction, nonsignificant

b. handedness main effect, significant; illumination main effect, nonsignificant; interaction, significant

c. handedness main effect, nonsignificant; illumination main effect, nonsignificant; interaction, significant

3. task difficulty, significant; anxiety level, significant; interaction, significant

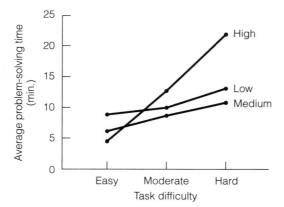

4. anxiety, significant; problem difficulty, significant; interaction, significant

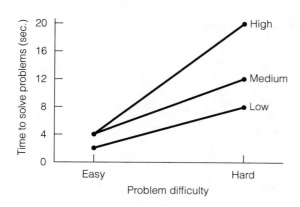

5. thrill seeking, significant; alcohol level, significant; interaction, significant

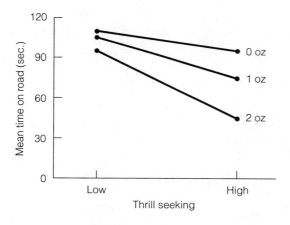

6. a. The handedness main effect was significant ($p < .05$); dextrals spent more time on target than sinistrals. The illumination main effect was significant ($p < .05$); performance improved with higher illumination levels. The interaction was not significant.

b. The handedness main effect was significant ($p < .05$); dextrals did better than sinistrals overall. The illumination main effect was not significant ($p > .05$). The handedness/illumination interaction was significant ($p < .01$); dextrals outperformed sinistrals at high and low levels of illumination but did worse at medium levels.

c. Neither main effect was significant ($p > .05$). The interaction effect was significant ($p < .01$); sinistrals improved as light levels increased, whereas dextrals got worse under the same conditions.

SELF-TEST

1. c

2. d

3. a. main effect (smoking), significant; main effect (nicotine), significant; interaction, significant

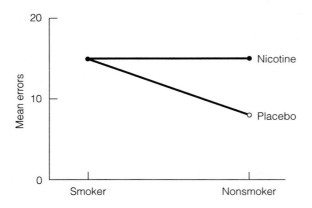

b. main effect (smoking), nonsignificant; main effect (nicotine), nonsignificant; interaction, significant

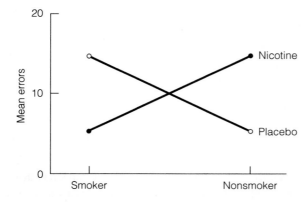

c. main effect (smoking), significant; main effect (nicotine), significant; interaction, nonsignificant

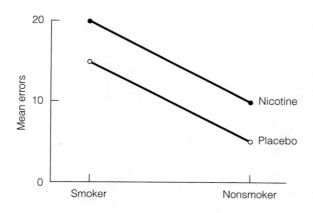

CHAPTER 13

Fill-in-the-blanks

(1) correlation
(2) linear correlation
(3) high
(4) low
(5) positive
(6) scatterplot
(7) negative
(8) downward
(9) zero
(10) absolute value
(11) causes
(12) sufficient
(13) mean
(14) −1 to +1
(15) positive
(16) inverse
(17) zero
(18) covariance
(19) covariance
(20) Pearson correlation
(21) lowers or reduces
(22) no relationship

(23) ρ (rho)
(24) zero
(25) E
(26) *df*
(27) zero
(28) reject
(29) relationship
(30) linear
(31) straight
(32) $Y = bX + a$ or $Y = a + bX$
(33) slope
(34) Y axis
(35) deviations
(36) 1.00
(37) multiple regression
(38) coefficient of determination
(39) r^2
(40) large
(41) significance
(42) compute
(43) ordinal
(44) ordinal

(45) rank
(46) ranks
(47) average
(48) point biserial
(49) two
(50) phi coefficient
(51) multiple regression
(52) general linear model
(53) relationships
(54) strength
(55) group
(56) −1 to +1
(57) rank
(58) 1
(59) $\overline{Y} - \left(\dfrac{rs_y}{s_x}\right)\overline{X}$
(60) algebraically

Problems

1. a. negatively correlated

   b. positively correlated

c. negatively correlated
d. not correlated
e. negatively correlated
f. not correlated
g. positively correlated

2.

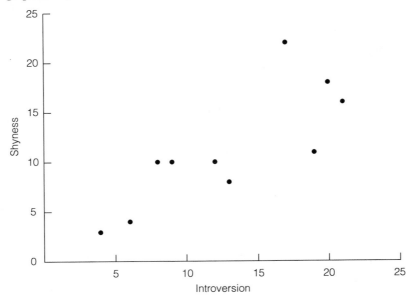

Scatterplot of introversion and shyness.

$r(8) = .81$, $p < .01$; there is a significant positive correlation between introversion and shyness. $r^2 = .66$.

3. $\hat{Y} = 0.79X + 1.01$. If $X = 15$, $\hat{Y} = 12.86$.

4. $r = .92$. $r(15) = .92$, $p < .01$. There is a significant positive correlation between first and last exam scores.
$\hat{Y} = 0.66X + 31.4$
If $X = 95$, $\hat{Y} = 94.1$ or 94. If $X = 55$, $\hat{Y} = 67.7$ or 68.

5. $r_S = .93$, $p < .01$. There is a significant positive relationship between the rankings.

6. $r(6) = .96$, $p < .01$. There is a significant positive relationship between time spent reading the paper and recognition of current events. $r^2 = .92$.

7. $r(7) = -.96$, $p < .01$. The length of the car is inversely related to its gas mileage.

8. $\hat{Y} = -5.63X + 31.33$. If $X = 4.3$ (4,300 pounds), $\hat{Y} = 7.12$ mpg.

9. $r_S = -.07$, $p > .05$. The correlation between the ratings is not significant.

10. $r_S = .96$, $p < .01$. There is a significant positive correlation between the ratings of the experimenters.

11. $r(8) = .84$, $p < .01$. There is a significant positive relationship for heart rates of subjects viewing different stimuli.

EXERCISES USING SPSS

1. `CORRELATIONS`
   ` /VARIABLES=time score`
   ` /PRINT=TWOTAIL NOSIG`
   ` /STATISTICS DESCRIPTIVES`
   ` /MISSING=PAIRWISE .`

Correlations

Descriptive Statistics

	Mean	Std. Deviation	N
TIME	26.8750	19.0746	8
SCORE	10.5000	5.0427	8

Correlations

		TIME	SCORE
TIME	Pearson Correlation	1.000	.962**
	Sig. (2-tailed)	.	.000
	N	8	8
SCORE	Pearson Correlation	.962**	1.000
	Sig. (2-tailed)	.000	.
	N	8	8

**. Correlation is significant at the 0.01 level (2-tailed).

2. `REGRESSION`
   ` /DESCRIPTIVES MEAN STDDEV CORR SIG N`
   ` /MISSING LISTWISE`
   ` /STATISTICS COEFF OUTS R ANOVA`
   ` /CRITERIA=PIN(.05) POUT(.10)`
   ` /NOORIGIN`
   ` /DEPENDENT score`
   ` /METHOD=ENTER time   .`

Regression

Descriptive Statistics

	Mean	Std. Deviation	N
SCORE	10.5000	5.0427	8
TIME	26.8750	19.0746	8

Correlations

		SCORE	TIME
Pearson Correlation	SCORE	1.000	.962
	TIME	.962	1.000
Sig. (1-tailed)	SCORE	.	.000
	TIME	.000	.
N	SCORE	8	8
	TIME	8	8

Variables Entered/Removed[b]

Model	Variables Entered	Variables Removed	Method
1	TIME[a]	.	Enter

a. All requested variables entered.

b. Dependent Variable: SCORE

Model Summary

Model	R	R Square	Adjusted R Square	Std. Error of the Estimate
1	.962[a]	.925	.912	1.4935

a. Predictors: (Constant), TIME

ANOVA[b]

Model		Sum of Squares	df	Mean Square	F	Sig.
1	Regression	164.616	1	164.616	73.796	.000[a]
	Residual	13.384	6	2.231		
	Total	178.000	7			

a. Predictors: (Constant), TIME

b. Dependent Variable: SCORE

Coefficients[a]

Model		Unstandardized Coefficients		Standardized Coefficients	t	Sig.
		B	Std. Error	Beta		
1	(Constant)	3.667	.955		3.842	.009
	TIME	.254	.030	.962	8.590	.000

a. Dependent Variable: SCORE

$$SCORE = 3.667 + 0.254 \ (TIME)$$

```
GRAPH
  /SCATTERPLOT(BIVAR)=time WITH score
  /MISSING=LISTWISE .
```

Graph

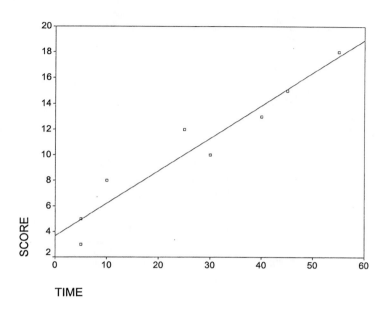

3.
```
FORMATS a (F8.2).
FORMATS b (F8.2).
NONPAR CORR
  /VARIABLES=b a
  /PRINT=SPEARMAN TWOTAIL NOSIG
  /MISSING=PAIRWISE .
```

Nonparametric Correlations

Correlations

			B	A
Spearman's rho	B	Correlation Coefficient	1.000	-.098
		Sig. (2-tailed)	.	.817
		N	8	8
	A	Correlation Coefficient	-.098	1.000
		Sig. (2-tailed)	.817	.
		N	8	8

```
GRAPH
  /SCATTERPLOT(BIVAR)=raterb WITH ratera
  /MISSING=LISTWISE .
```

Graph

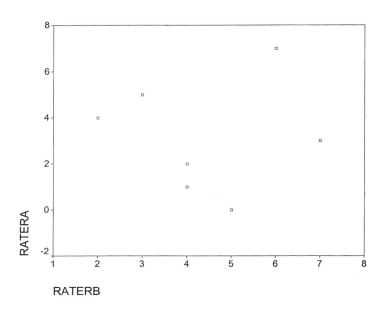

SELF-TEST

1. e, f, d, g, i, a, h, b, j, c
2. $r(6) = .89, p < .01$. There is a significant, positive relationship between math and science ACT scores.
3. $\hat{Y} = 0.93X + 1.50$
   science ACT = 32.19 or 32
4. $r_S = .78, p < .05$. There is a significant, positive relationship between the attractiveness ratings of husbands and wives.

CHAPTER 14

Fill-in-the-blanks

(1) parametric
(2) nonparametric
(3) distribution-free
(4) nominal
(5) frequencies
(6) Chi square
(7) goodness-of-fit
(8) squared

(9) equally distributed
(10) previous research
(11) summed
(12) $K - 1$
(13) levels
(14) research hypothesis
(15) confirmation
(16) power

(17) replication
(18) two
(19) independence
(20) two-sample
(21) independent
(22) contingency
(23) research
(24) marginal

(25) N (29) independent   (33) four

(26) subtraction   (30) occurrence   (34) expected

(27) $(R - 1)(C - 1)$ (31) nonoccurrence   (35) negative

(28) frequency   (32) 5

Problems

1. a. 20.77   9.23
      24.23   10.77

Only one value had to be computed; the remaining three could be found by subtraction.

b. 23.77   14.85   12.38
    24.23   15.15   12.62

It was necessary to compute two expected values; four were found by subtraction.

c. 16.85   33.29   22.86
    9.23   18.24   12.53
   15.92   31.47   21.61

It was necessary to compute four values; five were found by subtraction.

2. a. $\chi^2 (1, N = 65) = 13.32, p < .01$.

b. $\chi^2 (2, N = 103) = 1.60, p > .05$.

c. $\chi^2 (4, N = 182) = 17.77, p < .01$.

3. $\chi^2 (1, N = 132) = 11.68, p < .01$. Left-handers were less likely to be aphasic than right-handers.

4. $\chi^2 (1, N = 204) = 3.53, p > .05$. Parental alcoholism was not significantly related to alcoholism of the participants in the study.

5. $\chi^2 (1, N = 50) = 25.92, p < .01$. The monkey had generalized its learned response from objects to pictures of objects.

6. $\chi^2 (2, N = 160) = 1.91, p > .05$. Introversion–extraversion did not affect brand preference.

7. $\chi^2 (4, N = 170) = 103.11, p < .01$. The grade assignment significantly departed from a normal distribution.

8. $\chi^2 (1, N = 60) = 3.51, p > .05$. High- and low-self-esteem students did not differ on the test of attitudes toward risk taking.

9. $\chi^2 (1, N = 28) = 11.57, p < .01$. In physiological psychology, the professor scored significantly better than the departmental average.

10. $\chi^2 (1, N = 28) = 2.29, p > .05$. In statistics, the professor did not score better than the departmental average.

EXERCISES USING SPSS

1.
```
FORMATS item (F8.2).
NPAR TEST
  /CHISQUARE=item
  /EXPECTED=EQUAL
  /MISSING ANALYSIS.
```

NPar Tests

Chi-Square Test

Frequencies

ITEM

	Observed N	Expected N	Residual
.00	5	14.0	-9.0
1.00	23	14.0	9.0
Total	28		

Test Statistics

	ITEM
Chi-Square[a]	11.571
df	1
Asymp. Sig.	.001

a. 0 cells (.0%) have expected frequencies less than 5. The minimum expected cell frequency is 14.0.

This result—being above average on 23 of 28 evaluation items—is significantly different from a chance outcome, $\chi^2 (1, N = 28) = 11.57, p = .001$.

2.
```
FORMATS esteem (F8.2).
FORMATS risk (F8.2).
CROSSTABS
   /TABLES=esteem  BY risk
   /FORMAT= AVALUE TABLES
   /STATISTIC=CHISQ
   /CELLS= COUNT EXPECTED TOTAL
   /BARCHART .
```

Crosstabs

Case Processing Summary

	Cases					
	Valid		Missing		Total	
	N	Percent	N	Percent	N	Percent
ESTEEM * RISK	60	100.0%	0	.0%	60	100.0%

ESTEEM * RISK Crosstabulation

			RISK		Total
			1.00	2.00	
ESTEEM	1.00	Count	18	9	27
		Expected Count	14.4	12.6	27.0
		% of Total	30.0%	15.0%	45.0%
	2.00	Count	14	19	33
		Expected Count	17.6	15.4	33.0
		% of Total	23.3%	31.7%	55.0%
Total		Count	32	28	60
		Expected Count	32.0	28.0	60.0
		% of Total	53.3%	46.7%	100.0%

Chi-Square Tests

	Value	df	Asymp. Sig. (2-sided)	Exact Sig. (2-sided)	Exact Sig. (1-sided)
Pearson Chi-Square	3.506[b]	1	.061		
Continuity Correction[a]	2.600	1	.107		
Likelihood Ratio	3.552	1	.059		
Fisher's Exact Test				.074	.053
Linear-by-Linear Association	3.448	1	.063		
N of Valid Cases	60				

a. Computed only for a 2x2 table

b. 0 cells (.0%) have expected count less than 5. The minimum expected count is 12.60.

Students differing in self-esteem do not differ significantly in their risk-taking atttitude, χ^2 (1, $N = 60$) = 3.506, $p = .061$.

SELF-TEST

1. a, d, e, h

2. χ^2 (1, $N = 201$) = 18.49, $p < .01$. Republicans and Democrats differ in their opinions on increased entitlement spending: Democrats tend to favor it, whereas Republicans tend to oppose it.

3. χ^2 (2, $N = 80$) = 2.42, $p > .05$. The diets did not affect problem-solving ability significantly.

CHAPTER 15

Fill-in-the-blanks

(1) nonparametric
(2) distribution free
(3) assumptions
(4) interval
(5) *t* test for independent
(6) independent
(7) ordinal
(8) identical
(9) ranked
(10) U'
(11) populations
(12) H
(13) less
(14) *z* score

(15) 1.96
(16) dependent
(17) randomly
(18) ordinal
(19) identical
(20) difference
(21) 0
(22) rank-
(23) sign
(24) less
(25) smaller
(26) normal
(27) *z* score
(28) Mann–Whitney

(29) *F* test or one-way ANOVA
(30) ordinal
(31) ranked
(32) ranks
(33) chi square
(34) $K - 1$
(35) M–W
(36) ranking
(37) *N*
(38) positive
(39) U'
(40) 0
(41) absolute
(42) less

Problems

1. a. Mann–Whitney test

b. *t* test for dependent samples

   c. Kruskal–Wallis test

   d. Wilcoxon test

   e. Chi-square test of significance

2. $U' = 4, p = .02$. Only children were less willing to share toys with other children.

3. $H = 13.42, p < .01$. There were significant differences between the diets in their effects on handling scores.

   A vs. B: $U' = 12, p < .01$. Diet B made rats harder to handle than Diet A.

   A vs. C: $U = 47.5, p > .05$. Diets A and C did not differ in their effects.

   B vs. C: $U = 7, p < .01$. Diet B made rats more irritable than Diet C.

4. $U = 36.5, p > .05$. There was no difference in the speech patterns of the parents of schizophrenic children.

5. $T = 11, p = .05$. Attitudes toward risk taking were more positive after alcohol consumption.

6. $U' = 58.5, p > .05$. The groups did not differ in attitudes toward risk taking.

7. $T = 26.5, p > .05$. There were no differences in double-blind statements between the parents' letters.

8. $H = 10.20, p < .01$. The classes differed significantly.

   1 vs. 2: $U = 16, p = .01$. Class 1 had higher creativity scores than Class 2.

   1 vs. 3: $U = 12, p < .01$. Class 1 had higher scores than Class 3.

   2 vs. 3: $U = 44, p > .05$. Classes 2 and 3 did not differ.

EXERCISES USING SPSS

1.

```
FORMATS group (F8.2).
FORMATS share (F8.2).
NPAR TESTS
   /M-W= share   BY group(1 2)
   /MISSING ANALYSIS.
```

NPar Tests

Mann-Whitney Test

Ranks

	GROUP	N	Mean Rank	Sum of Ranks
SHARE	1.00	7	4.57	32.00
	2.00	6	9.83	59.00
	Total	13		

Test Statistics[b]

	SHARE
Mann-Whitney U	4.000
Wilcoxon W	32.000
Z	-2.449
Asymp. Sig. (2-tailed)	.014
Exact Sig. [2*(1-tailed Sig.)]	.014[a]

a. Not corrected for ties.

b. Grouping Variable: GROUP

```
EXAMINE
  VARIABLES=share BY group /PLOT=BOXPLOT/STATISTICS=NONE/NOTOTAL
  /MISSING=REPORT.
```

Explore

GROUP

Case Processing Summary

		Cases					
		Valid		Missing		Total	
	GROUP	N	Percent	N	Percent	N	Percent
SHARE	1.00	7	100.0%	0	.0%	7	100.0%
	2.00	6	100.0%	0	.0%	6	100.0%

SHARE

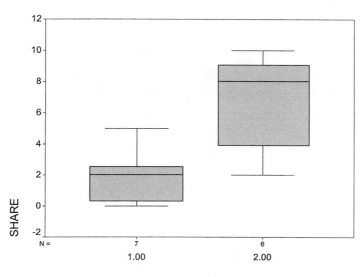

GROUP

The results were that the group of children with siblings indicated more willingness to share toys than the group of only children, $U = 4.0, p = .014$.

2.
```
  /COMPRESSED.
NPAR TEST
  /WILCOXON=schizo  WITH nonschiz (PAIRED)
  /MISSING ANALYSIS.
```

NPar Tests

Wilcoxon Signed Ranks Test

Ranks

		N	Mean Rank	Sum of Ranks
NONSCHIZ - SCHIZO	Negative Ranks	5[a]	5.30	26.50
	Positive Ranks	6[b]	6.58	39.50
	Ties	1[c]		
	Total	12		

a. NONSCHIZ < SCHIZO

b. NONSCHIZ > SCHIZO

c. SCHIZO = NONSCHIZ

Test Statistics[b]

	NONSCHIZ - SCHIZO
Z	-.582[a]
Asymp. Sig. (2-tailed)	.560

a. Based on negative ranks.

b. Wilcoxon Signed Ranks Test

```
EXAMINE
  VARIABLES=schizo nonschiz /COMPARE VARIABLE/PLOT=BOXPLOT/STATISTICS=NONE
/NOTOTAL
  /MISSING=LISTWISE .
```

Explore

Case Processing Summary

	Cases					
	Valid		Missing		Total	
	N	Percent	N	Percent	N	Percent
SCHIZO	12	100.0%	0	.0%	12	100.0%
NONSCHIZ	12	100.0%	0	.0%	12	100.0%

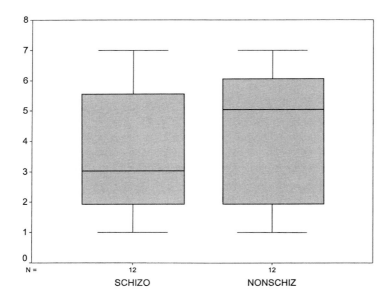

The results indicated that there were no differences in ratings of incompatible ideas and feelings in letters from parents of schizophrenic versus nonschizophrenic children by the Wilcoxon test, $T = 26.50$, $p = .56$.

3.
```
NPAR TESTS
  /K-W=creat   BY group(1 3)
  /MISSING ANALYSIS.
```

NPar Tests

Kruskal-Wallis Test

Ranks

	GROUP	N	Mean Rank
CREAT	1.00	10	22.70
	2.00	10	12.70
	3.00	10	11.10
	Total	30	

Test Statistics[a,b]

	CREAT
Chi-Square	10.212
df	2
Asymp. Sig.	.006

a. Kruskal Wallis Test

b. Grouping Variable: GROUP

```
EXAMINE
  VARIABLES=creat BY group /PLOT=BOXPLOT/STATISTICS=NONE/NOTOTAL
  /MISSING=REPORT.
```

Explore

GROUP

Case Processing Summary

		Cases					
		Valid		Missing		Total	
	GROUP	N	Percent	N	Percent	N	Percent
CREAT	1.00	10	100.0%	0	.0%	10	100.0%
	2.00	10	100.0%	0	.0%	10	100.0%
	3.00	10	100.0%	0	.0%	10	100.0%

CREAT

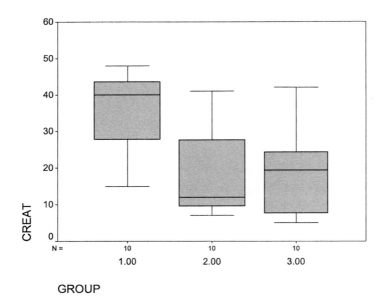

GROUP

```
NPAR TESTS
  /M-W= creat   BY group(1 2)
  /MISSING ANALYSIS.
```

NPar Tests

Mann-Whitney Test

Ranks

	GROUP	N	Mean Rank	Sum of Ranks
CREAT	1.00	10	13.90	139.00
	2.00	10	7.10	71.00
	Total	20		

Test Statistics[b]

	CREAT
Mann-Whitney U	16.000
Wilcoxon W	71.000
Z	-2.573
Asymp. Sig. (2-tailed)	.010
Exact Sig. [2*(1-tailed Sig.)]	.009[a]

a. Not corrected for ties.

b. Grouping Variable: GROUP

```
NPAR TESTS
  /M-W= creat   BY group(1 3)
  /MISSING ANALYSIS.
```

NPar Tests

Mann-Whitney Test

Ranks

	GROUP	N	Mean Rank	Sum of Ranks
CREAT	1.00	10	14.30	143.00
	3.00	10	6.70	67.00
	Total	20		

Test Statistics[b]

	CREAT
Mann-Whitney U	12.000
Wilcoxon W	67.000
Z	-2.874
Asymp. Sig. (2-tailed)	.004
Exact Sig. [2*(1-tailed Sig.)]	.003[a]

a. Not corrected for ties.

b. Grouping Variable: GROUP

```
NPAR TESTS
  /M-W= creat   BY group(2 3)
  /MISSING ANALYSIS.
```

NPar Tests

Mann-Whitney Test

Ranks

	GROUP	N	Mean Rank	Sum of Ranks
CREAT	2.00	10	11.10	111.00
	3.00	10	9.90	99.00
	Total	20		

Test Statistics[b]

	CREAT
Mann-Whitney U	44.000
Wilcoxon W	99.000
Z	-.454
Asymp. Sig. (2-tailed)	.650
Exact Sig. [2*(1-tailed Sig.)]	.684[a]

a. Not corrected for ties.

b. Grouping Variable: GROUP

The three classes differed in creativity test scores overall by the Kruskal–Wallis test: χ^2 (2, $N = 30$) = 10.21, $p = .006$. Pairwise comparisons using the Mann–Whitney procedure indicated that Class 1 was higher than Class 2, $U = 16.0$, $p = .01$; Class 1 was higher than Class 3, $U = 12.0$, $p = .004$; and Class 2 and Class 3 were not significantly different, $U = 44.0$, $p = .65$. The results can be summarized in terms of creativity scores as follows: Class 3 = Class 2 < Class 1.

SELF-TEST

1. c, a, b
2. $H = 9.42$, $p < .01$. The diets significantly affected the rats' latencies to leave the lighted platform.
   Group 1 vs. Group 2: $U' = 16.5$, $p > .05$. Groups 1 and 2 do not differ significantly in latency to leave the platform.
   Group 1 vs. Group 3: $U = 14$, $p > .05$. Groups 1 and 3 do not differ significantly in latency to leave the platform.
   Group 2 vs. Group 3: $U = 2.5$, $p < .01$. Group 3 had shorter latencies than Group 2.
3. $T = -11$, $p < .01$. Assetiveness training decreased the introversion score.

MATH–ALGEBRA REVIEW

1. 0.06
2. 0.51
3. 0.03
4. 29
5. 25
6. 27
7. 121
8. -130
9. 8.50
10. 7.13
11. -3.4
12. $X = 12$
13. $X = 21$
14. $X = 12$
15. $X = 2$

APPENDIX 4

GETTING STARTED USING SPSS

We believe that hands-on manipulation and calculation of numerical examples using a simple pocket calculator create an important, concrete skill foundation for initial learning and understanding of statistics. This foundation is reinforced by practice on several exercises, which are provided both in this study guide and in the textbook it accompanies. Once this foundation has been established, however, many instructors may want to introduce the solution of statistical problems using computers.

In today's research setting, statistical analysis is conducted using one or more of the statistical analysis programs or packages readily available at most universities. The SPSS Statistical Package for the Social Sciences is one of the most popular and complete of the statistical analysis programs. For this reason, we are going to introduce you to SPSS, show you some worked-out examples, and give you exercises from each chapter for computer solution. If more detailed information on using SPSS is desired, we recommend using a brief supplemental text such as *Ready, Set, Go! A Student Guide to SPSS 8.0 for Windows* by T. W. Pavkov and K. A. Pierce, 1999, Mountain View, CA: Mayfield. Although SPSS also has an extensive built-in tutorial, our experience has convinced us that the tutorial is more detailed than is desirable for a first-time user.

Preliminary Information

Versions. SPSS is an evolving product. Versions are available for mainframe computers and for PCs, and six versions of SPSS for Windows have been released. Our introduction to SPSS for Windows is based on Version 8.0. You should find that Version 7.0 and later versions perform similarly. Versions released before 7.0 have similar-appearing menus but may differ in the appearance and flexibility of their output.

Scope. Our goal here is to give you a basic introduction to SPSS. Once you get accustomed to the main features, you will find the program easy to use. However, like most computer application software, SPSS becomes easy to use *after* you learn how to use it. Many experienced users of SPSS have forgotten the feelings of confusion and frustration associated with first-time learning. We will make every effort to keep the potential problems for the neophyte in mind. Note that SPSS has many fancy features—"bells and whistles," as they're sometimes called. We will stick to basics and avoid the bells and whistles, and we suggest that anyone you get to assist you do the same.

Your computer knowledge. At this point, we need to make some assumptions about your basic computer skills. Specifically, we will assume that you are familiar with such basic computer concepts and operations as formatting a disk, naming and using files, the cursor, using a mouse, and basic Windows environment operations (e.g., starting an applications program such as a word processor, spreadsheet, or SPSS; opening a file; moving between directories; saving a file; printing a file; switching between windows). In case you are not familiar with these concepts and operations, consider using the *Ready, Set, Go!* text we mentioned earlier, working through the tutorial, and/or consulting your instructor for additional information. Also, one of the best ways to acquire the basic Windows concepts and learn operations—and SPSS concepts and operations as well—is to have someone familiar with SPSS lead you through it.

Installation of SPSS. We will also assume that SPSS is installed and available on the computer you will be using, which is often the case in university computing laboratories. If SPSS is not already installed on the computer, contact your instructor, lab monitor, or computer support personnel to determine how SPSS can be installed.

Starting an SPSS Session

Start SPSS by double clicking on the SPSS icon or program name in your Windows Desktop Start Menu. We will represent this sequence of point-and-click steps with the following convention: Start>Programs>SPSS 8.0 for Windows.

Once SPSS is started, what you see on the screen should be similar to what is shown here:

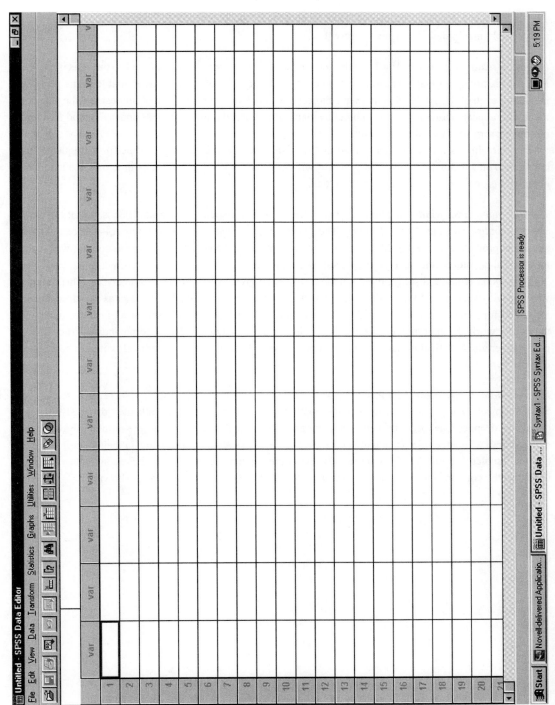

Data Editor window.

The figure shows the *Data Editor window*. The purpose of this window is to enter your data or to examine and possibly manipulate data already present.

Important features of the window. Note the second line beginning with File, Edit, and so on. This is the *Menu Bar.* At this time, you may want to take a quick, exploratory tour of the options available in the pull-down menus for each of the 10 SPSS main menu choices. Just click on the menu item of interest and the pull-down menu will appear, showing you the choices available. You should find the choices under *File* and *Edit* familiar to you from your use of other Windows applications.

The third line is a row of icons called the *Toolbar.* These icons allow you to perform frequently used commands on a menu. Several of the icons are self-explanatory. Hold the mouse pointer over the icon to find out what task can be performed by clicking on it.

The two other SPSS windows. There are two other windows associated with an SPSS session: the *Output Viewer window* and the *Syntax window.* The *Output Viewer window* displays output—the results of the statistical procedure you tell SPSS to perform for you. We will examine this window as soon as we have run a statistical procedure and have generated some output to look at.

The *Syntax window* displays the commands you have given SPSS to perform analyses. The simplified way we will work with SPSS will not require us to make extensive use of the Syntax window, but it is important for more advanced use of SPSS. (*Note:* It is important for SPSS users at all levels to understand that SPSS works by running commands written in the SPSS language. These commands instruct SPSS to perform certain statistical or data processing operations. We can cause the command syntax to be "pasted" into the Syntax window.)

Entering data. We will enter the following scores into the Data Editor: 8, 7, 6, 5, 4, 9, 11, 8, 5, 5, 8, 3, 5, 3, 5. The numbers were obtained from a crude reaction-time test that one of us calls the "dropped-ruler" test (a ruler is dropped unexpectedly between a student's thumb and forefinger, and the number above the student's thumb where the ruler is caught is his or her score). Enter the first data value in the first cell in the first column (labeled VAR00001). Press return (Enter) or the down arrow, then enter the second data value moving down the column, and so on. Once they are entered, the values should appear as shown:

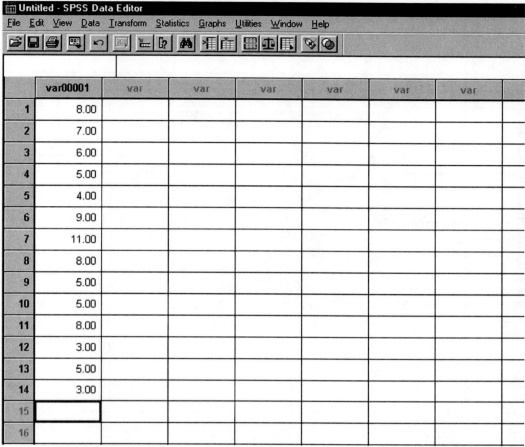

Data Editor window with data entered.

Other data can be entered in a similar manner. Note that data can also be entered into the Data Editor from preexisting data files. However, in order to keep things simple, we will not cover how to do this. *We will assume that you will be working with short examples and will be entering the data directly into the Data Editor.*

Variable names. SPSS uses default eight-character names until you change them. These variable names can consist of any letter or number but must begin with a letter. To change a variable name, double click on the existing variable name and fill in a new name in the dialog box that appears here:

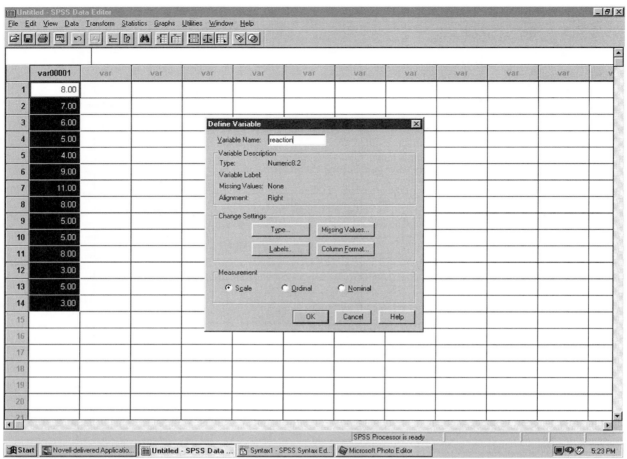

The Define Variable dialog box.

Change the first variable name to "reaction," then click OK. Repeat for other variables as necessary.

Changing settings to reveal your input. To keep our use of SPSS as simple as possible, we will recommend using the "Point-Click" method of instructing SPSS to perform the desired analysis. With this method, you will use the mouse to select various choices for your analysis and to cause the analysis to be run. The alternative to the Point-Click method is the Syntax method in which SPSS commands are pasted or typed into the Syntax Window and run to produce the desired analysis. The Syntax method allows us to see and run the commands that make SPSS work to produce output. Being familiar with how SPSS works—through syntax—is highly desirable for more advanced SPSS work but adds to the detail, so we will not emphasize it here.

No matter which method you use to produce your results—Point-Click or Syntax—errors can arise, and you will have the problem of correcting them. There is an old computer acronym—GIGO, which stands for "garbage in-garbage out"—that speaks to the problem of errors. Errors may be caused by data entry mistakes or by misinstructing SPSS on what to do. Either way, the resulting output may be incorrect. To help diagnose errors, we need to know the *input* to SPSS. This is the great shortcoming of the Point-Click method;

if you use it and find an error or an inconsistency, or are unsure about the instructions used to produce the output, you have no way of knowing the input commands that produced the output. A student comes with output in hand and asks the instructor, "Why didn't I get the right answer?" The difficulty is that there is no way to "debug" (correct) the problem unless we know the input. *For this reason and to keep you aware that commands drive SPSS, we recommend a change in base or default settings that will cause command syntax to be included in the output.* With this change, the output will show the exact commands that produced each result. If there are any problems with the answer, you will know what the input was for each result and will be able to make corrections accordingly.

Putting the syntax commands into the output. In the menu bar click Edit>Preferences>Viewer. Click the box for "Display commands in the log." The correct settings should now appear as follows:

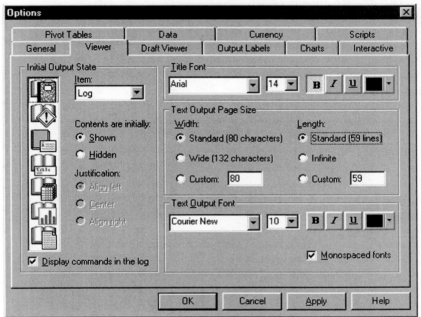

Options for Viewer (Output window) to display commands in the Output log (lower left).

Then click OK. Once this setting is saved, it will be in effect for subsequent SPSS sessions and will not need to be reset each time SPSS is started.

Running a Statistical Procedure

To run a statistical procedure in SPSS, use the Statistics items in the menu bar. Then choose the category of procedures, then the specific procedure. Fill in the dialog box and click OK. For example, suppose you want your data displayed as a frequency distribution. This process is summarized as follows: Statistics>Summarize>Frequencies. Highlight **reaction** and click the arrow to move it into the Variable(s) box. Click OK.

The Statistics and Summarize pull-down menus and the Frequencies dialog box are shown here:

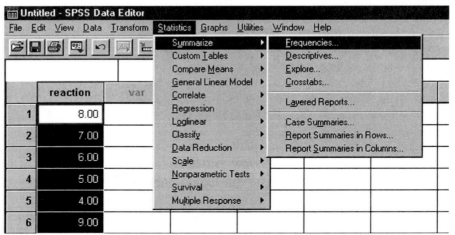

Statistics and Summarize menu choices.

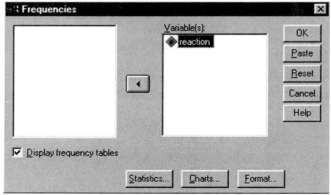

Frequencies dialog box.

The Output should appear showing the frequency distribution. For reference, the command syntax also should appear before the frequency distribution, as shown here:

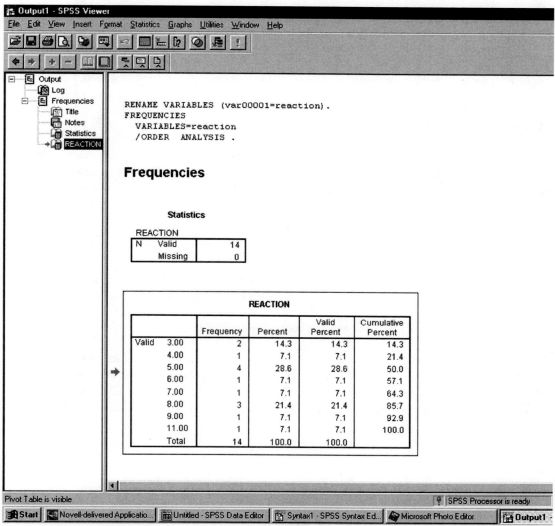

Output (SPSS Viewer) showing the frequency distribution and SPSS command syntax.

Note that the frequency distribution appears in ascending order, from the lowest score to the highest. In Chapter 3, we show you how to reverse the order, changing it to descending rather than ascending.

Printing the Output

If you would like to *print the output,* from the Output Viewer window, click File>Print (or click the printer icon in the Toolbar), just as in any other Windows application.

Switching Between Windows

To switch back to the Data Editor window, click Window>SPSS Data Editor in the menu bar. You can also switch windows by clicking the desired minimized window on the bottom row of the screen.

Computing a New Variable

Occasionally you will want to combine existing variables or to transform them to create a new variable. This new variable could also be a square root of an existing variable or the sum of several variables. To compute a new variable, you can use the Compute command found under Transform in the toolbar for the Data Editor window. Here is the sequence of steps:

1. Your data should be entered and your variables named.
2. From the Data Editor window,
      Transform>Compute.
      Enter the name for the new variable in the Target Variable box. Type the desired computation in the Numeric Expression box. You may use existing variable names, arithmetic symbols, and parentheses. >OK.
3. Switch back to the Data Editor and examine your computed variable.

Example: To create the sum of the questions from a rating scale, we have entered data for Q1, Q2, and Q3. SUMQ is the name of the new variable and is typed in the Target Variable box in the Compute Variable dialog box. In the Numeric Expression box, type Q1+Q2+Q3. Variable names can also be entered in the box by highlighting and clicking on the arrow. The Compute Variables dialog box should look as follows:

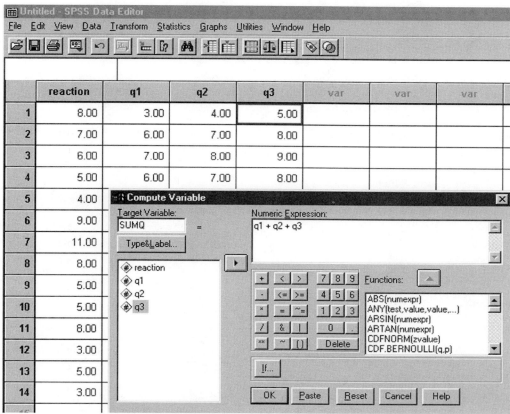

The completed Compute Variable dialog box.

Click OK and the new variable SUMQ will be calculated and will appear in the Data Editor window.

Saving and Recalling Data

To save your data file:

    File>Save as.

    Enter a filename ending in .sav (for example, EX1-1.sav) and specify the drive it should be saved to.

    >OK.

To open an existing SPSS data file:

    File>Open

    Click the file you want to open.

    >OK

You should now be ready to tackle the SPSS exercises at the end of each chapter. For further information on using SPSS, consult an SPSS user guide such as the one suggested at the beginning of this appendix.

HISTORY & GEOGRAPHY 406
THE POLAR REGIONS

Author:
Theresa K. Buskey, B.A., J.D.

Editor:
Alan Christopherson, M.S.

Assistant Editor:
Annette M. Walker, B.S.

Media Credits:
Page 3: © Ryan McVay, Digital Vision, Thinkstock; **4:** © Fuego, iStock, Thinkstock; **7:** © Joe Rainbow, iStock, Thinkstock; **9:** © MR1805, iStock, Thinkstock; **10:** © Achim BaquA, iStock, Thinkstock; **15:** © IPG Gutenberg UK Ltd, iStock, Thinkstock; **19:** © Photos.com, Thinkstock; **20:** © ad foto, iStock, Thinkstock; **23:** © nikolay100, iStock, Thinkstock; **24:** © USO, iStock, Thinkstock; **25:** © Jeff McGraw, iStock, Thinkstock; **26:** © Alby DeTweede, iStock, Thinkstock; **28:** © Maisna, iStock, Thinkstock; **29:** © ErikaMitchell, iStock, Thinkstock; **30:** © Rita Januskeviciute, iStock, Thinkstock; **31:** © Pierrette Guertin, iStock, Thinkstock; © egon faganel, iStock, Thinkstock; **32:** © Photon Photos, iStock, Thinkstock; **39:** © Nikolay Tsuguliev, iStock, Thinkstock; **41:** © MR1805, iStock, Thinkstock; **42:** © Dorling Kindersley Thinkstock; **43:** © Dorling Kindersley, Thinkstock; **44:** © Dorling Kindersley, Thinkstock; **45:** © WestWindGraphics, iStock, Thinkstock; **48:** © Antrey, iStock, Thinkstock; **49:** © Sebastian Kaulitzki, Hemera, Thinkstock; **51:** © pilipenkoD, iStock, Thinkstock; **52:** © axily, iStock, Thinkstock; **54:** © JanRoode, iStock, Thinkstock; **55:** © Australis Photography, iStock, Thinkstock.

Alpha Omega
PUBLICATIONS

804 N. 2nd Ave. E.
Rock Rapids, IA 51246-1759

THE POLAR REGIONS

In this **LIFEPAC®** you will learn about the two coldest places on earth — the polar regions. **You will learn many facts about the North Pole and the South Pole. You will learn how men explored these areas, what animals live there, and how people can survive there.**

Objectives

Read these objectives. The objectives tell you what you will be able to do when you have successfully completed this LIFEPAC. Each section will list according to the numbers below what objectives will be met in that section. When you have finished this LIFEPAC, you should be able to:

1.   Tell how the two polar regions are alike and how they are different.
2.   Describe glaciers and pack ice.
3.   Tell how icebergs are formed and why they are dangerous.
4.   Describe the land and oceans around the poles.
5.   Tell about the exploration of the polar regions.
6.   Identify and describe polar animals.
7.   Tell how Arctic people can live off their land.
8.   Tell how the polar regions are used today.

1. THE POLAR REGIONS: COLDEST PLACES IN THE WORLD

The two polar regions, the Arctic and Antarctic, are alike in many ways. The way they are most alike is that both have huge areas of year-round ice. The ice is the first thing you would notice about the poles if you saw them from outer space.

Objectives

Review these objectives. When you have completed this section, you should be able to:

1. Tell how the two polar regions are alike and how they are different.
2. Describe glaciers and pack ice.
3. Tell how icebergs are formed and why they are dangerous.
4. Describe the land and oceans around the poles.

Vocabulary

Study these new words. Learning the meanings of these words is a good study habit and will improve your understanding of this LIFEPAC.

floe (flō). A sheet of floating ice.

glacier (glā′ shər). A large mass of ice created by packed snow.

iceberg (īs′ berg′). A large mass of ice floating in the sea.

polar region (pō′ lər rē′ jən). The area near the North or South Pole.

radar (ra′ där). Instrument used for telling the distance and direction of unseen objects.

region (re′ jən). Any large part of the earth's surface.

Note: *All vocabulary words in this LIFEPAC appear in* **boldface** *print the first time they are used. If you are unsure of the meaning when you are reading, study the definitions given.*

Pronunciation Key: hat, āge, cãre, fär; let, ēqual, tėrm; it, īce; hot, ōpen, ôrder; oil; out; cup, pu̇t, rüle; child; long; thin; /ᵺ/ for then; /zh/ for measure; /u/ or /ə/ represents /a/ in about, /e/ in taken, /i/ in pencil, /o/ in lemon, and /u/ in circus.

The Polar Regions

Look at the globe in your classroom. Put your finger on the North Pole. All around the North Pole is water — the Arctic Ocean. Along the coast of the Arctic Ocean are the continents of North America, Europe, and Asia.

Through the northern part of these continents, a circle is marked on the globe. This line marks what is called the Arctic Circle. Find it on the map of the Northern Hemisphere.

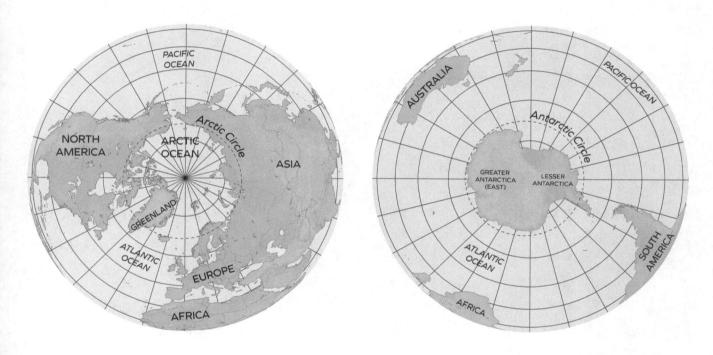

| Northern Hemisphere | Southern Hemisphere

Now look at the bottom of your globe. At the South Pole you will see a large piece of land. This is the continent of Antarctica, which is surrounded by oceans. The Atlantic, Pacific, and the Indian Oceans all flow together at the bottom of the earth. There is another circle around the continent of Antarctica. This line marks what is called the Antarctic Circle. Find it on the map of the Southern Hemisphere.

The top region of the world is an icy ocean. The bottom region of the world is an ice-covered piece of land. The two areas are alike in many ways. But God never makes any two things or places exactly the same, and the Arctic and Antarctic are different, too.

Complete this activity.

1.1 Write the names of the places marked on the globe.

a. _____

b. _____

c. _____

d. _____

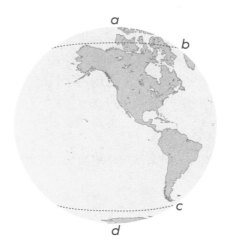

Our earth orbits (circles) the sun once a year. As it moves around the sun, the North Pole is always tilted toward the North Star. In summer the North Pole leans toward the sun. Inside the Arctic Circle, the sun can be seen all day and all night at least once a summer. The sun does not heat up the Arctic Circle ice because the sun's rays hit the earth at a slant. When you are closer to the North Pole, you will more often see the sun shining at midnight. If you were at the North Pole, you would see the midnight sun for six months! As you move south from the North Pole toward the Arctic Circle, the midnight sun is seen for fewer nights. Right on the Arctic Circle the sun shines all night only once a year (June 21).

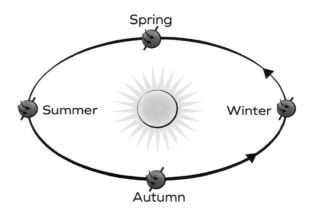

| Seasons in the Northern Hemisphere

South of the equator, seasons are exactly opposite to those north of the equator. When the North Pole has summer, the South Pole has winter. There are six months of darkness at the bottom of the world while the North Pole has sunshine day and night. The long days of darkness and light are one way that the Arctic and Antarctic are alike.

Another way the two polar regions are alike is very surprising. Neither area gets very much rain or snow! It is so cold at the poles that the air cannot hold much moisture.

Without moisture in the air, there cannot be much rain or snow. The two poles are dry enough to be called deserts. When it does snow, it never melts at the poles and will not melt for months on the edges of the polar regions. So, while there is often snow there; it is still unusual to see new-falling snow.

| Northern Lights (Aurora Borealis)

There are some very beautiful and unusual lights that can be seen during the polar nights in both the Arctic and Antarctic regions. They are called the Northern Lights (Aurora Borealis) or the Southern Lights (Aurora Australis). They shine like long, wavy strips across the dark sky. They can be dim or bright. They shine in many different colors. Sometimes they are unusually bright and can be seen far to the south of the Arctic.

The lights are caused by the sun and the earth together. Tiny pieces of the sun hit the earth all the time. Most of the time we cannot see these pieces; but sometimes, near the poles, the pieces light up as they hit the air around our earth. They do that because near the poles, the earth acts like the end of a magnet. A compass will point at the North or South Magnetic Pole from anywhere in the same hemisphere. This *magnetic field* makes the pieces of the sun light up. That way God allows people in the long polar darkness to see beautiful lights.

Complete these statements.

1.2   When the North Pole has summer, the South Pole has _____ .

1.3   In summer you can see the _____ at night in the Arctic region.

1.4   The sun doesn't heat up the polar lands because the sun's rays are

_____ .

1.5   The sun can be seen all day and night at least once during the summer inside

the _____ .

1.6   The beautiful lights seen during the polar darkness are called the

_____ in the Arctic.

1.7   The place where compasses point in the Antarctic is called the

_____ .

1.8   The poles are dry enough to be called _____ .

Ice and Icebergs

The first thing anyone would notice about the poles is that they are covered with ice all year around. Even with the sun shining all the time in the summer, it never gets warm enough to melt the ice at the poles. The ice may melt on the edge of the polar regions, but not in the center.

The ice on the edges changes through the year. As winter nears, more of the ocean freezes solid, making the polar "land" bigger. This same ice melts in the summer, and the area of solid ice gets smaller. From outer space it looks as if the poles grow and shrink each year!

This frozen ocean water is called *pack ice*. It freezes and is "packed" together by the wind and currents to form a large solid piece. Sometimes the waves and currents will cause cracks of water called *leads* to open up in the ice. Leads may not stay open very long, so ships that try to sail up a lead may suddenly be trapped if the ice moves. If pack ice stays frozen for a whole year, the salt in it seeps out. That means people can melt it and use it to drink.

The ice helps keep it cold at the poles. Ice reflects sunlight just like a mirror. That means the sunlight does not stay to make things warmer and melt the ice. The ice also makes it very bright for people who go there. They must wear sunglasses or a mask to protect their eyes. If they do not, they can get "snow blindness." That happens when a person's eyes are hurt by the brightness, so they cannot see.

When ice sheets cover a whole land, they are called continental **glaciers**. Glaciers are not, however, created of frozen sea water. The ice in these glaciers started as snow. Polar regions do not have much snow falling each year, but the snow that does fall never melts. It is packed down and forms thick ice. These continental glaciers often hide the land, so ice is all that people can see there. Other glaciers, called valley glaciers, only fill up valleys in cold areas, while nearby land is ice-free.

The icy glaciers are very heavy. Their weight causes them to move slowly downhill toward the ocean. The ice on a glacier often cracks or breaks as it moves. These cracks form deep holes called crevasses (kre vas'ez). They can be covered with a thin layer of snow or ice, so people cannot see them. Many polar explorers died when they fell into crevasses they did not see in time.

Over a long time, many glaciers will move into the ocean. The water and the waves hitting the glacier will cause pieces of the ice to break off. When a big piece breaks off, it is called calving. A huge piece of ice that calves off a glacier becomes an **iceberg**, a floating island of ice. Some can be the size of a city! Around Antarctica people often find icebergs that are 10 miles long! Icebergs will slowly melt in the water, like an ice cube. Sometimes they break apart into smaller pieces called ice **floes**.

Occasionally, ocean currents carry the icebergs into warmer waters. Only a small part of an iceberg shows above water. The part below the surface is many times larger than the part above. This makes icebergs very dangerous to ships which may get too close and hit the part underwater. Before **radar** was used, icebergs caused many shipwrecks.

The most famous iceberg accident happened in April of 1912. A new passenger ship named the *Titanic* had been built in Great Britain. It was one of the largest and most beautiful ships ever built. It had ball courts, a swimming pool, and a palm garden.

| The *Titanic* hit an iceberg.

| An iceberg

Enough rooms were available for two thousand, five hundred passengers. The builders believed the ship was unsinkable.

The ship sailed proudly from its British port across the Atlantic Ocean. Close to midnight on April 15, the cruiser came to a halt with a loud crash! The jagged point of an iceberg had torn a long hole down the side of the *Titanic*. The ship began to sink.

The ship owners were so sure the ship could not sink that they did not provide enough lifeboats for all the passengers. Only about 700 people of 2,200 were able to escape on the boats. Most of those were women and children. Because of that accident, ships now always carry enough lifeboats for all their passengers, and no one ever assumes a ship to be unsinkable!

For each statement put an *I* if it describes an iceberg, a *P* if it describes pack ice, or a *G* if it describes a glacier.

1.9 _____ caused the wreck of the *Titanic*

1.10 _____ created by packed down snow that never melts

1.11 _____ frozen sea water

1.12 _____ makes the poles look like they grow and shrink every year

1.13 _____ flows slowly downhill to the ocean

1.14 _____ many around Antarctica can be 10 miles long

1.15 _____ cracks form called leads with open water in them

1.16 _____ only a small part is above the water

1.17 _____ dangerous, deep holes called crevasses may be difficult to see

Answer *true* or *false*.

1.18 _____ Ice reflects sunlight like a mirror.

1.19 _____ Ice at the poles melts every summer.

1.20 _____ When a piece of a glacier breaks off to form an iceberg, it is called division.

1.21 _____ Pack ice stays salty all the time it is frozen.

Review the material in this section to prepare for the Self Test. The Self Test will check your understanding of this section. Any items you miss on this test will show you what areas you will need to restudy in order to prepare for the unit test.

SELF TEST 1

Match these items (2 points each answer).

1.01	_____ pack ice	a.	North Pole region
1.02	_____ icebergs	b.	South Pole region
1.03	_____ glacier	c.	frozen sea water
1.04	_____ Arctic	d.	snow packed down into ice
1.05	_____ Antarctic	e.	ice islands

Complete these statements (4 points each answer).

1.06 The area where the sun shines at least once all day and all night in June is

called the _____ .

1.07 The North Pole is on an ocean; the South Pole is on _____ .

1.08 The bright, wavy lights seen in Antarctica during the darkness are called the

_____ .

1.09 The place where a compass points to is called either the North or South

_____ Pole.

1.010 Both the South and North Poles are covered all year by _____ .

Write the correct letter in the blank (4 points each answer).

1.011 During summer at the South Pole, the season at the North Pole is _____ .
  a. fall   b. spring   c. winter

1.012 Ships now use _____ to warn them of icebergs.
  a. lights   b. radar   c. guns

1.013 Antarctica is a(n) _____ .
  a. island   b. continent   c. glacier

1.014 A crack of open water in the pack ice is called a _____ .
  a. crevasse   b. calf   c. lead

1.015 Glaciers move _____ .

    a. downhill   b. not at all   c. toward the sun

1.016 Many polar explorers died when they fell into a _____ they did not see on a glacier.

    a. crevasse   b. calf   c. lead

1.017 The poles look as if they get bigger and smaller each year because of _____ .

    a. icebergs   b. glaciers   c. pack ice

1.018 Smaller packs of ice are called _____ .

    a. floes   b. glaciers   c. icebergs

1.019 The *Titanic* sank after hitting _____ .

    a. pack ice   b. an iceberg   c. Antarctica

1.020 The sun does not heat up the polar regions because the rays hit the earth _____ .

    a. too slowly   b. too quickly   c. at a slant

Answer *true* or *false* (2 points each answer).

1.021 _____ Icebergs can be as big as a city.

1.022 _____ Antarctica is surrounded by oceans.

1.023 _____ There is no land in the Arctic Circle.

1.024 _____ Most of an iceberg is under the surface of the water.

1.025 _____ There are six months of darkness at the equator each winter.

Answer these questions (5 points each answer).

1.026 Why did the *Titanic* not have enough lifeboats?

_____

_____

_____

1.027   Why does the sun not set at the North Pole in the summer?

_____

_____

_____

1.028   In what ways are the North Pole and the South Pole alike?

_____

_____

_____

_____

_____

_____

1.029   How are icebergs formed?

_____

_____

_____

✓	**Teacher check:**	Initials	_____	80
	Score _____	Date _____		100

2. THE ARCTIC POLAR REGION: TOP OF THE WORLD

The North Pole is not on land as is the South Pole; but the Arctic region is much easier for people to reach than the Antarctic. That is because the northern edges of North America, Asia, and Europe all reach the Arctic Circle. People could just walk up there. In fact, people live within the Arctic Circle and have for thousands of years.

Reaching the North Pole was difficult, however. A person had to cross miles and miles of frozen ocean with no plants or animals for food, so the people who live in the Arctic did not go to the Pole. Instead, the first man to the North Pole was an explorer who carefully planned an expedition there.

Objectives

Review these objectives. When you have completed this section, you should be able to:

1. Tell how the two polar regions are alike and how they differ.
4. Describe the land and oceans around the poles.
5. Tell about the exploration of the polar regions.
6. Identify and describe polar animals.
7. Tell how Arctic people can live off their land.
8. Tell how the polar regions are used today.

Vocabulary

Study these new words. Learning the meanings of these words is a good study habit and will improve your understanding of this LIFEPAC.

ancient (ān' shənt). Belonging to times long past.

antler (ant' lər). Branched horn of a deer or deer-like animal.

blubber (blub' ər). The fat of whales and some other sea animals.

cache (kash). A hole or hiding place used for storing supplies and other necessary things in the wilderness.

harpoon (här pün'). A spear with a rope tied to it, used for catching whales and seals.

icebreaker (īs' brā kər). A strong boat used to break a channel through ice.

kayak (kī' ak). An Eskimo canoe made of skins stretched over a frame, with a hole in the middle where the user sits.

lichen (lī' kən). A plant that grows on rocks or tree trunks; grows in flat patches and looks somewhat like moss.

migration (mī gra' shən). A move from one place to another.

petroleum (pə trō' lē əm). An oily, dark-colored liquid that is found in the earth; gasoline, kerosene, and many other products are made from it.

predator (pred' i tər). An animal that lives by killing and eating other animals.

prey (prā). An animal hunted for food.

relative (rel' ə tiv). Belonging to the same family.

sinew (sin' yü). A tough, stringy part of the body that fastens muscles to the bones.

soapstone (sōp' stōn). A soft rock that feels soapy or oily when touched.

sod (sod). A layer of ground containing grass and its roots.

Pronunciation Key: hat, āge, cãre, fär; let, ēqual, tėrm; it, īce; hot, ōpen, ôrder; oil; out; cup, pu̇t, rüle; child; long; thin; /ŦH/ for then; /zh/ for measure; /u/ or /ə/ represents /a/ in about, /e/ in taken, /i/ in pencil, /o/ in lemon, and /u/ in circus.

Exploring the Arctic

The first European to explore the Arctic was a man from **ancient** Greece. He sailed north of Scotland 300 years before Jesus was born! He found an Arctic island there and wrote about it, but no one believed him. They were sure that there was only ice in the north!

Most of the Europeans did not learn about the Arctic until the Age of Exploration, 1,800 years later. At that time, the people of Europe explored much of the world while trying to get to China because they could make so much money trading with that country. America was in their way if they sailed west from Europe to reach China. They tried to find the "Northwest Passage," a way around America to the north, and learned about the Arctic as they searched.

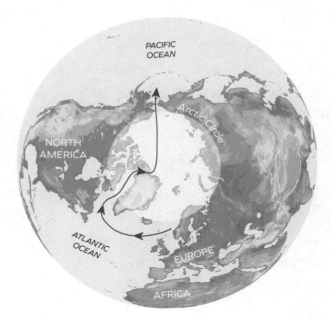

| Northwest Passage

The explorers spent many years sailing along the coast of northern Canada to find a way around the continent. The pack ice made it dangerous because the ice could put holes in or crush their wooden sailing ships. In spite of the dangers, the explorers made many important discoveries. Very often new places were named for the man who found them. It is an old custom that the leader of an expedition can name any new land, rivers, or bays he finds.

One famous explorer was Henry Hudson. He made four different trips to North America between 1607 and 1611. He sailed further north than any other explorer in 1607 when he reached a group of islands that are about even with the top of Greenland. He was forced to turn back by the ice.

On later voyages, he found Hudson Straight between Baffin Island and Canada. He also discovered Hudson Bay, the largest bay in North America. Can you find it on the map above? (Check another map if you need help.) Hudson never did find the Northwest Passage.

When the explorer found Hudson Bay in 1610, his ship was trapped by the ice and had to stay all winter. In the spring, Hudson wanted to continue, but his men refused. They left Hudson, his son, and a few other men behind in a small boat to die and sailed back to Europe. Hudson was never seen again.

Many men tried, and failed, to find the Northwest Passage. Many died. One of the most famous failures was led by Sir John Franklin of England. His well-equipped expedition sailed in 1845 and disappeared! The many ships that went searching for him learned a great deal about the Arctic region. One of these search parties was led by Sir Robert McClure in 1850. His ship was stopped by the ice in the Northwest Passage, but he and his men crossed the rest of the way walking on the ice. They were the first to cross the Passage.

However, the first ship to sail through the Northwest Passage was the *Gjöa* of Norway. That expedition was led by Roald Amundsen of Norway. It did not happen until 1906, three hundred years after Henry Hudson tried! The Northwest Passage was just too dangerous for regular trade and travel, but exploring it taught us a great deal about the North American Arctic.

Match the names.

2.1 _____ Henry Hudson

2.2 _____ John Franklin

2.3 _____ Robert McClure

2.4 _____ Roald Amundsen

a. his expedition disappeared in 1845

b. made four trips looking for the Passage in the 1600s

c. first man to sail through the Passage

d. first to cross the Passage; part by ship, part on foot

Complete these statements.

2.5 The first European known to have explored the Arctic came from ancient

_____ .

2.6 The largest bay in North America is named for _____ .

2.7 Expeditions searched the northern shores of Canada for the

_____ , a way around America.

2.8   The first ship sailed around America to the north in _____ .

2.9   The main danger to the wooden ships of the early Arctic explorers was the

_____ .

Robert E. Peary was a famous American Arctic explorer. He was an officer in the U.S. Navy when he became interested in the Arctic. In 1891, he led an expedition to northern Greenland proving it was an island. He made three more trips into the region to try to reach the North Pole. Each time he got a little further north before he had to turn back. He finally made it on the third trip in 1909.

| Robert Peary

Peary's expedition to the North Pole started from Ellesmere Island, north of Canada. They traveled using Eskimo dogs to pull their supplies on sleds. The harsh trip forced most of his men to turn back. Eventually, however, Peary, Matthew Henson (his African-American assistant), and four Eskimos reached the pole. They brought back carefully recorded notes of what they saw and did. These notes were very important. Another man claimed to have gotten to the pole a year before Peary, but he had no proof. An investigation proved that Peary had indeed been there first. Peary recorded many facts that only someone who had been to the North Pole would know.

The first man to fly an airplane over the North Pole was also an American. Richard E. Byrd was a navy man, too, who eventually became a rear admiral. He began commanding airplane flights in the Arctic in 1925. The next year, he and Floyd Bennett became the first men to fly over the North Pole. Byrd then switched his attention to the South Pole and worked to explore that unknown continent for the rest of his life.

The *U.S.S. Nautilus* reached the North Pole in 1958. It was the first ship to do so, and it only made it by going <u>under</u> the ice. The *Nautilus* was a submarine. One last "first" for the North Pole was in 1978. In that year, Naomi Uemura of Japan became the first man to reach the pole alone by dogsled.

| A dogsled team

 Answer these questions.

2.10   Who were the first men to reach the North Pole?

_____

_____

2.11   What was the name of the first ship to reach the North Pole, and what was unusual about that trip?_____

_____

2.12   Why were Robert Peary's notes from his trip to the North Pole so important?

_____

_____

_____

2.13   Who were the first men to fly over the North Pole?

_____

2.14   What did Peary prove about Greenland on his expedition there in 1891?

_____

2.15   How did Robert Peary and Naomi Uemura carry their supplies to the North Pole? _____

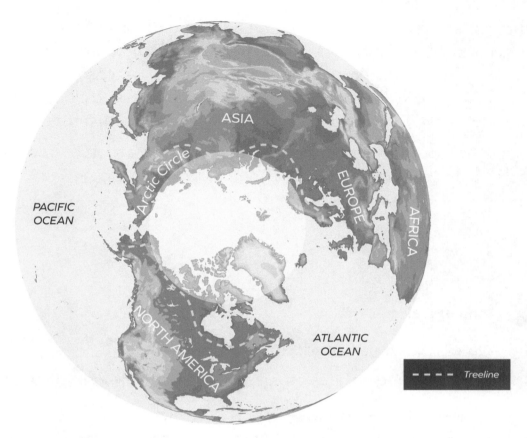

| The Arctic Circle with the treeline.
It is more difficult for things to grow beyond the treeline.

The Arctic Region

The Arctic includes the cold area around the North Pole and the Arctic Ocean. The Arctic region is larger than just the Arctic Circle. Most scientists call the area north of the treeline Arctic. Trees will not grow when the temperatures get too cold. The forests of the continents stop when they get too far north or too high up a mountain. (It gets colder as you go higher in altitude, too.) The place where the trees stop is called the *treeline*.

The area north of the treeline is not an empty ice field. In fact, the only ice-covered land is central Greenland, which is covered year-round by a continental glacier. The land of the Arctic is around the edges of the Arctic Circle and is usually covered with tundra. A tundra is a cold, almost treeless plain covered with moss and grass-like plants called *sedges*.

Tundras do not get very much rain or snow. However, they are very wet in the summertime because, three feet or so below the surface, the ground is always frozen. This *permafrost* is a layer of ice with the hardness of stone that keeps water from soaking into the earth beneath it. Permafrost can be thousands of feet thick. In the summer the ground on top thaws out when the sun shines and the snow that did fall melts. But the melted snow cannot drain into the ground; it just soaks the topsoil. It would be like pouring a bucket of water on a rug laid on a concrete floor. There is no place for the water to go, except to form lakes and puddles on top of the ground until it freezes again or dries up.

Winter on the tundra is long and harsh. The summers are short and cool. In spite of this, God has created special plants and animals that can live and grow there.

Map exercises.

2.16 What is the name of the largest Arctic island? _____

2.17 Is the Arctic region bigger than or smaller than the inside of the Arctic Circle?
_____

2.18 Name the three continents that touch the Arctic Circle.
_____

Complete each statement.

2.19 The frozen ground underneath the Arctic soil is called
_____ .

2.20 The treeless plains of the Arctic are called _____ .

2.21 The summer soil on the tundra is very _____ .

2.22 The place where the forest stops because of the cold is called the
_____ .

2.23 Greenland is covered by a _____ .

Plant Life

In some parts of the Arctic the ground is covered with bright-colored flowers during the short summer. These little plants have very short stems. They must stay close to the ground, because the earth is warmer than the biting winds that blow above it. Even some rocks have plants growing on them. These rock plants are called **lichens**. Lichens will grow right on the bare rocks.

| Moss growing on a rock

Yellow reindeer moss is really a lichen. It grows slowly, but often grows over six inches (15 cm) tall. It is spongy and full of water. This plant is the summer food for reindeer.

Trees are seldom seen on the tundra. Only in the protected valleys or along riverbanks are small trees able to grow. Rivers come into the Arctic from the warmer south. The places along their banks are a little bit warmer than the rest of the tundra. This means trees can grow there. Otherwise only a few clusters of bushes grow sparingly. Berries are the only fruit that grows in the Arctic.

Each summer the ice and snow will melt, allowing the animals to find food and the plants to flower. The moisture from the snow stays toward the top of the ground's surface. Plant roots can use it for their growth. Even so, in many places the soil is too poor for plant growth. Less than half of the tundra has plants growing on it.

Answer *true* or *false*.

2.24 _____ Trees never grow anywhere on the tundra.

2.25 _____ Berries are the only fruit that grows on the tundra.

2.26 _____ Lichens are plants that grow on rocks.

2.27 _____ Flowers cannot bloom on the tundra.

2.28 _____ Plant roots draw water from deep underground on the tundra.

Animal Life

The polar bear is the king of Arctic animals. It is the world's largest meat-eating land animal. Polar bears were perfectly designed to hunt seals out on the ice. They are excellent swimmers, and the coldest water does not bother them. They just jump into any leads that open in the pack ice and swim across. They are quiet enough to sneak up on a sleeping seal and strong enough to kill it with one blow. They have a very strong sense of smell, which they use to find **prey** out on the ice.

| Polar bears playing

Polar bears live most of their lives out on the pack ice. Males go to the land only when the ice is gone. The females, however, will dig themselves into a den of snow on land for the winter. There, the mother bears have their cubs, usually twins.

Bears will eat fish, birds' eggs, seaweed, and dead whales, but they would rather have a meal of seal or walrus. The Arctic fox will often trail the bears onto the ice to eat their leftover food. The fox also eats rabbits, lemmings, and voles.

The lemmings and voles are the rats and mice of the Arctic. The lemmings have very short tails. They live underground in summer. Because the topsoil freezes in the winter, they cannot burrow underground then, so they live under the snow during the colder months. They eat plants and roots. If they find plenty of food, they will have extra large families that year.

In a year with plenty of food, millions of lemmings will be roaming the tundra. The owls and foxes have more food than they can eat. They will have extra babies in the years when there are so many lemmings. However, the tundra does not have enough food for millions of lemmings. They rush across the tundra looking for food. They are eaten by **predators** or starve to death. Some try to swim across lakes or rivers and drown. The few that remain continue to have families, and in a few years the Arctic will experience another lemming boom.

Caribou (kar' i bü) and their **relative**, the reindeer, are grass-eating deer of the Arctic. The caribou are now found mostly in North America. They are larger than reindeer. Caribou live well on the tundra in the Arctic summer. Large herds feed on the grass and lichens. When fall comes, they move south to winter feeding grounds. They dig through the snow with their sharp hoofs for food. Their hollow fur creates a cushion of air around them that helps them to stay warm. In the spring they return north to the summer pastures, where their calves are born. An hour or so after being born, the calves are able to follow the herd toward the Arctic Ocean.

| Caribou

Most of the world's reindeer live in Europe and Asia. Some of these reindeer are not wild. They have been tamed by herdsmen who protect them from wolves and lead the **migrations** each spring and fall. In the spring the herdsmen lead the reindeer north to the Arctic Ocean. The calves are born on the journey and soon follow their mothers northward. During the days of the midnight sun, the reindeer graze on the tundra plants. When the ground freezes over, they move south again. In winter pastures the reindeer dig out moss to eat through drifts of snow three feet (1 meter) deep.

The greatest enemy of the reindeer and caribou is the wolf. Wolves kill because they are hungry. They hunt in packs and look for herds of caribou or reindeer. They try to find deer that are weak or sick. They use teamwork to chase the animal until it is too weak to fight.

The biggest animal on the tundra is the musk ox, which looks like a shaggy buffalo. They eat twigs and grass. Their huge feet paw through the snow to reach food in winter. Musk oxen have long, thick fur to keep them warm. They also have a soft underfur that makes some of the best wool in the world. Some people have begun to keep herds of musk oxen for their wool.

When musk oxen are in danger, they form a circle around their calves. The bigger oxen face out. Their heads are lowered, and their horns are ready to fight. This is a very good way to fight wolves, but a very poor way to fight men with rifles. The Arctic oxen almost disappeared as hunters killed them off in the 1800s. Today they are starting to recover and are found in Greenland and North America.

In summer, many birds visit the Arctic. Most of them are water birds, such as geese, ducks, swans, loons, and Arctic terns. Flying in for the summer, they raise their young and return south for the winter. The snowy owl and the ptarmigan (tär' me gen) stay all year. God has provided protection for these birds against their enemies. The color of the snowy owl matches the snow. The ptarmigan's summer feathers change to white when it gets colder and it, too, matches the snow.

| Musk oxen

The smallest animals of the Arctic are the flies and the mosquitoes. Mosquitoes and black flies love the wet summer tundra. Thick swarms of large, hungry bugs bite both men and animals. The reindeer try to escape the mosquitoes by running to higher pastures, but the only real help comes with the snow and cold, when the pesky swarms die off for another season.

Complete this activity. Study the following list of Arctic animals. After each animal's name, write a food the animal likes to eat.

2.29

a. polar bear _____   b. Arctic fox _____

c. lemming _____   d. vole _____

e. owl _____   f. caribou _____

g. reindeer _____   h. wolf _____

i. musk ox _____

Complete each statement.

2.30 Two all-year-round birds of the Arctic are the a. _____

and the b. _____ .

2.31 Three feathered visitors during the summer are _____ ,

_____ , and _____ .

2.32 The world's largest land meat-eater is the _____ .

2.33 Every few years on the tundra there is an abundance of food and millions of

_____ cover the land.

Complete these activities.

2.34 The following puzzle is a jumble of letters called a **BRAIN GAME**. You may read up and down, forward and backward, or crisscross at an angle to find the names of Arctic animals. Circle the names you can find.

bear	caribou	fox	hare
lemming	mosquito	musk ox	owl
ptarmigan	reindeer	seal	vole
walrus	wolf	wolverine	

P	T	A	R	M	I	G	A	N	E
C	R	R	E	E	D	N	I	E	R
A	W	O	L	F	P	U	N	R	A
X	A	X	R	E	I	I	N	D	H
O	L	O	C	A	R	I	B	O	U
K	R	F	X	E	N	B	P	Q	V
S	U	Z	V	O	L	E	E	S	L
U	S	L	W	O	M	S	E	A	L
M	O	S	Q	U	I	T	O	B	R
W	G	L	E	M	M	I	N	G	G

2.35   Choose an animal of the Arctic, and look it up online or in an encyclopedia. Write a report about this animal. Draw a picture to go with your report.

✓ **Teacher check:**

Initials _____   Date _____

Human Life

One of the surprises of the Arctic is that many people live there. Some people have lived there for thousands of years. Eskimo and Lapp people lived in the Arctic long before electric heaters, snowmobiles, and modern houses. You will learn about how these clever people survived the Arctic and how they live today.

The Lapps. In an extremely northern part of Europe you will find a place called Lapland. It is not a country, but parts of four countries. The people who live there are called Lapps by outsiders. They call themselves *Sami*.

The Lapps of these four countries lived there long before the countries of Norway, Sweden, Finland, and Russia were created. There were several kinds of Lapp people. Some lived by the ocean and lived mostly on fish. Another group lived along the warmer rivers. These people did a little farming, hunting, and fishing to live. But the best known of the Lapp people were the nomads who raised reindeer.

The Lapps survived in their harsh homeland by domesticating the reindeer God created to live in the Arctic. The Lapps

| Reindeer

were able to get everything they needed from the deer. They ate mostly meat, milk, and cheese. Their clothes were made from reindeer skins and wool. Their tents were also made from deer skins. They are known for the beautifully decorated woolen clothing they made.

The Lapps protected the herds, moving with them as they migrated from summer to winter pastures. They used trained reindeer to pull sleds carrying their supplies. During the winter, the herds moved south of the treeline. The Lapps would live nearby in homes made of logs or **sod**.

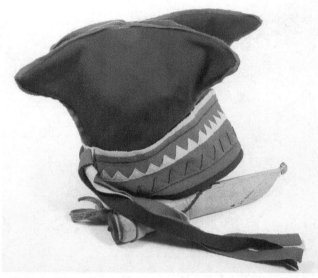

| Blue four winds hat and knife from Lapland

The Lapps were very careful not to waste anything they got from the reindeer. Milk was taken from the reindeer to drink or make cheese. Meat was taken for food. The blood was frozen in chunks and used for soup and pancakes. Knives and belt buckles were carved from the bones and **antlers**. The **sinews** were used as sewing thread. Cleaned-out stomachs were used to carry milk or cheese. Every part of a dead reindeer was used.

Winter clothing was made from layers of deer skin. The inside layer would be worn with the fur facing in toward the person's skin. The second layer was worn with the fur facing out. Boots were also made of fur, lined with grass that had been gathered during the short summer. Every evening the grass would be taken out and dried by the fire, so it would be ready to use again the next day. Thus, a Lapp could be warm and comfortable in even the coldest weather.

Lapps today. Today only a few of the Lapp people still follow the herds. Those few use modern tools on their ancient migration. They use snowmobiles to herd the reindeer and rifles to kill the wolves that chase them. Even helicopters and radios are used to locate and move the reindeer.

Most of the Lapp people now live on small farms in one of the four nations of Lapland. They raise crops and animals, including a few reindeer, to meet their needs. The sale of reindeer meat is an important source of income for the Lapp people.

Complete the following.

2.36 List four parts of a reindeer and how the Lapps use it.

a. _____   _____

b. _____   _____

c. _____   _____

d. _____   _____

2.37 What are the four countries of Lapland?

_____

2.38 What do the Lapp people call themselves? _____ .

2.39 How did Lapps move their supplies from place to place?

_____

2.40 What modern things do the Lapps use when they herd reindeer today?

_____

Eskimos. Eskimos are Arctic people who live in Russia, Canada, Alaska, and Greenland. They were called Eskimos by other Native American people who lived south of them. The name means "eaters of raw meat." Eskimos call themselves *Inuit*, (in' yü et) which simply means "people" in their language.

| Igloos

The Eskimos did eat raw meat. However, there was a reason. They had no wood to burn for fires. The little bit of wood they found was too important to burn. It had to be used for other things. The only fire they had was **blubber** lamps. These burned low and gave off only a little heat. It took a long time to cook a meal over one. So, the Eskimos often ate their meat without cooking it.

HISTORY & GEOGRAPHY 406

LIFEPAC TEST

NAME _____

DATE _____

SCORE _____

$$\frac{80}{100}$$

HISTORY & GEOGRAPHY 406: LIFEPAC TEST

Write an _N_ in the blank if the statement or thing is from the North Pole region and an _S_ if it is from the South Pole region (2 points each answer).

1. _____ Arctic

2. _____ Antarctic

3. _____ polar bears

4. _____ penguins

5. _____ Amundsen-Scott

6. _____ people have homes there

7. _____ colder area because of higher altitude and being on land

8. _____ _Terra Australis Incognita_

9. _____ Robert Peary was the first to the pole.

10. _____ was not fully explored until about 1958

Match these items (2 points each answer).

11. _____ musk ox
12. _____ whale
13. _____ lemming
14. _____ snowy owl
15. _____ polar bear
16. _____ penguin
17. _____ caribou
18. _____ lichen
19. _____ tundra
20. _____ mosquito

a. hunted by the Eskimo with sealskin floats on harpoons

b. treeless plains of the Arctic

c. plant that grows on rocks

d. mice of the Arctic

e. bird that lives year-round in the Arctic

f. swarms attack animals and people in the Arctic summer

g. swimming bird that cannot fly

h. made to hunt seals on the ice

i. grass-eating deer of the Arctic

j. protect themselves by forming a circle with the calves in the middle

Put the correct answer in the blank (4 points each answer).

21. The wavy lights that can be seen in the darkness of the Arctic are called the _____ .

22. The Inuit who live in North America were called "eaters of raw flesh," or _____ , by other Native Americans.

23. James Cook was sent to explore the southern ocean in 1772 and his ship became the first to cross the _____ .

24. When it is summer at the North Pole, it is _____ at the South.

25. The nomadic reindeer herders of northern Europe are called the _____ .

26. The man who made four trips to the Arctic to find the Northwest Passage and instead found North America's largest bay was _____ .

27. The hardest part of spending the winter in Antarctica was _____ .

28. Antarctica and Greenland are covered by _____ .

29. Leads are cracks of open water that form in the _____ , the frozen sea water around the poles.

30. In the Southern Hemisphere, a compass will point at the _____

_____ .

Circle the correct answer (2 points each answer).

31. Men hunted (whales, musk oxen, seals) around Antarctica for their valuable fur.

32. The first ship to reach the North Pole was a submarine called the (*Nautilus*, *Titanic*, *Franklin*).

33. Before the invention of the snowmobile, most successful expeditions and the Eskimos used (reindeer, horses, dogs) to pull supply sleds.

34. Huge islands of ice that calve off of glaciers are called (floes, icebergs, crevasses).

35. Both of the polar regions can be called (rain forests, deserts, continental glaciers).

36. The ice on a glacier comes from (layers of frozen rain, frozen lakes and oceans, packed snow).

37. The first man to sail through the Northwest Passage was (Robert Peary, James Cook, Roald Amundsen).

38. The first man to fly over both the North and South Poles was (Richard Byrd, Robert Scott, Ernest Shackleton).

39. Glaciers (melt in the summer, move downhill, stay in one place and grow bigger each year).

40. The first successful expedition to the South Pole traveled (east, west, south) across the Ross Ice Shelf.

Eskimos were also nomads, but they did not domesticate any animals except dogs, which they used to pull their sleds and help with the hunting. They were hunter/gatherers, living off whatever they found or killed. Like the Lapps, they were very careful to make good use of every part of the animals they killed.

Eskimos lived in tents made of animal skins during the summer. In the winter they lived in sod houses or houses made of snow. We call the snow houses *igloos*, but to the Eskimos, that word meant any home. They could build an igloo out of snow bricks in

| Snow shoes

just a couple of hours. Snow is full of air spaces, which helps it hold in warmth. With just a blubber lamp for heat, an igloo could be 65° warmer than the air outside!

The Eskimos made very clever things from the bones, antlers, and wood they had. They invented the **harpoon**, which was used to hunt seals and whales. They built boats from wood or bone covered with animal skins. They invented the **kayak** for one man to use for hunting the ocean and among the pack ice. Eskimo sleds could be built from wood, bone, or even animal skins wrapped around frozen fish! Dishes were made from carved **soapstone**, bones, or musk ox horns. They wore two layers of skins, one fur side in, the other facing out, just like the Lapps, to stay warm.

Eskimos had to be good hunters to survive. In the winter, seals did not come out onto the ice. They only came up for air at holes they chewed in the ice. Eskimos would use their dogs to find the air-holes, then wait patiently until the seal came back to breathe and kill it with a harpoon. In the summer, the seals would lie out on the ice enjoying the sun. The hunter would have to slowly creep up on a seal to kill it.

| Sled

The Eskimos would use their dogs and spears to hunt polar bears, musk oxen, and caribou. Sometimes they would kill caribou from their boats as the animals crossed the rivers on their migration.

The Eskimos even hunted whales. From their boats, they would throw harpoons that were attached to floats made of inflated seal skins. The whale would grow tired from dragging the floats under water. When it slowed down and came up to the surface, the Eskimos could keep hitting it with more harpoons or spears until they killed it.

During the summer months, the Eskimos were able to gather berries and roots to eat. They also collected grasses to line their boots or make baskets. Often the food they found or killed during the summer was put into a **cache** for use during the long winter. A cache was created by digging down to the permafrost and building a rock lined pit there. The top would be covered with a pile of rocks to keep out the animals. It was as good as a freezer! The food would stay frozen there until the family needed it.

Eskimos did not have a government or laws. They learned early in life to help each other in order to survive. They always shared food, since it was often so hard to find. They usually moved around in small groups looking for food. Sometimes they would get together with other groups to hunt for larger animals such as whales. The men did the hunting and home building, and also made weapons, sleds, and boats. The women cooked, made the clothes, and took care of the children.

Eskimos today. Today, most Eskimos live in modern houses built by the government of their country. Many still hunt or fish for some of their food and income. They use rifles and snowmobiles when they go. They sell some of the fish they catch or the beautiful things they make for extra money. In Alaska, many of the people have received money from the oil discovered in that state. However, there are not many jobs for people in the Arctic. Often they must have help from the government in order to survive. The Arctic is so different from the rest of the world that the way of life in the south does not work well in the north.

| Inuit village in Greenland

Complete these sentences.

2.41 Eskimos invented the a. _____ and the b. _____ .

2.42 The Eskimos called any home an _____ .

2.43 "Eskimo" means _____ .

2.44 Eskimos call themselves _____ , which means *people*.

2.45 The only animals domesticated by the Eskimos were _____ .

2.46 Because it was so hard to find, Eskimos always shared _____ .

2.47 The only fire Eskimos had was _____ .

Answer these questions.

2.48 How did an Eskimo make a cache?

_____

_____

2.49 How did an Eskimo hunt seals in the winter?

_____

_____

2.50 How did Eskimos hunt whales?

_____

_____

_____

The Arctic Today

The Arctic region has many minerals that are important to people. Iron, lead, coal, copper, gold, and tin are all mined in different parts of this cold land. Large amounts of **petroleum** (oil) have been discovered in the Arctic in Russia, Alaska, and Canada. People live and work in the Arctic to remove these valuable minerals and sell them.

The oil in Alaska, for example, is very important to the United States. The main source of the oil is near Prudhoe Bay on Alaska's north coast. It was discovered in 1968. Plans were quickly made to build a pipeline to bring the oil to an ice-free port so it could be shipped south.

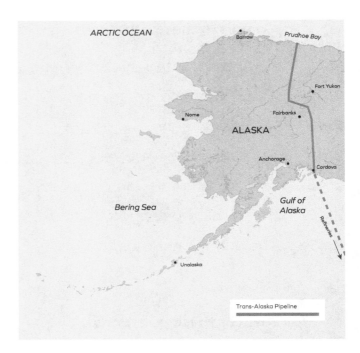

| Alaska Pipeline

Oil companies spent billions of dollars to build the Trans-Alaska Pipeline System (TAPS) in the mid-1970s. It had to be built above the ground in the northern section because of the permafrost. The warm oil in the pipes would have melted the permafrost and caused the ground to sink. That would have broken the pipes and caused an oil spill. The pipeline was completed in 1977. It brings oil to the seaport of Valdez on Alaska's south coast. From there the oil is taken by huge tankers to refineries along the west coast of the United States. If you live in western America, your family car may have Alaskan gasoline in its tank.

Russia has more land in the Arctic than any other nation. The Russian Arctic in Asia and the area just south of it are called Siberia. It is such an empty, harsh place that it has been used as a penal colony for many years. The old Russian rulers and the modern communist Soviets would send criminals and people who disagreed with the government to live there. However, many people were also sent there to remove minerals, harvest trees from the forests, and build cities.

Russia has a huge port city right in Lapland, within the Arctic Circle. Murmansk is the largest city north of the Arctic Circle. The port is kept ice-free by the warm waters of the Gulf Stream coming up around Norway and Sweden from the South Atlantic. Huge **ice-breakers** work to keep a path open so ships can reach the port. The port ships out fish, minerals, and lumber to Russia and the rest of the world.

The Arctic is also the shortest way for airlines to fly between some cities on different continents. The flight from London to Tokyo, for example, is 1,400 miles shorter if flown across the top of the world instead of the old route south across Europe and Asia. The polar route from San Francisco to Norway is several hours shorter than the same flight going across the United States and the Pacific Ocean. Thus, man is making use of the Arctic in various ways even though it is a hard place to live.

Answer *true* or *false*.

2.51 _____ The Trans-Alaska Pipeline was built underground.

2.52 _____ Murmansk, Russia is the largest city north of the Arctic Circle.

2.53 _____ Siberia was used as a penal colony.

2.54 _____ There are no valuable minerals in the Arctic.

2.55 _____ The Trans-Alaska Pipeline carries oil to Los Angeles, California.

2.56 _____ Murmansk's harbor is only ice-free three months of the year.

Review the material in this section to prepare for the Self Test. The Self Test will check your understanding of this section and will review the other section. Any items you miss on this test will show you what areas you will need to restudy in order to prepare for the unit test.

SELF TEST 2

Put the correct answer in the blank (4 points each answer).

2.01   The area around the North Pole is called the _____ region.

2.02   The area around the South Pole is called the _____ region.

2.03   In the northern hemisphere, a compass will point at the _____

_____ .

2.04   The forests do not grow north of the _____ .

2.05   The treeless plains of the Arctic are called _____ .

Match the following (2 points each answer).

2.06   _____ Henry Hudson

2.07   _____ John Franklin

2.08   _____ Roald Amundsen

2.09   _____ Robert Peary

2.010 _____ Richard Byrd

a. first to sail around America to the north

b. Arctic expedition disappeared in 1845

c. first to the North Pole

d. first to fly an airplane over the North Pole

e. discovered the largest bay in North America

Answer these questions in complete sentences (5 points each answer).

2.011 How did the Eskimos hunt whales?

_____

_____

_____

2.012 How are the regions around the North and South Pole alike?

_____

_____

_____

Answer these questions in complete sentences (5 points each answer).

Northwest Passage	*Nautilus*	permafrost	lichens
pack ice	glacier	icebergs	petroleum
Siberia	Southern Lights		

2.013   The frozen sea water around the polar regions is _____ .

2.014   _____ are plants that grow on rocks.

2.015   The northern route around America is the _____ .

2.016   The first ship to reach the North Pole was a submarine, the

_____ .

2.017   Ground that is always frozen is _____ .

2.018   The Russian Arctic is called _____ .

2.019   The darkness in Antarctica is sometimes brightened by the

_____ .

2.020   The Trans-Alaska Pipeline was built to move _____ .

2.021   Greenland is covered by a continental _____ .

2.022   The huge islands that calve off from a glacier are called _____ .

Put an _E_ beside each statement that is true of the Eskimos and an _L_ beside the statements that are true of Lapps. Some will be true of both (2 points each numbered answer).

2.023   _____   domesticated reindeer

2.024   _____   invented the harpoon and kayak

2.025   _____   nomads

2.026   _____   Inuit

2.027   _____   wore two layers of fur, one facing in, the other out

2.028   _____   use snowmobiles and rifles today

2.029   _____   Sami

2.030   _____   Norway, Sweden, and Finland

2.031 _____ Alaska, Canada, and Greenland

2.032 _____ "eaters of raw meat"

Answer *true* or *false* (1 point each answer).

2.033 _____ A lead is a deep crack in a glacier.

2.034 _____ Antarctica is an island.

2.035 _____ The polar bear is the world's largest land meat-eater.

2.036 _____ Musk oxen run away to escape predators.

2.037 _____ There are no flies or mosquitoes on the tundra.

2.038 _____ Snowy owls and Arctic foxes eat lemmings.

2.039 _____ No animals live in the Arctic all year.

2.040 _____ An igloo is a home that can be made of snow.

2.041 _____ Polar bears live most of their life out on the pack ice.

2.042 _____ The only animals to be domesticated by the Eskimos were dogs.

Teacher check:

Score _____

Initials _____

Date _____

80

100

3. THE ANTARCTIC POLAR REGION: BOTTOM OF THE WORLD

Antarctica is the last place on our planet that people explored, named, and put on a map. The oceans around Antarctica are very rough, wild, and dangerous. Even if a ship survived the ocean, it would face seas full of ice as it got closer to the southern continent. Brave men tried it anyway, and many died; but they slowly made Antarctica give up its secrets.

Objectives

Review these objectives. When you have completed this section, you should be able to:

1. Tell how the two polar regions are alike and how they differ.
4. Describe the land and oceans around the poles.
5. Tell about the exploration of the polar regions.
6. Identify and describe polar animals.
8. Tell how the polar regions are used today.

Vocabulary

Study these new words. Learning the meanings of these words is a good study habit and will improve your understanding of this LIFEPAC.

blizzard (bliz′ ərd). A blinding snowstorm with a very strong wind and very great cold.
diary (dī′ ə rē). A book in which each day a person writes down what has happened.
down (doun). Very soft, tiny feathers.
extinction (ek stingk′ shən). A bringing to an end; dying out; no longer existing.
frostbite (frôst′ bīt). An injury to a part of the body caused by freezing.

moss (môs). Very small, soft, green plants that grow close together like a carpet on the ground, rocks, or trees.

plankton (plangk′ tən). Small living things that float or drift in water, especially at or near the surface; provides food for fish.

Pronunciation Key: hat, āge, cãre, fär; let, ēqual, tėrm; it, īce; hot, ōpen, ôrder; **oil**; out; cup, put, rüle; **ch**ild; long; **th**in; /ŦH/ for **th**en; /zh/ for measure; /u/ or /ə/ represents /a/ in about, /e/ in taken, /i/ in pencil, /o/ in lemon, and /u/ in circus.

Exploration and Discovery

It is amazing to us how little people knew about the world before the Age of Exploration (A.D. 1500-1700). Well-educated people knew the world was round, but they did not know what was on the other side of it. Christopher Columbus accidentally found America when he sailed across the ocean in 1492. From that time on, men began to explore and map the lands outside of Europe. The very last place discovered and mapped was Antarctica. It was truly the last place on earth!

Captain James Cook was the man who began the exploration of the Antarctic region. Captain Cook was a British navy officer who was sent on an expedition to explore the unknown southern ocean.

Maps of his day were blank around the South Pole. No one knew what was there. Some people believed there was land at the bottom of the world. They called it *Terra Australis Incognita*. (That is Latin for "unknown southern land.")

Cook sailed in 1772 with instructions to go as far south as he could. He sailed south until ice blocked his path. His ship was the first to cross the Antarctic Circle. Then he sailed all the way around Antarctica, getting as close as the ice would allow. It was dangerous. The wooden ship could easily have been crushed and sunk by the heavy icebergs. He never got close enough to see the continent, but he did prove that there was no land out further in the ocean. He also proved that it would be a cold, ice-covered land if it was there. His ship found many small islands, and he reported seeing lots of whales and seals.

Many men came to the region after Cook because of the seals and whales. Seals had fur that was very valuable in Europe and China. Men came to the islands around Antarctica and began killing the seals for their fur or their oil (which was used as a fuel).

These men killed all of the seals they could find on an island. They also hunted whales for their meat and oil. They killed so many animals that many islands no longer had any seals left, and the whales became very hard to find.

| Sailing ship and whale

Other men came to learn and explore, however. These men particularly wanted to know if there was a continent at the South Pole, or just islands covered with ice. Whenever they found land, they would draw a picture of it, put it on a map, and give it a name. Often they did not know if it was an island or part of a big continent. They only knew it was an island if they could sail around it, and ice often stopped them.

Sometime around 1820, someone saw the continent of Antarctica for the first time. Three different men claimed to have been the first to see it. We do not know which one was first because even they were not sure of what they were seeing. We also do not know who was the first person to set foot on the continent. Perhaps it was the men hunting seals and whales. They often did not tell about what they found because they wanted to keep the places they hunted secret.

Put the correct word(s) in the blank.

3.1   Before the Age of Exploration, maps of the bottom of the world showed

_____ .

3.2   The first person to explore the Antarctic region was _____

_____ .

3.3   Many men came to the Antarctic region to hunt for whales and _____ .

3.4   What three things did an explorer do when he found land in Antarctica?

a. _____

b. _____

c. _____

Answer *true* or *false*.

3.5   _____   People called the land they thought might be at the South Pole *Terra Australis Incognita*.

3.6   _____   The hunters wanted the teeth and meat of the seals.

3.7   _____   No one knows who the first person to cross the Antarctic Circle was.

3.8   _____   Antarctica was the last place on earth to be explored and mapped.

Slowly, the explorers found different parts of the continent and mapped them. They could only work during the short summer months. The areas they found and mapped have the names the founders gave them. In 1823 James Weddell sailed further south than anyone had before. He found a large gulf, which is named the Weddell Sea. John Biscoe named Enderby Land after the whaling company that owned his ship. The Ross Ice Shelf and Ross Sea were named for British explorer, James Ross, who found them around 1840. Ross also named two volcanoes *Erebus* and *Terror* after his ships.

Slowly a map of the edges of the continent was made. People began to realize that it was indeed a continent. Then they began to talk about exploring the land. But that would require breaking through the ice that always floated around Antarctica, landing on it, and bringing in enough supplies to live while they explored. There were two places people wanted to reach on the continent. One was the South Pole.

| A ship stuck in Antarctic ice

The other was the South Magnetic Pole. The second is the place where compasses point in the Southern Hemisphere.

The first people to stay all winter in Antarctica did it on ships trapped in the ice. The first was the *Belgica* which was trapped from March 1898 to March 1899. Other ships began staying all winter to study the weather and other things about Antarctica. It was risky, because sometimes the boats could not be set free from the ice in the summer! One clever group melted an opening to the ocean by laying down a path of garbage between their trapped ship and the sea. The sun warmed the garbage and melted the ice!

| An early Antarctic explorer outside a hut

Eventually, men began building small huts and spending winters on the mainland. From these bases, as soon as summer arrived, they could set out on foot or on sleds pulled by dogs, to explore their surroundings. These stays were very difficult. Fierce winds and unbelievably cold temperatures made life miserable. The men had to constantly watch for **frostbite**.

The hardest part of the winter was many long days of darkness. During the darkness, the men were stuck together inside the small huts because of the **blizzards** outside. The explorers quickly learned that people became very angry and sometimes insane during that time. The better leaders worked hard to keep their men busy and happy during those difficult days.

The first man to begin serious exploration of the Antarctic inland was Robert Falcon Scott, the most well known of the explorers. He was an Englishman who wanted to be the first man to reach the South Pole. He began looking for a way in 1902, working his way south from the Ross Ice Shelf. He was forced to turn back because of illness and lack of food.

Ernest Shackleton, a member of Scott's party, tried again in 1907. He reached the Magnetic South Pole and came within 97 miles of the South Pole itself before he turned back. But Shackleton got close enough that everyone was now certain the South Pole was on land, not ice over the ocean.

Complete these statements.

3.9 The two places on Antarctica that people wanted to reach were

a. _____ and b. _____ .

3.10 The first group of men to spend the winter in Antarctica did it on _____ .

3.11 The hardest part of spending the winter in Antarctica was the _____

_____ .

3.12 The Ross Sea is named for the _____ explorer, John Ross.

3.13 Men who spent the winter would set out to explore on foot or with sleds pulled

by _____ .

3.14 The first man to reach the South Magnetic Pole was _____

_____ .

3.15 The first man to seriously explore the inland areas of Antarctica was

_____ .

In 1911 two teams set off to try to reach the South Pole. The team from Norway was led by Roald Amundsen (the first man to sail the Northwest Passage). He had hoped to be the first man to reach the North Pole. He switched at the last minute to try for the South Pole because he heard that Peary had already reached the northern one. The British team was lead by Robert Scott and left about the same time. It became a race. Both men knew the other team was trying. However, they did not have radio or any other way of talking to each other, so neither team knew where the other was.

| Roald Amundsen and his team at the South Pole

Amundsen used only sled dogs to pull his supplies. He planned well and made good use of the animals. Scott did not plan as well as Amundsen. Scott used ponies and motor sleds (which were new inventions). They could not pull his supplies all the way to the pole. Scott and his men had to pull their supply sleds themselves toward the end of the trip. This made Scott and his men work hard and they became tired quickly.

Amundsen's team arrived at the Pole first on December 14, 1911. He left a tent and a flag there along with a message for Robert Scott. Scott and his four men arrived a month later to find Amundsen had beaten him. Bitterly disappointed, he and his tired, discouraged group headed back.

The reason Scott is better known than Amundsen is because Scott and all of his team died trying to get back to their camp. Scott and two of the men managed to get within 11 miles of their supply of food. They were forced to stop by a blizzard and froze to death waiting for it to end. It was eight months later when their bodies were found inside the tent where they died. The searchers also found Scott's records and **diary** there. He had written in it every day right up until he died.

In 1929 the same dangerous journey to the Pole which took Amundsen three months was completed in about 16 hours by American Admiral Richard Byrd. He was the first man to fly an airplane over the South Pole, having already been the first over the North Pole. Before World War II, Richard Byrd led three more large American expeditions to do experiments and explore Antarctica. He led two more after the war, one of which was "Operation Highjump," that mapped an area of Antarctica which was as large as Germany and France combined.

It was the arrival of airplanes that finally allowed large areas of the continent to be searched and mapped. By about 1958, most of the continent of Antarctica was mapped and known. Then people began to wonder what to do with it.

Several countries had claimed land in Antarctica, and some had claimed the same land. In 1959 twelve countries signed the Antarctic Treaty. They agreed to ignore the claims and treat the continent as everyone's land. Several countries have

| A plane equipped for landing in snow

not totally given up their claims. They just agreed not to do anything about it. The countries agreed to use the continent only for peaceful, scientific research and to share what they learn. This treaty still controls the use of Antarctica today, and several more nations have signed it.

Answer each question.

3.16 What were the names of the two men who raced to the South Pole in 1911 and what country were they from?

a. _____   from _____

b. _____   from _____

3.17 What happened to Robert Scott?

_____

_____

3.18 Who was the first man to fly over both the South and the North Poles?

_____

3.19 By about what year was most of Antarctica mapped? _____

3.20 What did the countries agree to in the Antarctic Treaty?

_____

_____

_____

_____

3.21 Who was the first man to reach the South Pole?

_____

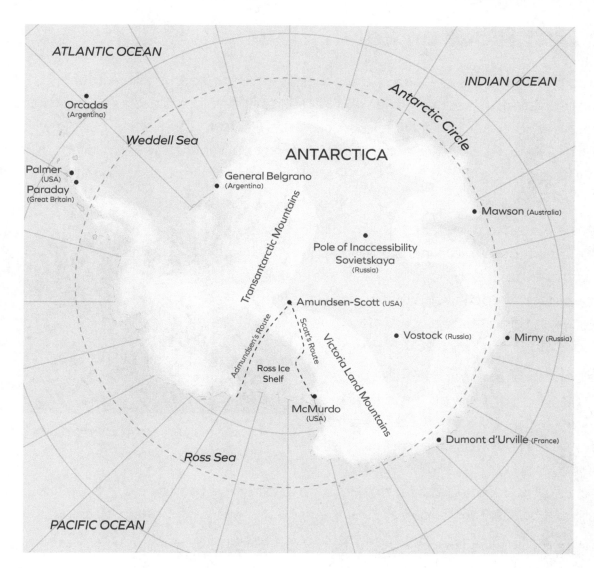

 Map exercises.

3.22 Circle the Antarctic Peninsula.

3.23 Draw a line along the path taken by the first man to the South Pole.

3.24 Put a box around the point that is farthest away from the ocean.

3.25 Label the map where West and East Antarctica are.

3.26 Draw an arrow that points south (anywhere).

Teacher check:

Initials _____   Date _____

The Last Place on Earth

The map of Antarctica shows the continent of Antarctica as we know it today. The dots are research stations set up by different countries. There are people at the stations all year round. The largest is McMurdo Base on Ross Island. A thousand people will be there in the summer doing science work. Close to two hundred will stay there during the winter. The oldest station is Orcadas, which is an Argentine station. It has been in operation since 1903.

Notice the Russian station, *Sovietskaya*, at the Pole of Inaccessibility. This is the point furthest from the ocean. That makes it the hardest place to reach. It has also recorded the lowest temperature on earth. It got down to 129° (F) <u>below</u> zero!

At the bottom of the map is the Ross Ice Shelf. This is one of several ice-covered bays. The ice comes from the continental glacier pushing out from the land. The ice is as solid as the ice-covered land. Both

| Scientists live year round on Antarctica conducting research.

Amundsen and Scott went over the Ross Ice Shelf going to the pole. It is the closest a ship can get to the South Pole, and all their supplies were brought in by ships.

Notice the mountains, Transantarctic and Victoria Land, that run across the middle of Antarctica. These divide the continent into West (or Lesser) Antarctica and East (or Greater) Antarctica. East Antarctica is the larger side and is south of Asia, which is called the eastern part of the world. The smaller part, including the Antarctic Peninsula, is south of the Americas, in the west.

There is one <u>very</u> strange thing about this map. There is no north and south marked on the map. That is because *everything* going in towards the pole is south and every direction going away from the pole is north! If you stood at the South Pole, you would go north no matter which way you took a step.

Antarctica is about as big as the United States and Mexico put together. It seems to grow bigger in the winter because of the pack ice around it. The ice around the continent will grow to be as large as half the land. Ice is a very big part of Antarctica.

Antarctica is a large, icy desert. It is almost as dry as the Sahara, the world's biggest desert, in Africa. It is so dry because it is so cold. Remember that cold air cannot hold very much water. However, when it does snow, the snow never melts. It just piles up deeper and deeper, and it makes thick ice over most of the land. The ice of this continental glacier is often a mile or more deep!

Antarctica is colder than the North Pole because it is higher in altitude than the North Pole. Its deep ice raises the altitude much higher than the North Pole, which is near the level of the ocean. Temperatures always get colder as you go higher in altitude. Antarctica is also colder because it is on land. Oceans make warm places cooler and cold places warmer. The ocean under and around the North Pole keeps the temperatures warmer than they are at the South Pole.

| Most of an iceberg's mass is under the water.

Most of the fresh (drinkable) water in the world is frozen as ice in Antarctica. The ice does not stay in one place, either. It moves slowly downhill, as glaciers, to the ocean. In some place it may move a mile or more in a year. Eventually, the ice will reach the ocean. Some of it will push out over the top of the ocean, making an ice shelf. Pieces of it will calve off into the water as icebergs. The icebergs will drift away and melt. That is the only way the water gets back to the sea from Antarctica, because it never melts on the land.

The fresh water melting around Antarctica makes the ocean water less-salty than in other parts of the world. This cold, less-salty water goes out away from the continent until it runs into warmer, saltier water coming from the north. The colder water sinks down under the warmer water. This is the point that scientist say the Antarctic region ends. It is called the *Antarctic Convergence* or *Polar Front*. It is further out than the Antarctic Circle. It is where the water and weather change. It is inside the Polar Front that we can talk about life in the Antarctic region.

Match these words with their description.

3.27 _____ Antarctica   a. ice pushed together to be solid

3.28 _____ Antarctic Convergence   b. most is frozen as Antarctic ice

3.29 _____ pack ice   c. big as the U.S. and Mexico

3.30 _____ fresh water   d. edge of the colder, fresher water
                                          from Antarctica

Answer these questions.

3.31 Why is Antarctica so dry? _____

3.32 What happens to the snow that does fall? _____

_____

3.33 Where does the ice move?_____

_____

3.34 What are the two reasons Antarctica is colder than the Arctic?

a. _____

b. _____

Life in Antarctica

Plants. The only plants that grow on the land in Antarctica are **moss** and lichens. The most important plant in Antarctica is the **plankton** that grows in the ocean. It grows well when the water is still and the sun shines all day and night.

Animals. There are no land animals in Antarctica. All the animals there come from the ocean and visit the land. The most important animal of the Antarctic is the small, shrimp-like krill. The krill eats the plankton growing in the ocean. It is important because almost all the other animals eat the krill. Penguins, whales, and seals all eat krill. Even some of the birds eat them. Without the krill there would be very little to eat in Antarctica and almost no animals living there.

The biggest krill-eaters are whales. Whales are the largest animals in the ocean. They are mammals, not fish. That means that they breathe air and do not lay eggs. Many different kinds of whales live in the oceans around Antarctica.

| Antarctic krill floating in the water

The whales that eat krill do not have teeth. Instead they have *baleen* in their mouths. Baleen is long, hard strips that act like a strainer. The whale takes in a mouthful of water, and it goes through the baleen. Any krill in the water is trapped and swallowed, while the water goes back out.

Men have hunted whales for hundreds of years. Whale meat is used for food. Whales have a thick layer of fat, or blubber, that can be melted down to make oil. The oil is used to light lamps and keep engine parts from rubbing together. Other parts of the whale can also be used for many things.

However, in the early part of the 1900s, too many whales were killed. People became afraid that all the whales would die. Most countries no longer hunt whales. A few still do, but they do not kill as many as they once did. There are more whales now, but many people are still afraid they may all die if we are not careful.

Complete each sentence.

3.35 The most important animal in Antarctica is the _____ .

3.36 There are _____ land animals in Antarctica.

3.37 Whales use _____ to strain krill out of the water.

3.38 The only land plants in Antarctica are _____ and _____ .

3.39 Whale oil is made from the whale's _____ .

The animal most people think of when talking about Antarctica is the penguin. Penguins only live south of the equator. Several different kinds live in and around Antarctica. The biggest ones stand nearly 4 feet tall and can weigh almost 100 pounds. The smallest kinds are only about one foot tall.

Penguins are large birds that swim very well but cannot fly. They are very odd looking on land. They have black backs and wings with white fronts. They look rather like fat, little men in suits as they waddle over the ice.

God designed penguins to live in the cold south. They have a thick layer of blubber that keeps them warm. Their feathers are very tightly packed and overlap each other to make another thick cover. They also have a layer of woolly **down** under the feathers. The feathers themselves are coated with a type of oil that makes them waterproof.

The penguins eat krill or fish and are at home in the ocean. They come up on the land or ice to lay their eggs and raise the chicks (baby penguins). The animals nest together in a huge group that is called a rookery. They usually make shallow nests on the ground out of rocks or mud. There are no animals on land that can harm a penguin. Some birds will steal eggs or baby chicks, but the adults have no land enemies.

The Emperor Penguin is a most remarkable Antarctic animal. The mother lays her egg on the ice right before winter begins. She gives it to the father who puts it on his foot and covers it up with his belly. The mother goes away for two months to live in the ocean, eat, and get fat. The fathers all huddle together to keep warm and protect the eggs during the winter. They <u>do not eat at all</u> during this time. They live off the fat in their bodies.

When the baby hatches, the father feeds it with a milk-like liquid he makes in his throat. Soon after the chick hatches, the mother returns and takes over feeding the baby. The hungry daddy goes out to the ocean to find some food. He will return after about three weeks. Then the two parents take turns going out to get food and returning to feed the chick.

| Penguins

Seals also live around Antarctica. Many, many seals were killed by greedy men in the 1800s. Several kinds came close to **extinction**. The seals were killed until there were so few left that it was not worth the time to come and hunt for them.

Seals have increased in number in this century. Many of the islands that the seal hunters emptied have seals on them again. Most of the seals eat krill and fish, but one kind of seal is known as a killer. The Leopard Seal eats penguins and other seals. It and the Killer Whale are the main predators of the animals of Antarctica, particularly penguins.

Several kinds of birds come south to nest in the Antarctic region. Most of these birds nest on the Antarctic islands and fly long distances to come there each spring. The albatross is a huge bird that only comes to land to lay eggs. The wings of an albatross can be more than 11 feet across! Petrels also live out over the ocean, where they eat by scooping food off the surface or diving for it. The skua, (skyü' ə) are very mean birds that steal penguin eggs and chicks. Penguins are very careful when a skua is nearby.

Match the animal with its description.

3.40	_____ skua	a. live only south of the equator
3.41	_____ penguin	b. hunted almost to extinction
3.42	_____ seal	c. can have 11-foot wingspan
3.43	_____ petrel	d. mean birds, eat penguin eggs
3.44	_____ albatross	e. eats off the surface of the ocean or by diving

Complete the following.

3.45 List some of the ways God designed penguins to live in the cold.

a. _____

b. _____

c. _____

d. _____

3.46 Penguins nest in a large group called a _____ .

3.47   Describe how the Emperor Penguin father takes care of the egg after it is laid.

_____

_____

_____

People. Unlike in the Arctic, no humans have their homes in Antarctica, but many people live there for a short time to work on the bases that have been built there. Most of the people who come to Antarctica are scientists. They study the weather, animals, glaciers, and the air around our earth. Some scientists drill into the ice to find out about the weather long ago. They can do that because the ice never melts. They can count down the layers of ice to see how much snow fell ten, twenty, or a hundred years ago!

People who work in Antarctica must be very careful. They dress in many layers of warm clothes. They must never go very far from shelter because a blizzard can start any time. When they take a trip away from their base they always take plenty of extra food, in case they are forced to stop by a storm.

People staying in Antarctica must be careful not to do any damage while they are there. Garbage will just freeze and stay there forever if it is dropped outside. A footprint on the moss may stay there for ten years! So, the scientists try to burn all of their garbage or send it back to their countries where it can be put in a landfill. They also are careful where they walk and work.

| Antarctica

The bases are built to keep the people warm and comfortable even during the harsh winter. The buildings must keep out both the cold and the snow that blows everywhere. Also, remember that the ice on Antarctica moves. That means that the buildings move, too. An American base, Amundsen-Scott, was built on the South Pole in 1957. Since that time it has moved and is now more than 1,000 yards away from the Pole! All of the bases are eventually buried by the ice, as it builds up each year. Then they have to be rebuilt.

Today people explore Antarctica using snowmobiles. They are faster and can pull heavier loads than dogs can. Only a few of the bases still have sled dogs. They like to have the dogs for company! It is easier to bring in supplies today, also. Icebreaker ships can cut through the pack ice to bring in supplies every summer. Airplanes can bring in people and supplies, too.

| Emperor penguin and cruise ship

In fact, it has become so easy to get to Antarctica that many people just come to visit. There are companies in South America that have vacations to Antarctica! You can pay and take a ship down there. Some people take their own boats down to see the continent. Perhaps some day you will take a vacation to Antarctica, the last place on earth!

Complete these statements.

3.48   Today people explore Antarctica not with dogsleds, but with

_____ .

3.49   Most of the people who go to Antarctica are _____ .

3.50   Buildings do not stay in one place because the ice _____ .

3.51   Supplies can be brought to Antarctica by _____ or by

_____ .

3.52   Many people now visit Antarctica on _____ .

3.53   Garbage dropped in Antarctica will _____ and stay forever.

Do this activity.

3.54 Do a one-page report on a polar explorer. You can choose: Robert Scott, Roald Amundsen, Ernest Shackleton, Richard Byrd, James Cook, Robert Peary, or another one you may find.

✓ **Teacher check:**

Initials _____ Date _____

Before you take this last Self Test, you may want to do one or more of these self checks.

1. _____ Read the objectives. See if you can do them.
2. _____ Restudy the material related to any objectives that you cannot do.
3. _____ Use the **SQ3R** study procedure to review the material:
   a. **S**can the sections.
   b. **Q**uestion yourself.
   c. **R**ead to answer your questions.
   d. **R**ecite the answers to yourself.
   e. **R**eview areas you did not understand.
4. _____ Review all vocabulary, activities, and Self Tests, writing a correct answer for every wrong answer.

SELF TEST 3

Match these people with the statement that describes them (2 points each answer).

3.01 _____ Robert Peary

3.02 _____ Richard Byrd

3.03 _____ Robert Scott

3.04 _____ Roald Amundsen

3.05 _____ Henry Hudson

3.06 _____ James Cook

3.07 _____ Ernest Shackleton

a. first to the North Pole

b. first to the South Pole

c. second to South Pole, died on the way out

d. first across the Antarctic Circle

e. first to South Magnetic Pole

f. first to fly across North and South Poles

g. made four trips to the Arctic in the 1600s

Answer *true* or *false* (2 points each answer).

3.08 _____ Antarctica was not fully explored until about 1958.

3.09 _____ People take vacations in Antarctica today.

3.010 _____ The first people to spend the winter in Antarctica stayed on ships frozen in the ice.

3.011 _____ The North Pole is on land.

3.012 _____ The coldest temperature ever recorded was in Antarctica.

3.013 _____ Most of the fresh water in the world is frozen as ice in Antarctica.

3.014 _____ A crevasse is a space of open water in the pack ice around the poles.

3.015 _____ Glaciers move slowly downhill.

3.016 _____ The countries that work in Antarctica have agreed to only use it for peaceful research.

3.017 _____ The ice at the poles reflects sunlight away and that helps keep it cold there.

Answer these questions (5 points each answer).

3.018 In what ways are the Arctic and Antarctic alike?

_____

_____

_____

_____

3.019 In what ways are the Arctic and Antarctic different?

_____

_____

_____

_____

Write the correct answer in the blank (4 points each answer).

3.020 *Terra Australis Incognita* is Latin for _____ .

3.021 Men came to the islands of the Antarctic to hunt _____ for
their valuable fur.

3.022 The hardest part of staying in Antarctica all winter was _____
_____ .

3.023 The first successful expeditions to both the North and South Poles used
_____ to carry their supplies.

3.024 If you stood at the South Pole and took a step towards the Antarctic Peninsula,
you would be going (what direction?) _____ .

3.025 _____ are birds that swim but cannot
fly and are found only south of the equator.

3.026 The nomads of northern Europe who domesticated reindeer are called
_____ .

3.027 Inuit is the name the _____ hunter/gatherers of Arctic North
America, call themselves.

3.028 Greenland and Antarctica are covered with a thick layer of ice called a

_____ .

Choose the correct answer from the list below (3 points each answer).

seal	Siberia	musk ox
krill	pack ice	iceberg
Northwest Passage	Operation Highjump	Amundsen-Scott
Antarctic Convergence		

3.029 The most important animal of the Antarctic is the _____ which many of the other animals eat.

3.030 The _____ is the way around North America through the Arctic.

3.031 _____ is America's base near the South Pole.

3.032 The point in the ocean where the cold, less-salty Antarctic water meets the warmer, saltier water from the north is called the _____

_____ .

3.033 _____ defend themselves by forming a circle with the calves in the center and the big ones facing out.

3.034 _____ was led by Admiral Byrd after World War II and mapped a huge part of Antarctica.

3.035 Frozen sea water around the poles is called _____ .

3.036 The _Titanic_ sank when it hit _____ .

3.037 Polar bears were created to hunt _____ out on the ice.

3.038 _____ was the Russian Arctic area that was used as a penal colony.

✔ **Teacher check:** Initials _____ Score _____ Date _____ 80 / 100

Before you take the LIFEPAC Test, you may want to do one or more of these self checks.

1. _____ Read the objectives. See if you can do them.
2. _____ Restudy the material related to any objectives that you cannot do.
3. _____ Use the **SQ3R** study procedure to review the material.
4. _____ Review activities, Self Tests, and LIFEPAC vocabulary words.
5. _____ Restudy areas of weakness indicated by the last Self Test.